LOVE
LESSONS

LOVE
LESSONS

♥

A Guide to Transforming Relationships

♥

Dr. Brenda Wade

AND

Brenda Lane Richardson

Amistad

NEW YORK, NEW YORK

Amistad Press, Inc.
1271 Avenue of the Americas
New York, NY 10020

Distributed by:
Penguin USA
375 Hudson Street
New York, NY 10014

Designed by Stanley S. Drate/Folio Graphics Co. Inc.
Produced by March Tenth, Inc.

1   2   3   4   5   6   7   8   9   10

Library of Congress Cataloging-in-Publication Data

Wade, Brenda.
   Love lessons : a guide to transforming relationships / by Brenda
Wade and Brenda Lane Richardson.
      p.   cm.
   Includes Index.
   ISBN 1-56743-005-8 : $24.95
   1. Marital psychotherapy—Popular works.   2. Marital
psychotherapy—Case studies.   I. Richardson, Brenda Lane.   1948–
II. Title.
RC488.5.W3   1993
616.89'156—dc20   92-36240
                                                                        CIP

Acknowledgments

We are forever indebted to the five couples who tolerated long hours of exhausting interviews and who, in the end, worked fearlessly in therapeutic sessions so we could put Step 12 into practice, "to carry this message to others."

Our thanks to our publisher, Charles Harris, for believing deeply in our vision, to our editor, Malaika Adero for her support, insight, and keen professionalism, and finally, to Marie Brown, literary agent extraordinaire.

For my dearly loved teachers: Kena, Kai, Tat, my family, Chow Chow, and Sai Baba.

—BRENDA WADE

♥

For my lover, playmate, best friend, and husband—Mark Richardson

—BRENDA LANE RICHARDSON

Contents

Preface

Every experience is a lesson, every loss a gain.
—SATYA SAI BABA

Although I have been a family therapist with a private practice in San Francisco for fourteen years, I was startled by the magnitude of the response I received when, in 1989, I began hosting the nationally syndicated television show, "Can This Marriage Be Saved?" The show, produced by Group 'W' Productions, was canceled eventually, but two years later, former viewers continue to stop me at airports, in restaurants, and in various public locations. They either remember the show or have seen me during one of my more recent appearances on "Good Morning America," "The Home Show," "Oprah Winfrey," or "Donahue." People usually ask me about couples who have been featured on my show and the rapid changes they saw occur as I counseled them in the studio. Then they ask me questions about their own lives and issues, hoping I can steer them quickly in the right direction.

The show may also have been familiar to so many because it was named for and based upon a magazine feature in *Ladies Home Journal* called "Can This Marriage Be Saved?" It is the longest running feature series in any women's magazine.

Whatever their reason for remembering me, I am grateful, because it is they who gave me the determination to begin this book. When the moment has allowed, I've tried to at least leave people I met on the street with comforting words. But I always begin by telling them that I, like millions of other people, including thousands of other family therapists, have suffered the pain of divorce.

That may be a sad comment on the state of romantic affairs in today's world, but the good news is that I, like many others (including hundreds of the couples I've counseled), now have a deeper understanding of myself and relationships in general skills generally as a result of working through my personal issues. I had to confront and change my negative behaviors and character flaws that interfered with my ability to have healthy love relationships.

The strangers I talk to in airports are among the millions who so desperately want change in their own relationships. You're obviously much like them, which is why you're reading this book. You believe in the power of love and you have the will to make it better. You're right not to give up easily. Whether you're in a relationship now, hope to be in one, or have ended one, you will continue to have the same problems in various disguises unless you learn to look closely at yourself. Nothing offers a better opportunity for looking at yourself than being a part of a love relationship, but even wanting a new relationship helps.

Once we're in relationships, they often seem impossible to maintain, because we focus on our partner's shortcomings and lose interest in correcting our own. One of the first lessons of love is to see our partner—whether present or past—as someone who has enabled us to examine who we are and how we interact. Our partners are our teachers.

If you can learn to fully understand why you chose to love that individual and work to bring about change in yourself, your relationships will change for the better, while at the same time, a wonderful process of self-transformation will occur.

This book offers me the opportunity to share my thoughts and expertise in ways that I cannot during the brief encounters with people who stop me in public or even during my television appearances. My approach to the subject of love relationships is effective, practical, and forthright; I do not simply offer theory or soundbites. I put my ideas to work on real people, and with *Love Lessons,* I'd like to show you how.

My coauthor, Brenda Richardson, and I advertised in newspapers around the country and offered couples free therapy in exchange for the use of their stories. Brenda, an award-winning, veteran journalist, spent many hours with our subjects, observing them as couples, interviewing them individually, sometimes even going through old photo albums with them to stir their memories. She used a method of compiling emotional family history that we will share with you in this book. Although we've changed the names and certain biographical details of the couples to protect their privacy, I can assure you they are real people, not composite sketches. I am forever indebted to these five couples for their candor, their courage, and their generosity of spirit. They offered a way for me to demonstrate, rather than simply tell you, how change in relationships occurs.

We chose the couples for specific reasons and with certain qualities in mind. I have often heard people offer financial difficulties as an excuse for the problems in their marriages. Let me assure you, good relationships are seldom dependent on material possessions; but financial hardships can mask deeper problems. For that reason, I was particularly interested in the Kinkaids, who are quite wealthy. The other couples in the book are not as financially fit as they, but they are materially comfortable. They include a college instructor, a medical researcher, a social worker, a homemaker, and a salesperson.

With the same hope of ridding ourselves of distractions, I looked for another common denominator in the couples who agreed to participate. None of these individuals, except for one woman (who revealed at the end of a long interview session that she'd been raped as a child), come from family backgrounds filled with repeated trauma. I was concerned that a family history of violence or blatant abuse might also lead us away from the real reasons their relationships were failing.

Almost everyone, even from the best of family environments, needs to do some emotional homework if they want healthy relationships. And the time to do so is now. The reasons for that are twofold.

First, most of us are the first generation out of the basic survival mode. Our parents and grandparents lived during world wars and the Depression, and most of them were caught up in simply trying to earn enough money for food and shelter for their families. There was little time to worry or talk about how they felt about their lives and their relationships. Years and a generation or two later, though, the consequence of neglecting the health of their emotions is evidenced in all the troubled relationships around us. We all yearn for inner happiness whether or not we take the time to seek it.

Second, the current wave of advances in mental health treatment coincides with technological and industrial advances that have created available time and energy that individuals and couples need to do inner work.

One of the most important characteristics we sought in our five couples was that each of the individuals not only have some insight into what they felt, but that they were also capable of talking about those feelings.

One note of caution, though: Don't be misled by what these couples have in common. You will find that their experiences are quite unique. As they share their stories in their distinctive and original voices, you'll begin to feel that they could well be you, your next-door neighbors, or your cousins or uncles. They come from various parts of the country and range in ages from twenty-five to fifty. Their problems include poor communication, general unhappiness, emotional abuse, addictive behavior, conflicts over money, and sexual dysfunction, problems which could surely be found among your friends and neighbors if they spoke truthfully.

I wanted this to be a book that anyone who cares about love can learn from. It is a book filled with the drama and conflicts that we all have in our lives, and the pain most of us have felt at one time or another in love. Simply put, it is the story of five couples who have everything they want in life—except what really matters: a happy love life. It shows how therapy can transform their lives and their love relationships to something better and more fulfilling.

We'll take you quietly and unobtrusively into their bedrooms, seat you at their kitchen tables, walk you through their pasts, their lives today, and even into their futures. *Love Lessons* will give you an opportunity to witness them in therapy, grow as they grow, and benefit from the step-by-step exercises and techniques explained in each chapter. I'm certain that by the end of the book you will understand better even your most troubling problems and find positive ways to solve them.

A Note to Readers

Before I introduce you to my approach for helping people in love relationships, I want to prepare you to meet five of the most heroic couples I have had the pleasure of knowing. They have put themselves on the line, allowing us into every facet of their lives, because they want happy and successful marriages.

Their problems include poor communication, arguments over money, sex, children, jobs, in-laws, and addictions. We'll travel via their stories, as far away as the Kenyan countryside, Minsk, Quebec City, Israel, and a Peruvian beach. We'll sit oh so quietly in their homes, which are located in Massachusetts, California, Illinois, Georgia, and New York. And, finally, we'll weep, then celebrate with them during their therapy sessions.

As you come to know them better, you'll come to understand yourself, your mates (past and present), realize why you were attracted to one another, and learn how to make that knowledge work for you. These couples have allowed us to create one of the first of its kind: a self-help book that's actually easy to understand and fun to read.

I urge you to sit back and enjoy the ride.

LOVE
LESSONS

———— ♥ ————

1 THE POWER OF LOVE

An old myth relates this tale. A handsome young man, with dark and curling hair, stood beneath the window of his beloved, strumming softly on his lute. The music beckoned her to the window. He raised his song of love in a clear and strong voice: "Dearest love, thou art more beautiful than the newly budded rose or a brilliant sky." By now his lovely lady was leaning from the window, soft lips parted as she longed for him. He sang on: "I love thee truly, from the deepest well of my soul, I pledge my heart and my very life to thee. Happily would I die for thee. I pray only that God grant that I love thee still more."

As the story goes, years later, when this young swain met with death and he reached the heavenly throne, the master asked him, "Did you love me while you lived on earth?" The young man cried, "Oh yes! I loved my beloved with all my heart and soul. Through that love divine I touch thee my lord."

Through love you touch the divine in yourself. Love can bring out the best in us. The ennobling, transforming power of love is often overlooked these days. We certainly don't think of love as the spiritual path that the troubadour in the story recognized. The lovers of old committed deeds of daring and courage to prove their love. They refined their basic instincts as they opened them-

1

selves to the uplifting qualities of the finest human sentiments. They strove to express the beauty of their heartfelt experiences through outpourings of song, poetry, and prose.

Is it possible to claim some of the magic and radiance of the old tradition of romantic love in today's world? At this point, when half of all unions dissolve in divorce, and economic and career concerns stamp out the joy and poetry of loving another, it is difficult. More baffling still is how, even when we really try to make our togetherness hold, we find we lack the skills and understanding to do so.

To form a lasting and growing bond of love there are several threads that must be simultaneously woven together. The first thread recaptures the beauty and magic of love, thereby lifting us above cynicism and jaded attitudes. Consistently maintaining a positive view of our partners and celebrating what is wonderful in them can keep a marriage vibrant. It is so important, in fact, that I have developed a set of exercises to help you bring the best forward in your relationship. The second step clears the blocks to our ability to love freely. Those blocks of course come from the bad examples we followed and earliest lessons we learned—and must unlearn—in relating to others.

The people who raised us taught what they knew about love and what they knew had been passed on from their parents. When you fell in love, all that was passed down to you was brought to the fore. If there were gaps in the way you were nurtured or wounds that remained unhealed, they all come into play. But, if you allow it to, love can motivate you to heal those wounds and close the gaps, help you acquire greater maturity. You can become kinder, more generous, patient, and playful.

There are specific behaviors and methods of interacting that can hurt or enhance our ties with others. We have to recognize what they are. This may seem obvious to some people but a mystery to others. Most of us don't have any routine way of investing in or addressing our partners' or our own emotional needs. In a recent interview published in the *San Francisco Chronicle*, Professor David Olson of the University of Minnesota summarized the problem: "We assume that if people are going to do well in a career, they're going to invest time and money in education. But we don't assume that with marriage. . . . We shouldn't be surprised [that so many marriages are unhappy]; if you don't invest anything, what can you expect?"

Most of us know that couples counseling or marital therapy is readily available, but relatively few couples find their way into a professional's office. In large part this is due to the old stigma attached to therapy, the notion that it's for crazy people. Many people do not view therapy as a way of cultivating love. Instead, they consider it a sign of failure. An important and unique feature of *Love Lessons* is the inclusion of verbatim dialogue between couples and therapist. For many of you, this may be your first opportunity to see how therapy works and it will demystify the process for you. I hope it will inspire you to give yourself some *Love Lessons* with a qualified professional.

Most couples, including those who share their life stories with us in *Love Lessons,* find themselves feeling stuck at some point in their relationships. No matter what they do, it seems, they continue in a vicious cycle of anger and hurtful behavior toward one another. You will see that one of the techniques I use to assist our couples in moving forward involves releasing pent-up fury in a safe and productive way. Often the emotions expressed date back to childhood and involve the parents of each spouse. I cannot emphasize enough that simply getting in touch with repressed feelings and venting them does not lead to resolution of the issues. (But it does help free up misdirected feelings. The energy it takes to keep them locked up can now be used to enhance healing.) We must be careful not to fall into the "blame game," where we conveniently excuse our behavior by saying, "It's my parents' fault that I'm this way." Many people believe their family patterns can't be broken. Yes they can. To break out of your negative family legacy you must go beyond expressing feelings to actually understanding how even your childhood disappointments and trauma have contributed to your life. I once heard Oprah Winfrey speak eloquently about the sexual abuse she suffered in childhood. She said, "But I can't regret anything I've experienced in my life because all of it made me who I am today." She was right. Today she is a courageous, warm, inspiring person admired by millions.

After facing our pasts and understanding how our experiences both hurt and enhance us, we come to the critical point of letting go, forgiving, so that we don't continue to drag the past forward to ruin our future. The type of therapy that I practice focuses on developing new images and tools for successful, happy love lives.

I will also expose you to new skills necessary for resolving life's inevitable challenges while sustaining a relationship. I include exercises in solving problems as a twosome. But to achieve positive results you must be inspired to develop more self-knowledge and emotional maturity. The rewards are not only a satisfying marriage but improved health, longer life, a higher level of productivity, and greater contribution to the community. Most of us would and could have lasting happy marriages by committing ourselves to the task wholeheartedly. In those exercises for twosomes, both partners need to make a commitment. To succeed, persistence is required. So please begin by programming this thought: I will persist until I succeed. Repeat this phrase out loud, and as we proceed, keep this thought in mind. This is usually the first technique I offer a couple in marital therapy.

Growth is an ongoing part of your life and is even more necessary in the dynamic ebb and flow of two people sharing their lives. To make inner change you must first understand yourself. One way of doing this is to look extensively at your family history, paying special attention to the details of emotional patterns. We learn how to be in love by watching our family members. What you believe controls what you think, which dictates how you feel, which then manifests as behavior. But this hierarchy can be short-circuited and changed at any point. The most effective personal change comes from altering the highest rung of our consciousness, understanding, and beliefs. As above so below.

The Twelve Steps from Alcoholics Anonymous offer a great way to gain and support self-understanding and emotional maturity. So we'll work with a special version of the Twelve Steps, modified for the healing of relationships. The Twelve Steps bring the elevating realm of spirituality to life in a practical and beautiful way. They encourage you to take responsibility for your circumstances and to see yourselves as the architects of your own life. This includes being willing to apologize and make amends when you have erred and hurt someone. The steps break down the walls of self-centeredness that keep love out. They serve as an antidote to the poison of narcissism that leads us to believe we are entitled to have it our way and that life should be lived only on our terms. The steps point toward a balanced and whole existence that champions service to others and the pursuit of a meaningful spiritual life. Service and spiritual pursuits lead you to the ability to have compassion and empathy for others. The Twelve Steps are the keys to our process of healing.

You must learn to share your feelings, ask for what you need, and to take care of yourself so your partner isn't overloaded. I teach some exercises that show how.

My course in *Love Lessons* is as follows:

➤ You will read the stories of each of our five couples and see the patterns of events and themes that occurred in their families. Then you'll read of the problems they are confronting in their marriages.

➤ Then I'll share excerpts from each of the couples' actual therapy sessions. In witnessing them in their healing work you will find ideas and inspiration to speed your own healing.

➤ Each chapter presents at least one of the Twelve Steps and explains how that step relates to the marriage under discussion. My explanation includes how you can make use of and interpret the step.

➤ There are exercises at the end of every chapter. They give you the opportunity to try out your new tools for working through problems—before you need them in life—and lead to deeper self-discovery. Practice means improvement in all kinds of learning; romantic partnerships are no different. Practicing the exercises will make all the difference for you and your loved ones.

Others have turned their circumstances and behavior around to create happy marriages. You can too.

➤ Daily loving attention to your partner will keep your love fresh and vibrant. In each chapter I've included a series of items I call "love-savers."

Love can teach you to value and care for yourself, which is essential to loving and caring for a mate. Begin by believing your lover is or has been in your life so you can grow and be a better human being. Here's something new to say to yourself: "As I leave behind my flaws and foibles, I am more capable of a pure and devoted love. This love allows me to touch the divine in myself and in my beloved."

♥ EXERCISES ♥

The exercises at the end of each chapter always begin with breathing and relaxation, so that you really shift gears from the outer world to your inner world. Too often we work backwards, trying to heal what is inside us by working on the outside.

1. Breathe as deeply as possible into your abdomen; imagine that you are filling a balloon in your stomach as you breathe in. Do this as slowly as possible. Gently repeat to yourself, "I am releasing and I'm letting go," as you shed the tension from your body.

2. Purchase a notebook to use for all of the written exercises offered. The first item to write is a list of all your good qualities. When you finish there should be at least fifteen qualities on the list. Now write a similar list of all of your mate's positive traits. Remember, at least fifteen items should appear.

3. Be certain that you praise yourself every day by reminding yourself of your fine points, and do the same for your partner. If you are single right now, write a list of the qualities you would like to have in an ideal mate.

4. Affirmation: I will persist until I succeed. I am a success. Repeat these affirmations over and over. You must believe that you can succeed at love, and this will help you imprint the idea of success on your subconscious.

The exercises build on one another, so keep your notebook handy. Continue to praise yourself and your mate daily. If you focus on the negatives and tear either yourself or your mate down that is exactly what you accomplish—tearing down, depleting yourself and your love. Building, boosting, being positive—over and over, return to these basic building blocks.

♥ | *The first "love saver" tip:*
Hug your partner at least once a day.

2 FROM GENERATION TO GENERATION

Rebecca settles into a high winged-back chair. In this elegantly appointed office, wearing her chic black suit, she appears to have it all. This slightly built, raven-haired woman is clearly in charge in her hushed suite of offices. "I've been considering a divorce," says Rebecca, a petite thirty-six-year-old who is one of the most highly paid attorneys in Chicago. "I've never been unhappier," she adds.

Above her head, on the wall behind her, Rebecca's magna cum laude and Phi Beta Kappa degrees from the Yale University School of Law speaks volumes. They are the same documents that helped Rebecca land a partnership with her prestigious law firm and also helped place her at the legal helm of one of the largest corporate mergers of the decade. She works for the pleasure and excitement of it all. Thanks to a substantial family trust, she could retire today and continue a life of creature comforts.

She has two homes. One is a spacious condominium with a view of the city and a staff of three; the other, an antique-filled cottage in the woods.

From her office chair Rebecca gestures toward a framed photo on her desk. "That's Frank, of course," she says, briskly indicating a tall, blonde man with a kind smile and bright blue eyes.

Then, as she points to a little boy perched on Frank's shoulders, Rebecca's voice softens appreciably. "And that's our Kevin. We call him Kevin-from-Heaven."

Frank, age thirty-nine, she explains, has the self-confidence that commands attention when they enter one of the many political and corporate social affairs connected with her job. She said he is not flirtatious, but that women are drawn to him because they find the contradiction between his rugged athletic appearance and his gentle and sensitive manner so arresting.

That quality in particular interested Rebecca when they met ten years ago. Her mother had been in the hospital dying of cancer and Frank was the grief counselor assigned to her family's case. At Rebecca's instigation, they married two months after the funeral.

But if her husband is so charming and her life picture-perfect, why is Rebecca so unhappy?

"Frank saves all of his charm for the hospital," she says. "By the time he gets home the real Frank begins to emerge. He's emotionally abusive and has a terrible temper. Just last week we were all sitting at the kitchen table, getting ready to go to the country, and he blew up, for no reason. He called me a bitch, right in front of Kevin. I don't think I can take it anymore."

She reaches for a tissue from a porcelain box. Her eyes are wet and her nose pinkish, but she isn't crying. "I have several allergies," she explains before continuing on the subject of her marriage. "For a long time I tried to be the perfect wife. When something failed, I thought, I'm not doing well enough. I have to be better. Then something in me just snapped. I realized that Frank wants me to make up for everything his mother didn't give him. I can't do it. No one can ever make up for that. So I became rigid. I said, 'This is it. I'm not going to try anymore.' I went from being what I'd always been to just the opposite."

During the preliminary interviews she said that she and Frank had volunteered to work with me because they were desperate. She shook her head. "I have to be honest with you. For the last few years we've spent fifty thousand dollars a year on therapy and marriage counseling. It was like putting a Band-Aid on a bleeding ulcer. Dr. Wade's chances of improving our relationship are less than . . ." She holds up the tip of a clear, buffed fingernail, "one tenth the size of this."

When I met Frank Kinkaid, he seemed as defeated as his wife. In fact, when I inquired about their sex life, he sadly smiled and asked, "What sex life?" After a pause, he added, "It's practically nonexistent. She doesn't like me to put my hands on her. She's one of the coldest, angriest women I know. She has only wanted to have sex when she's ovulating."

When I saw them together, a fuller picture of their relationship emerged. During the first part of our therapy session together, Rebecca refused to allow Frank to touch her. She was in pain and angered beyond words. She felt there was absolutely nothing he could do to be forgiven for the unhappiness he'd already caused her. Frank felt that he could not turn to her for comfort.

Our other four couples were also feeling stymied and close to giving up. I explained to all of them that the problems they were experiencing were a direct result of their family histories.

Though you were probably unaware of it, you chose your partner with exquisite care. You may think you fell in love with those eyes, or that figure, or that zest for life or sense of humor, or his or her great intelligence. But it was probably your partner's pain. The truth is that your inner pain could be a one-of-a-kind emotional key that fits precisely into your partner's emotional lock. That is why we often feel such powerful emotional magnetism at the start of our love relationships. As strangers, Frank and Rebecca could have found each other across a crowded room. Their emotional antennae would have led them right into one another's arms.

It was the same for you when you fell in love. On one level you took in that which was immediately apparent. On another, deep feelings and long forgotten memories were stirred. Each of you unknowingly sensed that the other person would be a good vehicle for taking you back in time, reopening the past, and taking on unfinished business.

Marriage is the perfect place for raising up buried issues. No other institution has a way of setting off such dynamics. How often I've heard couples say, "It was so different before we got married." When people go through a marriage ceremony, they don't just exchange vows, they also exchange scripts. In addition to the vows it's as if they unconsciously say, "Psst, read this. It's the part I'm going to need you to act out for me."

Over the years personalized family themes merge with our ancestral lines, and we unconsciously find lovers who are tailor-made for the parts. Unless there is some major intervention, some transforming process in our lives, the roles continue on and on.

The therapy I employ doesn't simplify life. After all, human beings don't just function physically. Nor do we just function intellectually or emotionally. We're not just brains or bodies or feelings. We are all this and more. We are the intangible spirit that elevates us to the level of humanness and makes us more than animals.

The stamp our ancestors left on us cannot be ignored. We are the products of many generations of familial patterns. Intergenerational patterns are like architectural drawings you never see, yet they form the basis for the building, which is, in essence, your relationship. One of the most valuable tools I use in therapy is an examination of the individuals' family histories. Living in ignorance of your generational history, is like buying a home without looking beyond its facade. Just as you can restore and renovate a building, you can restore and begin making informed choices about your relationships.

Family history fuels those unconscious feelings that give rise to our expectations of ourselves and our partners. The way we think and behave is a result of these patterns. The miscommunication, misinterpretation of a partner's motives, and the malcontent that mars a relationship come from old emotional models.

Simply understanding them is not enough. Once patterns are identified, you need other tools to change them. The tools are emotional, behavioral, intellectual, and spiritual. It is attention to the ongoing process of change that brings about the deep and lasting transformation.

When we followed up on the progress of our five couples one year later, we found that those who had continued in more traditional marriage counseling made modest gains. But the couples who combined support groups with the more traditional marriage counseling made tremendous gains. People tend to need ongoing support to continue a forward momentum in the healing of their relationships. Dialogue with others who are also healing can create an external system of checks and balances. Support groups offer participants vital emotional support that delivers the message: You're not alone, there's hope and help. Left to your own devices, and alone with your mate, you may fail to see how you contribute to the problems and fall back into the old scripts. So I do recommend group therapy for thoroughly working out problems. I have found great success with taking an intergenerational approach to relationship issues, along with an amalgam of cognitive, emotional, and communication techniques, as well as an innovative application of the Twelve Step programs. Simple? Not quite. Effective? Yes!

The Twelve Steps originated with Alcoholics Anonymous. But I always say they are rather like aspirin, which was originally prescribed for easing physical pain. Later, aspirin was found to have far wider benefits, including preventing strokes and heart attacks. The Twelve Steps, as millions of non-drinking adherents have discovered, can enable any of us to move on with our lives after we've reached a general awareness of certain problems, even when they don't include addictive behavior.

For those of you familiar with the Twelve Steps, this is an opportunity for you to see them in a new light. If the steps are new to you I am delighted to introduce them as adapted for use with couples.

THE TWELVE STEPS TO HEALTHY RELATIONSHIPS

1. We admitted we were powerless over our relationships—that our lives had become unmanageable.

2. We came to believe that a power greater than ourselves could restore us to sanity.

3. We made a decision to turn our will and our relationships over to the care of God, as we understand God.

4. We made a fearless and searching moral inventory of ourselves.

5. We admitted to God, to ourselves, and to our partners the exact nature of our wrongs.

6. We are entirely ready to have God remove all our defects of character.

7. We humbly asked God to remove our shortcomings.

8. We made a list of all persons we had harmed, our mates in particular, and became willing to make amends to them all.

9. We made direct amends to such people wherever possible, except when to do so would injure them or others.

10. We continued to take personal inventory, and when we were wrong promptly admitted it.

11. We sought through prayer and meditation to improve our conscious contact with God as we understand God, praying only for knowledge of God's will for us and the power to carry that out.

12. Having had a spiritual awakening as a result of these steps, we tried to carry this message to others and to practice these principles in all our affairs.

As you can see, the Twelve Steps encourage followers to concentrate on taking a personal examination, to stop pointing fingers outward, and to "let go," i.e., stop trying to control the behavior of loved ones. They also enable us to move on from the "I want it to work" to the "I can make a difference" stage.

There is an emphasis on spirituality in the Twelve Steps that some of you may object to. But while I am not advocating religion per se, I am encouraging you to discover your own way of addressing your spiritual needs. In your case spiritual could mean communing with Mother Nature or learning to trust your intuition; those are as valid as the choice of an established religion. Whatever your choice of spiritual practice, it can help you develop and strengthen yourself. Even scientific research confirms the importance of integrating spirituality in our lives. A twenty-year study at Harvard University concluded that treatment programs that accepted the premise of the existence of a higher power had a much lower rate of relapse in addiction treatment than those that did not encourage spirituality. The researchers concluded that the difference between the successful and the unsuccessful programs was attributable to the "mysterious component" of some programs that could best be described as spiritual.

I've witnessed that couples with the deepest healing also had a spiritual life together. And finally, in another study at the University of Colorado, hundreds of couples were asked to rate the levels of satisfaction in their unions after twenty years of marriage. Those who responded that their marriages were satisfactory had certain factors in common, including a shared spiritual life.

MAKING CHANGES

STEP **1** ♥ **We admitted we were powerless over our relationships—that our lives had become unmanageable.**

This step had special significance for Frank and Rebecca, who had spent tens of thousands of dollars on therapy, to no avail. They certainly knew what the problems between them were, and through the therapeutic experience they also knew how they felt. What was missing? How to change. To change they first had to stop struggling. This first of the transforming Twelve Steps paves the way for the change. This means, you feel you've done the best you can with your relationships and they are not working the way you want them to, that it's time to get help. Please remember, it's unrealistic to expect yourself to be an expert on how to make relationships work, since none of us gets any real preparation. What we get instead is a family legacy of patterns that don't work.

For now, you're surrendering; that's really what step one is. You stop struggling on your own, take your attention off external distractions, and return to a place where you focus on yourself. This is your chance to start over. You have an opportunity to make real change.

When you are overly focused on someone else you are robbed of full command of your creative energies. It's like a novice sculptor whacking away at a beautiful piece of alabaster without pausing long enough to perceive what shape is suggested by the stone itself or by his consciousness, his muse. You usually don't need to look far to find the voice of wisdom; it is within you and you need it in the transformation process. How do you tap into your inner wisdom? Our first exercise provides a tool.

Sit quietly and repeat to yourself, three times, each one of the Twelve Steps. As you repeat the words allow yourself to feel a deeper sense of surrender. We will offer an explanation of each step at the end of each chapter.

♥ EXERCISES ♥

---

1. Let's turn our energies to creating an inner garden. Like any gardener hoping for a great harvest, we must prepare our "mental" soil.

   ➤ Sit comfortably anywhere you can be alone. Locking yourself in a bedroom, office, or bathroom is fine.

   ➤ Begin breathing, as slowly as you possibly can, deeply into the abdomen.

   ➤ Mentally, instruct your muscles to let go. It's mind over matter; be very gentle with yourself.

➤ As your body begins to relax, imagine a strong bright beam of sunlight pouring down on your head. Its warmth helps to relax your muscles. See the sunlight washing down, around and through each part of your body, starting with your head and working down to your toes.

➤ If your mind drifts to some specific thought, bring it back to the light, letting the thought pass. We are often not trained to focus in this way, so gently keep bringing your attention back to the light so that your mind can become clear and quiet.

➤ Do this for two to five minutes.

2. Centering has brought the sunlight together with fresh soil. Now it's time to plant seeds of thought. Keep in mind that what you think controls how you feel. The way you feel controls what you do.

This inner gardening exercise is designed to:

—Help you relax. You can't surrender unless you relax. Tension can interfere with intimacy.

—Clear your mind to make room for new thoughts, leading to healthier interactions.

—Reenergize you. Energy is necessary for growth.

—Change the way you think about yourself and your relationship.

➤ Program your subconscious by repeating the following to yourself, ten times—as often as possible, especially just before sleep: "Every day, in every way, I appreciate and approve of myself, more and more. The more I give love to myself, the more love I have to give." Use the power of repetition to imprint deeply on your subconscious mind.

(One tip: Write this affirmation in your appointment book or tape it to your bathroom mirror or closet door as a reminder.)

➤ Imagine self-appreciation in every cell of your body. Work to feel this as deeply as possible by imagining you're drawing this approval into your heart.

➤ Picture your life, especially your relationships, as they would look if you really loved and approved of yourself. Notice that the life in the picture is happier because you're loving yourself. What actions are you taking in the picture? Strive to do this in your daily life by writing down the actions you imagine.

Does focusing on yourself seem an odd way to start planting the seeds for a healthy relationship? Well, if you can't appreciate and approve of yourself, how can you truly give that to your partner? We simply can't give what we don't have. Furthermore, our negative feelings for ourselves actually lead us to expect negative feelings and behavior toward us from others and to interpret others' behavior toward us as negative no matter what. We can rig any relationship so that in time we receive treatment that we secretly think we deserve.

So start here by creating a healthier sense of self. Your relationships are only as healthy and as calm as you are, and as loving as you are to yourself.

♥ *Our second "love saver" tip:*
Each day, say, "I love you" to yourself and then to your partner.

3

CHANGING OLD
WAYS INTO NEW

Sometimes a person's intergenerational history is as difficult to trace as a trail of salt in the snow, especially in contemporary American culture, where family histories are seldom recorded. People are fortunate if they have a loquacious elder to inform them about their roots. They are even lucky if they have a relative who punitively blurts out the family secrets in a fit of anger.

Since most people are left in the dark, I tell clients that they should begin to collect whatever details are available, adding to their own childhood memories. I urge you to do the same. But even if your parents or relatives prove to be uncooperative about discussing family history, you can move on and heal without it by making logical assumptions and educated guesses based on your own beliefs and behaviors. Lost history in and of itself is a signal that a family was plagued with traumas and chaos. Careful examination of family history is critical. We can't change until we examine and understand what we are changing. The past that shaped us emotionally and psychologically gives rise to behaviors and beliefs we act out. Learning better ways to function is much easier when we can see the entire picture.

At the end of this chapter we'll show you how to begin recording the information you do gather and how to compile an

18

emotional family tree. As you trace along the faint trails you'll begin to feel the love relationships you've had thus far were almost inevitable.

Rebecca Kinkaid's maternal roots date back to the landing of the Mayflower, so familial pride served to keep stories about her illustrious ancestors alive in the family. Less is known about her paternal history, in part because they were German immigrants and left much of the family behind once they set sail for America.

Family Themes: There are two concurrent themes in both Rebecca and Frank's families. The women unconsciously believe that men will let them down. The men believe women do not respect them and will humiliate them.

For reference purposes we have listed the family members. Continue to refer to this chart as needed.

Rebecca's family

Maternal grandparents: ELIZABETH
WILLIAM

Paternal grandparents: SAMUEL
MARTHE

Rebecca's mother: ALICE
father: VICTOR

Frank's family

Frank's mother: ELLEN

Frank's father: DOUGLAS

I'll begin Rebecca's history with her grandparents. Here we see recurring circumstances such as pregnancies that were used as leverage in relationships. There are also adulterous liaisons and fierce battles over money. This isn't unusual, given that generational patterns run throughout all families; e.g., issues such as incest, public scandal, etc. Be aware, though, that the patterns are not always negative. The positive side of Rebecca's family story includes achievement at Ivy League universities, intellectual superiority, and career successes. With that said, let's look at Rebecca's maternal grandparents.

ELIZABETH: a beautiful and determined former office clerk, born in 1892 in a Chicago slum
WILLIAM: a patent attorney, born in 1890 to a family of old wealth in a Chicago suburb

Elizabeth was married and divorced at an early age. Her first husband had the ancestral credentials and old money Elizabeth was seeking to better her life, but he proved to be a drunk. After leaving him, Elizabeth worked as a clerk in a law office, where she met and fell in love with William, a young and single patent attorney with familial roots dating back to the Mayflower. They began a clandestine affair.

Before long, Elizabeth announced she was pregnant. William's mother resisted the union, calling Elizabeth a gold digger. But there was little time to argue. William had to choose between a scandal or a wife. The wedding took place four months into the pregnancy.

Although Elizabeth had the financial security she'd hoped for, it was not a happy marriage. The couple got along so poorly when their baby girl was born, they couldn't even agree on what to call her. In fact, she went by the name of "Little One" for the first eight years of her life, and was only given a proper name when school administrators insisted upon it. This child would grow up to be Rebecca's mother. She was named Alice.

Neither Alice, born in 1920 in Chicago, or the subsequent birth of her siblings would solidify Elizabeth and William's marriage. Their unhappy union ended many years later, when William suffered a heart attack and died in his mistress's bed.

Rebecca's mother had the wherewithal to pick up and travel to Wellesley College during the height of the country's depression. After graduation, thanks to a string of academic achievements, she landed some substantial jobs in New Haven, Connecticut. For the next several years she remained involved in New Haven's political scene and initiated some of the city's most vital social legislation.

It was in New Haven that she met Rebecca's father, Victor. His parents were:

SAMUEL: born in 1870; arrived in America in the late 1880s from Germany
MARTHE: born in 1870; traveled to America with Samuel, as his wife

Rebecca's paternal grandfather, Samuel, a German immigrant, lived virtually two different lives; his later years bore almost no resemblance to his early life. After arriving in Connecticut he spent the next decade struggling in poverty. Determined to succeed in his new land, Samuel used every spare penny—sometimes depriving his growing family of essentials, such as properly fitting shoes—to invest in real estate. One of those children, who would be Rebecca's father, would always carry a reminder of the family's early hardships: painful bunions and calluses. He was Samuel and Marthe's oldest child, Victor, who was born in 1889 in New Haven. The first of four children, he was believed to be highly intelligent from infancy.

Samuel wasn't around much to father Victor or any of his children. He was busy funding and juggling increasingly large real estate investments. His gambling paid off, though; he became a wealthy man. Unfortunately, his wife, Marthe, did not survive to enjoy the rewards of his efforts. She died giving birth to their fourth child.

After Marthe's death Samuel kept the three youngest children, all girls, with him, while he sent Rebecca's father to live with his own parents a few blocks away. The reasons for this are not known, but perhaps as the oldest child, Victor was deemed most useful to the grandparents. But while Rebecca's grandfather, his daughters, and his new wife lived a lavish life only a few blocks away, Victor and his grandparents struggled to make ends meet. Samuel proved to be harsh and rigid in his behavior toward his son.

Blind though he may have been to Victor's needs, Samuel had too much business savvy to ignore the boy's obvious genius. From an early age, Victor was first in every class. Samuel agreed to send

Victor to Yale, where the young man earned a Phi Beta Kappa key and graduated magna cum laude from the school of law.

Victor earned much success in the field of international law and lived abroad for many years. When he returned to his hometown, in Connecticut, he was introduced to Alice, Rebecca's mother, who was busy working away in the New Haven city council. They fell in love. But she worried that her blue-blooded family would never approve of Victor. Not only was he the son of immigrants, but he had, by now, been married and divorced. (Her siblings seemed to have conveniently forgotten that the family matriarch, Elizabeth, had also been through a divorce before marrying their father.) Alice realized her family would never accept Victor, but she wasn't willing to give him up. She knew he was brilliant and capable and her heart went out to him. His difficult past made him seem like a wounded bird.

When Alice took Victor home to announce wedding plans, her family didn't surprise her. They were wary of him. They said that at thirty-one years her senior, he was far too old for her. They blanched at his background and warned Alice he was only interested in her inheritance. They convinced her to sign a secret will that would disinherit him. But even with that concession, one brother still refused to attend the wedding.

Alice and Victor had a tempestuous union, just as her parents had had. They relocated to the Chicago suburbs at the start of their marriage so Alice could be close to her family. She had to quit her job to make the move but received many attractive offers in Chicago. The problem then was that she could not accept the offers because Victor refused to let her work outside the home. Although he spent days and sometimes weeks at a time traveling for business, he wanted her home and believed that it was the appropriate choice for the wife of a prominent attorney.

When Rebecca's mother asked to join Victor on business trips he refused. At first he claimed it was due to the high cost of travel accommodations. Then he argued that it would be a waste of money for her to fly first class with him. He insisted he had to go first class or risk embarrassing the rich and powerful clients he worked for, and that she couldn't fly tourist because one of his business associates might recognize her there.

Their arguments often centered around money. By then Victor was a millionaire, but he hated spending. He waited until months after the wedding to give her a wedding ring. He had been determined to locate the gold band that had been removed from his mother's hand. He claimed his reasons for choosing his mother's rather than a new ring were purely sentimental. Alice didn't quite believe him. After all, this was the same man who complained if Alice bought an expensive cut of meat or if she had her hair done at a beauty parlor.

Then there was this other, more persistent problem. Try as they might, Alice could not get pregnant. Alone in the house, missing her career, pining for children, she felt desperate. She turned to a fertility specialist for help and he prescribed the drug DES. They waited for signs of pregnancy. Then Alice made a shocking discovery. She was unpacking Victor's suitcase one day and found two identical pendants for women. One pendant had a card with her name on it; the other was apparently for another woman.

When she confronted Victor with the evidence he admitted his affair. Alice left him and returned to her family home. Victor called her New Year's Eve, begging Alice to see him and to spend one more night with him. She succumbed and the morning after, they said adieu. A month later, however, Alice discovered she was finally pregnant.

Overjoyed, Victor promised Alice that if she would just come back to him, he'd be faithful this time. So the two began another life together. That September, one of the two most important characters in this drama was born:

REBECCA: born in September 1955 in Chicago, the oldest of four children

Alice and Victor would have three more children, all girls. Victor seemed so happy about their growing family that after the birth of their second child he agreed to wear a wedding ring. In fact, his gift to Alice for Christmas 1957 was a wedding band— for himself. At last, it must have seemed to Alice, they were finally married.

By the early eighties, Alice was dying of an inoperable cancer. Ironically, one of the doctors on the staff at the hospital where Alice was admitted was Victor's first wife. The doctor, in fact, dropped in to pay her respects to Alice. Alice thanked her for coming, then introduced the doctor to a friend, Ruth, who was visiting her. Ruth had lived across the street from them for twenty-five years, Alice explained to her husband's ex-wife. Then Alice smiled from her bed and added, "Doctor, Ruth is my best friend, and she has something in common with you and me. She has been in love with Victor for twenty-five years."

Three weeks after Alice's death, Ruth moved in with Victor. Rebecca discovered her new stepmother had filed for divorce the week after doctors announced Alice was dying. That is also when she realized her father had been having an affair with Ruth for decades. It pained her especially that Alice had died with this knowledge. Ruth and Victor married less than a year later. It still infuriates Rebecca to know that Victor is married and extremely generous with their former neighbor, now his wife, as if he had, like his father, divided his life in two.

♥

Did you notice the other generational patterns in this family? For one, over and over again, there is a family member who appears to have a "golden touch." This was first displayed by the immigrant, Grandfather Samuel, then Victor himself, and now Rebecca. It's obviously far more than a case of good luck. There's a strain of great intelligence that runs through the family.

There was certainly no lack of chutzpah on the maternal side either. First, there was Rebecca's grandmother, Elizabeth, who was determined not to die poor. And next her daughter, Alice, who barely missed being born out of wedlock and into disgrace. She must have grown up with some sense that a marriage between her parents might never have happened had it not been for her. Inevitably there is anger and guilt connected to a birth that creates so much unhappiness. Her childhood couldn't have been very happy. What is there to say about parents who were so locked in conflict that for eight years they couldn't agree on a name for their firstborn? None of this held her back, though. When it came to her career Alice was a woman decades ahead of her time. Armed with her belongings and her mother's sense of determination, she cut a swathe through New Haven's local and established politics. Bravo, Alice.

It's not surprising she felt a certain kinship with Victor, the boy who'd been treated like an orphan (for so had she, in a way), but who had risen to the top, careerwise. Notice that her family accused Victor of "gold digging," just as her mother had been.

Also, Alice learned that the man she'd chosen would be unfaithful in their marriage, just as her father had been in his.

As for Victor, he seemed to have never recovered from the loss of his mother nor his father's emotional abandonment. Women passed in and out of his life as he searched for a replacement for his mother. Perhaps he felt at peace, having followed so very closely in his father's footsteps by remarrying and heaping luxuries on his second wife, just as his father had.

Finally, Rebecca's conception brought them back together, just as her own mother's birth had provided the reason for her parents to marry.

REBECCA'S CHILDHOOD AND LIFE BEFORE MARRIAGE

Rebecca remembers her mother as being patient and fun loving, a parent who devoted her life to her four daughters. "I took her for granted," said Rebecca. But not so with her father. She would race to the door when Victor returned from one of his frequent business trips. "He'd walk in the door calling, 'Where are my girls,'" said Rebecca. "He really loved his daughters, and we adored him."

The four sisters competed heavily for his attention, but it was Rebecca who figured out ways to capture his heart. Early mornings she'd rise to make his coffee, grab the newspaper from the doorway, and slip into her parents' room to greet them. In the evenings she stirred her father's martinis. It afforded an opportunity for this oldest child to talk to the man she worshiped.

Among other stories, Victor told his daughter about his first love, a woman he'd known in college, who was "the most brilliant woman he'd ever known." She sat listening quietly, realizing that above all, for her father, intellectual accomplishment in a woman was of utmost importance. She asked him more about his first wife, the physician, and why they'd divorced. "He said it was because she didn't want to have children," Rebecca recalled. Later she would learn, while rifling through his files, that his first wife had divorced him on the grounds of adultery, but his message about not having children did not escape Rebecca and would eventually impact her adult life.

Victor also told Rebecca about his impoverished childhood. In fact, stories of his past and his constant reminders that they were not "rich like the girls at my school, was drummed into me," said Rebecca. She was warned by her parents that they had to spend modestly because everything might come to an end and they'd be indigent. It made for a confusing message in the face of chauffeured limousine rides, a year of French schooling in Switzerland, presentation in the debutante ball, and swelling trust funds for each of the children.

Money continued to be the most rancorous subject between her parents. "When we were little we kids used to tiptoe out and listen to them fight," said Rebecca. "We were always afraid that my father was so old that he'd have a heart attack and die while they argued. That fear always haunted us. Most of my friends didn't have fathers as old as mine. He was in his sixties when I was born. Mommy usually ended up being more concerned about his blood pressure and went along with what he wanted."

The one issue Rebecca watched her mother refuse to give in on entirely was work. Since Victor didn't "allow" her to work for money, she volunteered at an antipoverty program on the south side of Chicago. "Sometimes I got the feeling that she was sneaking out to these volunteer positions," said Rebecca. "Daddy wanted her to be home with us."

Sneaking might have been the easier choice; Victor wasn't the kind of man you wanted to cross. "He was known for his terrible temper," said Rebecca. "In restaurants, if he didn't get the check soon enough, he'd blow up and embarrass us."

Members of the family learned early on that life would go smoother if they gave Victor what he wanted. That included educational success for his daughters. Following in Victor's footsteps, the young women studied the classics as undergraduates at Yale, and Rebecca's younger sisters eventually earned Ph.D.s and went into academic and artistic fields. But Rebecca outshone them all. After receiving her undergraduate degree, with significant honors, law school beckoned. She was offered a prestigious fellowship to study overseas, but she turned it down. She still worried about her father's health and advancing years.

Rebecca chose corporate law and climbed high in her field. After her mother's death and Victor's subsequent remarriage, the daughters, including Rebecca, tried without success to accept their new stepmother, Ruth.

"She's a stupid woman," said Rebecca, anger flashing through her eyes. "My sisters and my parents and I used to sit around and talk about linguistics and history. But this is the kind of woman whose greatest disappointment was when her favorite department store went out of business."

"She also spent weeks wondering why the Pope came to the States and visited migrant workers when there were any number of dignitaries he could meet. I'd say the family conversations shifted down several grades after my mother died."

Most of all, Rebecca resented her father's generosity toward Ruth. "It was very unfair, the way he treated my mother. She wouldn't have even dared to go to a hairdresser. He would have accused her of wasting money. He gives Ruth anything she wants. And she's so castrating. I once asked Daddy why he didn't take the interest from my trust fund and give it to my sisters. I don't need the money, but they're academics, they could use it. Daddy said, 'Please, I don't want to even talk about it. It makes Ruth so jealous.'"

The one benefit Ruth has provided for her stepdaughters is a new source of amusement. "When she's not around we play a game imagining what means we would use to murder her," said Rebecca, this time laughing girlishly. "We keep trying to come up with untraceable additives to put in her food."

In the meantime, shortly after her mother's death and just before Ruth moved in with Victor, Rebecca had started a relationship with Frank, the seemingly gentle and well read grief counselor who had comforted her family during Alice's hospitalization.

On a physical and intellectual level, her attraction to him is quite understandable. He's not only tall, strong, and charming, but intellectually gifted as well. But there were the less obvious factors for this young woman with a large trust fund, and all the proper WASP credentials. Let's take a look at his family history and find out what those factors were.

FRANK'S BACKGROUND

The information on Frank Kinkaid's family history is limited. So we have to skip his grandparents and look at his parents' generation. Even then we can only offer scanty details about them.

Frank's mother is Ellen, the daughter of a Methodist minister, born in 1929 in a small town in Missouri. We do know that Ellen had two brothers, both of whom worked their way through Harvard University.

Ellen graduated from a small women's college. The little we do know of her points to a certain disdain for a clergyman's meager salary and simple life. She seemed determined not to have to rely on a man for money, and to earn a living for herself, quite a goal for a woman in those times.

But she was traditional in one sense. She did want to get married. And of all the men she met when she began her career as an administrator at a department store in Chicago, only one young sailor seemed to share her desire for the good life. His name was Douglas: born in 1928 in Chicago, where his parents ran a small restaurant. Douglas had enlisted in the Navy before he could complete his studies at the University of Chicago. When he was back in Chicago on leave he dressed in elegant suits and wore silk ties. They'd met at a party while he was searching for work, hoping to quit the Navy for good.

Shortly after Ellen and Douglas's wedding, however, he reenlisted. His plans to find high-paying work in civilian life had met with failure. Ellen remained in Chicago, where she juggled the responsibilities of her job, and soon their two sons. Frank, born in October 1953, was their youngest.

Even with two children, and her husband stationed thousands of miles away, Ellen continued an upward spiral in her career. You can imagine the magnitude of her accomplishments when you picture the conservative world of the fifties. On the other hand, although Douglas tried various civilian jobs, he had little success. He continued to reenlist, but he developed alcoholism and was debilitated by it. This made it difficult for him to become an officer.

Douglas had the violent temper typical of many alcoholics. When Frank's parents were together they argued frequently, often over money and his inability to earn a lot of it. The arguments once got so fierce, Frank recalls that Douglas threatened his mother with a knife. One of their worst arguments concerned the man Ellen worked for. Douglas accused her of having an affair with him. There is some reason to believe this may have been the case.

Ellen eventually quit her job to remain home with their young sons, but a few years later, when she realized Douglas would never able to find a job that could support her in the style she'd hoped for, she went back to school, earned two master's degrees, and began teaching English in a private college. Although she would never earn a large income, she enjoyed the security and the opportunity to be surrounded by people of her educational level. The rancor in her marriage continued, and in the late sixties Douglas filed for divorce. Frank was a teenager by now, left alone with his mother in their small home in the suburbs. His older brother had joined the Navy.

The house Frank shared with his mother was a sad testimony to all the dreams and hopes Ellen had had when she married. She and Frank ran out of money before it was completed. Although it was habitable, the basement remained unfinished and the two bedrooms were separated by a flimsy, makeshift wall.

Douglas remarried and settled in the South, where he was finally promoted to officer. He would not have long to enjoy it though. He was quietly discharged after it was learned that he'd padded his expense accounts. His illness ran its course and he died of a heart attack before Frank graduated from Harvard. At the funeral, when Frank was handed the folded stars and stripes that had been draped over his father's coffin, it drove home the disappointment of the marriage he'd witnessed between his mother and father.

FRANK'S CHILDHOOD AND SINGLE LIFE

"I remember at five or six years old getting the sense that it was unusual that my mother worked," said Frank, "but I was proud of her. It was the early sixties and she was pulling down twenty and thirty thousand dollars a year. I can remember when she came home evenings. She wore high heels, and they made a certain sound against the floor, the sound of a woman who knows how to walk in them. She was blonde, pretty, and I want to say cold, but that's an adult Frank talking. I remember more about what I was supposed to be feeling than what I actually felt. She certainly wasn't warm. There was very little physical affection."

He was about ten when he realized that his dad was an intelligent and well-manicured drunk. "I was a little scared of him," Frank said, "but after he pulled that knife on my mother, about a week later I had an argument with a kid and threatened him with a knife. I suppose I'd made up my mind who I was going to be like."

In his early teens, Frank said, "I began noticing that a lot of my friends had fathers in the military who were younger than my dad, but they had higher ranking positions." Despite some disappointment in him, Frank idolized his father. When Douglas was home he took his son to baseball games, car races, and constructed plastic models of ships. Their time together was limited, but it was a relationship Frank treasured.

"When I started prep school he took me to his favorite men's store and introduced me to his tailor. . . . I had a sense that my parents were classier, more cosmopolitan than most of the other service people, who seemed more homespun. That idea also might have come from my mother, who had a way of making snide remarks about other families."

The sine qua non in their household was to earn good grades. Frank's mother encouraged him in school but seemed to take little interest in him otherwise. He felt that she didn't respect him. He remembered being at a store downhill from their home in the suburbs, and as he stood around "shooting the bull" with some older boys, he heard his mother screaming his name. "She could have easily walked down the hill to get me, but she just kept yelling for me. The guys started teasing, saying, 'Frank, your mommy wants you.' That wouldn't stand out in my mind except for the fact that it was typical of the way she treated me."

In that same vein, Frank said he joined a local church during his teens, and was up front one Sunday morning with his youth group when he heard his mother's voice at the back of the church. Apparently someone had casually asked her if she knew a certain person, an acquaintance from the neighborhood. Mention of this woman made Ellen furious. That's when Frank heard his mother saying quite loudly, "Of course I know who she is. That bitch stole my husband."

Frank said of the incident, "I'd say she was not being very respectful of my feelings." For these reasons, as well as similar incidents, he said that when his parents divorced, he blamed his mother. "I tended to excuse my dad's behavior, saying that she drove him to it."

With his older brother away at school, fourteen-year-old Frank was alone with his mother, their rooms separated only by thin walls. He fell asleep many nights listening to his mother sob. But that's not what he most remembers about those days.

"She used to get dressed and undressed in her room, with the door open," Frank said. "I'd see her standing there nude. I was not turned on. She'd been abandoned by my father and it was an aggressive and hostile act. I was so angry with her for parading around naked, for having a house built where there was no privacy."

His fury at his mother never seemed to leave him. After Ellen retired she moved to London for a while. Frank went to visit her, but after a few days he lied and said he had to leave early. "My mother and I had lunch, I said goodbye and that I was headed for the airport," said Frank. "Later, walking past Harrods, I turned the corner and saw her again. She didn't see me and I kept walking. There we were in a foreign country, surrounded by strangers, but I had no desire to talk to her. I just passed her by."

After graduation from college, Frank went to officers training school, and then joined the Air Force, ending a year-long affair with a woman seventeen years his senior. "She was interested in me, gave me everything my parents had not," he said. During his four years in the military he began a series of affairs. "There must have been at least fifty different women," he said, "not counting the bar girls." He said he "objectified" these women. "It was a way of acting out my hostility toward my mother. My main idea was to get drunk and get laid. I had no interest in talking to women as people."

Frank held a series of jobs, from banking executive to director of a boys' school, before he became a grief counselor. When he met Rebecca's family, he was particularly moved by the closeness they demonstrated when Alice was dying.

He and Rebecca began dating three days after the funeral. After their engagement, Rebecca and her family insisted he sign a prenuptial agreement. "I hated it. But I loved her then and I do now," he said. "The question of whether or not we will continue in this marriage is all on her side."

♥

So what are we to make of Frank and Rebecca, and how do we—with all we know about them—define the aspects of their beings that bind them together? Love, of course, is one answer, but there is more. Let's begin by examining the hidden emotional connections.

When people begin families they generally seek—whether consciously or unconsciously—the familiar. Remember, the root word is family. Rebecca and Frank certainly followed this path. They were from families where the fathers were known for their bad tempers, and disputes over money and infidelity were key themes. As for Rebecca and Frank's mothers, they were professional dynamos at a time when career achievement for women was considered quite unusual.

Frank and Rebecca had both attended the finest Ivy League

institutions. That alone created an intellectual fit between these two Mid-Westerners.

It also appears that Frank, thanks to his mother's background, wasn't in the least intimidated by Rebecca's professional success. Rebecca, who'd seen her mother forced out of paying jobs and relegated to sneaking to volunteer positions, couldn't have tolerated a man who was anything but encouraging toward her career.

Then there was, dare I say it, the money. Let's face it, Frank must have been fascinated by Rebecca's wealth. Is that really so terrible? After all, Frank is the same man whose childhood home had been left incomplete due to a lack of funds. Who, better than he, could appreciate the security of a substantial trust fund?

This is not a criticism but a much needed tilting of the gender scales. Ask yourself, is a woman looked down upon for marrying a man of wealth? On the contrary, she is generally admired, especially if she is involved in some nurturing social pursuit, such as the one Frank chose of counseling grieving families.

What's more, Frank got another bonus when he married Rebecca. In one fell swoop he could replicate his mother with a high-achieving and, according to him, "cold" Rebecca, while at the same time gain an admirable father-in-law to replace his disappointing, addicted father.

As for Rebecca, not only did Frank have the intellectual skills she prizes, but more importantly, he happened to be in the right place at the right time—her mother's bedside. As someone who offered solace and a sense of peace, he was a wonderful emotional replacement for Rebecca's mother and a distraction from her father, who was already looking elsewhere for love.

All of this is fascinating, but I suggest that what attracted Frank and Rebecca was a combination of all those events and more, all adding up to forces generations old. The emotional losses experienced by their grandparents and parents didn't simply vanish because they fell in love. Despite what folks with "stiff upper lips" may advise, emotional deprivation is not something that you can simply put behind you. Left untreated, these hurts and losses are passed on down the line, like marathon runners handing over flaming batons.

On Rebecca's side, those forces were as human as Grand-

mother Elizabeth's desperation, which caused her to risk humiliation to be the bride of a rich man who could not love her. They
were forces as old as the first breath that the almost illegitimate,
long unnamed Alice drew in the rancor of her family life. As old
and as grief-filled as Alice must have felt when she realized she'd
started life with a father who was unfaithful and was ending it
with a husband who was no different. Victor also contributed the
pain of his childhood, the loss of a mother and the abandonment
of a father.

The lack of historical detail in Frank's family can only lead
us to assume that the past his parents buried deserved a funeral.
We do know that statistically at least one of Frank's grandfathers
was probably an alcoholic. As for his maternal side, research has
shown the spouses of alcoholics, like Frank's mother, frequently
come from alcoholic homes. We can also surmise that Douglas
inherited the disease from one of his parents. The loss of Ellen's,
as well as Douglas's, family history is itself typical of alcoholic
families, where there is too much chaos to keep track of family
stories or records and too much bitterness to want to remember.

We know little about Frank's mother's childhood. What we
do know about her is that even as a grown woman she was still so
angry that she played naughty girl to the end, cursing in church,
engaging, perhaps, in extramarital affairs. Finally, alone in a
house that symbolized her failed dreams, she violated sexual
boundaries with her pubescent son, intensifying his fury toward
her and all women.

Today, Frank is introspective enough to understand just which
parent he modeled himself after: his rageful, underachieving father. All children choose a parent, and once the choice is made,
whether consciously or unconsciously, stepping out of that role
requires more than even the best of intentions.

So when Frank packed up and went off to college, he took
more than his belongings with him. Much like his father did so
many years before, Frank hid his rage behind his arresting manner, with sincere and comforting words. His parents had passed
on an ugly legacy, but it was Frank's, and struggle with it he has,
in the guise of a marriage.

Frank and Rebecca fell in love and began to sense a certain indefinable something that made being together seem just right. But later, as the marriage began and they opened their mouths and spoke, much to their dismay, they let loose harsh rebukes drawn from hidden wells. Ten years into the marriage, listen as Frank speaks and ask yourself whether some of these same battles might have been waged in his household between his mother and father . . . or even more intriguingly, if Frank, as a boy, had been able to step into his father's shoes, whether he might have had some of these same battles with his mother.

FRANK TALKS ABOUT HIS MARRIAGE

"I don't sit around premeditating how I'm going to get Rebecca. She's every bit as violent as I am. The difference is that I'm much bigger and have the ability to physically intimidate her. That time I raised a chair over her head when we were arguing, I wanted to demonstrate how powerful my feelings were. Once I kicked her hand, but what she'd said was enormously provoking. She dismisses me as the person who can't afford to buy anything.

"A couple of weeks ago I kicked a box that was on the floor, but then I just left. That part of myself scares me. It happens out of the blue. There we are, cruising along pretty well, having fun with Kevin. Then all of a sudden something comes up and Rebecca's right there, pressing the best buttons she can press, screaming, 'You're not a provider, you're a wimp.'

"There were cutbacks last year at the hospital, and now I'm only a part-timer. I work on the weekends. I didn't ask for less work, but I'm forced to accept it. She knows I feel vulnerable about how little I make. I'll never be as hard a worker as she is. But who earns as much as she does? She makes six hundred thousand dollars a year. Our expenses are eighteen thousand dollars a month. I have to go to her for my allowance, and she's always throwing the financial inequalities in my face. When she's angry, she tells me to get out of the house, that it's hers.

"You know, she could have married any number of investment bankers or lawyers who make twice as much as she does. For some reason she chose me. Now she's angry with me for not being that way.

"I feel ashamed of not being a better provider. I feel emasculated. The man in our society is supposed to be the provider. I really don't like meanness and nastiness, especially when it's out of proportion. I don't mind if it's in the middle of a knockdown drag-out fight, but there's something about us. . . . We could be having a pleasant little dinner, and all of a sudden, out of nowhere, she tends to go cosmic on me. I'm either the greatest husband or the biggest sleazeball.

"Sometimes when I'm angry she acts like I'm going to kill her or beat her up. I wouldn't, not ever. I've pushed her, grabbed her, loomed over her, but if I could wave a wand I'd erase all those things. I don't want to be that person, but I find her hysteria emotionally provocative. I'm not trying to let myself off the hook. There's just something in Rebecca that almost says, 'Hit me.' If we were to add up the minutes when each of us was out of control, then she'd be the winner, hands-down.

"When my mother and father were arguing, my mother was afraid to stand up to him. But in Rebecca's family, nobody backs down from anything. Kevin has been around for these scenes and that makes it so much worse. I have this vivid memory of Kevin, crying, and Rebecca and I are screaming at each other. I don't know, maybe it was the time I made a mistake and let the guy clean the wrong rug, so we had to pay an extra hundred dollars, or when I got a parking spot that was closer to the apartment and it cost an extra sixty-five dollars a month. Whatever it was, we were arguing.

"I wasn't coming at her, but I admit, I pulled my fist back. Rebecca ran down to the lobby of our building in her nightgown. She called the police. I said to her later, 'I don't think you have any idea how embarrassing or painful it was that you called the cops.' I'm still angry with her for that. She was indulging in her own hysteria at Kevin's expense. I have a hard time accepting that she can't help herself. When she went through that door to the lobby that night, I wanted her back, inside. I felt embarrassed, like she was letting the world in on our secrets."

♥

Now that you've heard Frank, listen to Rebecca and ask yourself who she's really battling with.

REBECCA'S VIEWS OF THE MARRIAGE

"We've been married ten years now and most of it has been a struggle. What is it? Well, when I get home nights, after long days at the office, and he's just laying there on the couch, it disgusts me. He could go out and find full-time work if he wanted to and that infuriates me. So when I get home, I'll realize he hasn't done anything all day, hasn't watered the plants, hasn't even picked up the phone and ordered the groceries. I also realize I have some of my father's traits about money. I really yell at Frank about it.

"He doesn't spend money freely on himself but buys expensive things for Kevin and the household, things like TVs, VCRs, and services. There are three people on staff at our home, plus in the country a man watches the house and does the lawn. Frank likes to have things done for him. I'm angry at him and I'm angry at Ruth, my father's wife. They both came into the family at the same time and neither brought any material assets.

"What do I want from him? . . . I'd like him to get full-time work, to be a fully supportive member of this family. I'd like him to stop drinking and smoking dope and I don't want to be afraid of him. He threatens me, often. I just want him to stop hurting me. When I was made partner, the firm had a big dinner, and Frank came and told me that the night before, he'd kissed another woman, that he'd wanted to make love to her but that he hadn't. That really hurt, and why on the night of the dinner?

"My greatest disappointment in our marriage has nothing to do with him. When you're feeling angry sometimes you lose sight of your targets. My anger becomes diffused and I let go at him. A lot of it surrounds my problems with conceiving a baby. My mother took DES and it really messed me up. We decided to adopt, of course. I've tried implants, spent thousands of dollars. I was pregnant once but it was ectopic. It was terrible. I love Kevin. It was wonderful when we got him. But I want to give birth to a baby. I've been through a lot of physical pain. I really don't like Frank to touch me."

AND FRANK AGAIN . . .

"In Rebecca's family there's some kind of mystique surrounding her father. The guy is a genius. But they act like he can't boil water for himself. Rebecca feels she has to amuse him every second she's with him. She talks to him like she's a child. 'Daddy, I did this today' and 'Daddy, let me get that for you.' I've sometimes said, in more cutting moments, 'Don't you want to go to the bathroom with him and wipe him? That's the only way you'll feel you've done enough for him.'

"When we're all together, sometimes Victor will say something, and I swear, the guy is getting old. But his daughters treat it as if it's a pronouncement, something akin to the Berlin Wall opening. Since she reverts from the high-powered attorney to the little girl as soon as she enters his bedroom, this means I have to be a kid, too, because I'm married to her. It hurts me to watch her play kid, but the issue in our marriage is certainly feeling infantilized, belittled, unappreciated. I want her understanding and respect, her interest. I feel she dismisses my life."

♥

And so it seems, their problems had traveled down ancestral lines. Once again, fights over money, embarrassing scenes, fits of rage, and the issue of whether a union is truly a marriage without a birth have returned to haunt them. There is also a repeat of the troubling pattern in which the wife is not only earning more than the husband and masking his lack of success, but she is embittered by his failures. I call women like this "Ms. Star Wars." They are stars at work; battling at home.

The core theme in Rebecca's family is that men can wield power in the family by controlling the money, and they use that power to hurt and disappoint their wives. Rebecca put one foot outside that pattern by choosing a man who couldn't rule her with money. Initially it must have seemed to her that Frank could give her the nurturing and support her father couldn't. The secret expectation on her part was what her mother and grandmother taught her, that men can't be counted on.

Frank's message came from his mother. He was programmed to disappoint women; to view himself as somewhat lethal. With his pot smoking and heavy drinking he has also inherited the genetic and behavioral bent toward addiction.

Their troubles are so entrenched, so chameleonlike that we could be lulled into believing that traditional therapy will save them. But the Kinkaids have already explored that option. The time and money they spent purchased them a great deal of knowledge about why they act as they do, but they are still bewildered when it comes to how to change their behavior and break the patterns. What they have realized is that an end of their marriage would only mean they'd move their troubles (and their histories) to some new lover's doorstep.

MAKING CHANGES

STEP 2 ♥ **We came to believe that a power greater than ourselves could restore us to sanity.**

Rebecca and Frank express such despair over their marriage that this step in particular will comfort them. This step lifts our sights from the problem to a higher source of light and inspiration. Clearly Frank and Rebecca can benefit from such refocusing.

Step 2 follows hard on the heels of the surrender in Step 1. Your question might be, just what are you surrendering to?

The answer is, Spirituality, a recognition that there is something beyond our human abilities, something with the power to uplift us and our circumstances. Above all, something that nurtures the highest and best within us and urges us to express it.

The real significance of this step is revealed for most people after a great deal of quiet inner work. Remain open to the notion even if at first it seems foreign and strange. You don't even have to have faith, just be willing to contemplate your spirituality. Seek to discover your own "still small voice within."

Family History

This is also part of looking beyond the apparent complications and focusing on the underlying cause of the problems.

➤ Take out the notebook in which you plan to record your thoughts.

➤ The notebook should be kept at your bedside, where you can use it for this exercise and others, before you sleep. Use this notebook to record your memories about your own family and childhood.

➤ It will help to record the family history chronologically. Here are the key questions to answer for each generation.

Where did your ancestors live?
Unless you are a Native American still living on ancestral land, almost every one of us in this country has a history of immigration and migration that disrupted the family. That being the case, try and discover why they left.

What are the birth dates of the first family members you can trace?
Approximations are fine.

What are the key life events in the family?

Consider here major moves, jobs, others coming to live with the family, etc.
losses: illnesses, death, divorces, business failures, etc.
problems: alcoholism, obesity, gambling, infidelities, family fights, crises.

Briefly describe the changes, losses, or problems. Add anything else that you feel is important that affected the emotional life of your family.

What were the relationships of the couples of each generation like?

Were the roles the men played loving, angry, passive, domineering, or violent, etc.?

What were the roles the women played?

How did people solve problems in their love relationships? Did they withdraw, fight, escape, become silent, overspend, deny or pretend that it didn't happen?

What were holidays and special events like in your family? Which birthday parties do you recall? What about Chanukah, Christmas, and other holidays? Who was there with you? What was it like for you? Did you receive gifts? What were they? Don't forget funerals, weddings, vacations, report cards, school plays, bar mitzvahs, bat mitzvahs, confirmations, baptisms, graduations—your own or perhaps a sibling's.

Identify the patterns: Go back over your notes and put a red asterisk beside any issue or trait that repeats itself in your family. Also put an asterisk next to any pattern or trait you recognize in yourself, your life, or your relationships that matches a family pattern.

Take the overlapping patterns from the past and present and sort out those that work for you and are positive. Note those that work against you. In the next chapter we'll show you how to change the patterns. For now just keep the information handy and add to it as memories occur to you.

Awareness must precede action. Continue to relax and affirm yourself with the exercises from Chapter 1.

♥ | *Love saver:*
Be grateful for your mate (remember when you didn't have one?).

4 LOST FOR WORDS

I met Rebecca and Frank Kinkaid on a cold winter's Sunday afternoon in the heart of downtown Chicago. Except for me, the Kinkaids, and Brenda Richardson, who sat in a corner taking notes, the only other occupant in this skyscraper may have been the security guard a few dozen floors below us. Looking back, I like to imagine that the unhappy ghosts we released that day fled down the long hallways.

These excerpts are condensed from a four-hour session. My time with them was unusual in many respects. Generally, when I meet clients in my practice, I know very little about them. But with the Kinkaids, at the start of our first and only face-to-face meeting, I felt I knew the Kinkaids better than most clients. Before their arrival I had poured over their exhaustive case histories, which had been compiled by Brenda Richardson. By the time we sat down together we could move on directly to the serious task of working on their relationship.

It was a challenge. Despite my knowledge of their backgrounds, I was unprepared for the open and obvious harshness they showed each other. In fact, I felt their relationship was on such unsteady footing that they didn't have a moment to spare in idle conversation with me. The following picks up about a half hour into our session with the Kincaids, when I was concentrating on Rebecca. Frank sat a few feet away.

REBECCA: One very touchy subject with us is sex. I've always had this idea, way in the back of my head, that sex is dangerous.

DR. WADE: Where do you think you got that idea?

REBECCA: I don't know.

DR. WADE: Well, I would think that having a grandfather die in the arms of a mistress, and a paternal grandmother die in childbirth, might set you up to believe that, not to mention all the issues around pregnancy in your family, who *had* to get married and so on.

REBECCA: I didn't know anything about my grandfather and his mistress until I was twelve years old.

DR. WADE: Oh yes you did. It's what I call psychic memory. In any family an event like this would be pretty dramatic. The fact that you didn't "hear" about it, only says it was so charged it went underground. It was there, lurking about as one of the secrets in your home, and you can be sure you knew about it. You just knew better than to talk about it.

REBECCA: That's probably true.

DR. WADE: And because it wasn't explained, you picked it up in some confused way.

REBECCA: I knew from the time I was twelve or thirteen that I was going to have trouble having a baby.

DR. WADE: How did you know that?

REBECCA: I don't know, but it wasn't until I was thirty that I learned I had tubal adhesions and had had them for ten years.

DR. WADE: You knew about your infertility problems for the same reason you knew about your grandfather. You clearly intuit your family dynamics and are intuitive about yourself, too. We're going to need that today, in our work. But let's get back to the point. How does that affect your sexual relationship with Frank?

REBECCA: It's more or less nonexistent. My attitude is that I really don't want to. I used to want to have sex to have a baby, then that didn't turn out so well. So, I said, I just don't want to. There's no room in my life for this. It's unpleasant.

DR. WADE: So you never found sex pleasurable, even when you were having it for the purpose of procreation?

REBECCA: There have been times when I've had wonderful sex. At the start of my relationship with Frank it was fantastic. And when I was single I was quite promiscuous and I had a lot of relationships. But the one Frank and I had at the beginning was the best. But that didn't survive marriage.

DR. WADE: Yes, a lot of the old family dynamics begin to spill over when you get married. Well, it has been ten years and the sex has been . . . ?

REBECCA: Getting worse, and therapy hasn't helped. I should say that I began therapy in 1978 and I just stopped a month ago. We have both been in a lot of therapy.

FRANK: And we also tried marriage therapy with three different people, but then we pulled out for one reason or another.

DR. WADE: That's not surprising. You guys are so entrenched in this exquisite torment and it's so compelling because of your family histories. For either of you to let go of the set of dynamics you're playing out with one another is going to be quite challenging. And I don't hear a lot of motivation for change, despite the fact that you're here. Oh, it's clear that you guys have done a lot of work on yourselves, but you're so entrenched. My guess is that what still fuels the conflicts and is keeping the two of you so firmly in the same place is that you're both still so filled with rage. Until you experience and integrate that rage you're going to continue to be pretty stuck. Have you addressed that rage toward your parents in your separate therapies?

FRANK: Not in any effective way.

REBECCA: I think that's why I stopped the therapy recently. This last woman was too Freudian for me. She was trying to get me to deal with my father. But I now see that she'd had me work through everyone in my family except my father. He was next, so I stopped.

DR. WADE: Yes, he's the big one in your life. You're caught in the double bind of adoring him and, what . . . ?

REBECCA: I've had this adoration thing about my father as long as I can remember.

FRANK: It's not just familial. There's something about that man. He's a genius, the smartest man I've ever met.

REBECCA: He's a very gruff person on the outside. Inside, he has a heart of gold. My father was a distant object, something I've always been desperately devoted to. I've always lived to please him, would always search for ways.

DR. WADE: When you were a child, what would happen when you weren't trying to please him?

REBECCA: Well, if he was angry about something he'd show his displeasure. But if he lost his temper there was this fear he would die. He has a temper. He yells. He never spanked, was never violent.

DR. WADE: But when you did do what he liked?

REBECCA: He would show his pleasure in ways that were enormously gratifying. If I brought home good grades, I'd get hugs, kisses, smiles, it didn't matter. The littlest, tiniest bit of warmth and approval from him has always gone an enormously long way. It still does.

DR. WADE: So essentially your dad was this gruff, distant figure, and when you did something he liked, the gruff side changed?

REBECCA: Something like that.

DR. WADE: Well, help me to understand. Could you spontaneously count on his good will by simply being yourself, say walking into a room and saying good morning?

REBECCA: No, because walking into a room where he was meant I'd gone out and gotten the paper, gone down the hall and made his coffee and brought it to him. It never occurred to me to approach him in any other way.

DR. WADE: Children don't set the tone in a relationship. Your father set that tone. He wanted you to perform. That was the way he learned to finally get his father's attention. He outperformed all the others and was rewarded with a good education from his father.
　　Now, when he became the daddy, here's a guy, and you won't like this Rebecca, so prepare yourself. I would say your dad was this larger-than-life, brilliant, dynamic, attractive, powerful, and charismatic figure. He could be warm, but it wasn't his nature to simply tune into you as a person and be available to you. But if you performed, you'd get his love and good will.

REBECCA: My mother said that because of his childhood emotional deprivation he had to be brought out by anyone who wanted anything from him. And he loved little girls. He'd come in the door calling, "Where are my girls?" He was that way with his cat later on, which is probably why I love cats, too.

DR. WADE: Rebecca, do you realize what you're saying? Little girls, cats. You were on par with cats?

(Rebecca slumps a bit in her chair and looks down, without speaking.)

DR. WADE (her voice softening): I know this is difficult, but what we're working on is an awareness of the patterns and the experiences that you had. We have to accept them and integrate them, and then move on to take action that is appropriate and corrective. We want to change some of those dynamics you keep tripping over in your marriage. They come from these experiences. I wonder . . . are you familiar with the intermittent reinforcement experiments that Skinner did with rats and pigeons?

REBECCA: Yes.

DR. WADE: Then you know that he found the reinforcement schedule most effective for maintaining shaped behavior that was intermittent. The pigeons never knew when the next pellet was going to come, so they'd press and press and press the little lever, then finally, they'd get another pellet. Then they'd press and press and press again for awhile. Then later they'd get another pellet. Imagine how desperate those pigeons might have felt had they been human. You can understand that desperation. You pressed all your childhood. And you have been pressing on: achieving at the best schools, joining him as a colleague and enjoying tremendous success in your field, marrying a respectable man, and displaying a brain that could outthink the best. Yet the rage that all this pressing has provoked, and your anger toward your father, who only offered occasional pellets, that rage has in some way generalized toward men. It's keeping you at arm's length from any intimate relationship with your husband.

REBECCA: That Skinner experiment. I'd never thought of that before, but it was a lot like that.

DR. WADE: I get the distinct impression that you're enraged with your father. There's this wish that was never fulfilled. You never really got the love and acknowledgment from him that you deserved.

REBECCA: Yes, that's so true.

DR. WADE: Well, it's the perfect marriage for you. You could have done a lot worse. You could have picked somebody where you could have exploded to bits long ago, but you've got your co-rages delicately balanced. She lashes out at you, Frank, you act out, she runs off, but just for a while.

FRANK: It's the only way we communicate.

DR. WADE: It's really quite Machiavellian. Frank, in Rebecca, you got your mother. You remember her as being cold and disrespectful toward you. You say the same about Rebecca. The script in your family is that women are cold, angry bitches. To make sure you keep the drama going, you say to your mother, who is really Rebecca, "I can get back at you by being just like my dad."
     And Rebecca, you finally have a chance to get back at your dad, who Frank represents, because you've got him just where you want him right now. You get to beat him over the head and keep him down and humiliate him. The script in your family, Rebecca, was that men will disappoint you. Your grandfather disappointed your grandmother, your father disappointed your mother. And there was always the fear that he'd cop out on you, Rebecca, that he would die, especially if he didn't get what he wanted. Then, according to the message in your family, you'd lose everything. So Frank and Rebecca, the task before us is to get your mother and father from between you. It will require more strength than either of you knew you had . . . Frank, would you please move your chair back a bit. Rebecca, would you come forward. I want Frank to see and hear you and be part of this experience. (With Rebecca remaining in her chair, Dr. Wade pulls two empty armchairs in front of Rebecca.)

DR. WADE: Now, Rebecca, which parent shall we start with?

REBECCA (quickly): My mother.

DR. WADE (patting one of the empty chairs and placing a pillow in the seat): Okay, here she is.

REBECCA: There?

DR. WADE: Umm hmm. Okay, you've brought her back from the dead. She's sitting in that chair and you know that nothing you can say will hurt her. What do you want to say?

REBECCA: For the last four years I've wanted to hurt you the way you hurt me.

DR. WADE: Tell her how she hurt you.

REBECCA: She made me infertile.

DR. WADE: Tell her.

REBECCA: You were only concerned about your own satisfaction, about keeping your marriage together. You didn't give a damn about what you did to me with that drug. Did you ask any questions about DES, whether it could hurt your baby? Did you care? (She begins sobbing.)

DR. WADE: It's okay to let yourself experience the feeling.

REBECCA: I'm afraid.

DR. WADE: It will help if you let go of some of that anger, just let it go. It's all right. You won't hurt her. Tell her how you feel.

REBECCA (screaming): I hate you (lowering her voice, sounding almost childlike), but I love you too, Mommy. (She continues sobbing.)

DR. WADE: Okay. Frank is sitting next to you. Is there anyway he can assist you? Comfort you?

REBECCA (screaming): No!

DR. WADE: If he tried to assist you what would you say?

REBECCA: I'd tell him to go away.

DR. WADE: Okay, tell him.

REBECCA: Go away!

DR. WADE (removing Rebecca's glasses and placing them on a table): You need to take these off for a while. I think you're more vulnerable without them.

REBECCA (gesturing toward Frank): I can't see him.

DR. WADE: That's okay, because we know who you really see over there. So tell Frank how angry you feel.

REBECCA: You make me sick. I hate you! I want to hurt you!

DR. WADE: Do you notice the difference in how direct you can be in your anger with Frank. When it was toward your mom it was so different.

REBECCA: He's there.

DR. WADE: Yes, but only as a stand-in.

REBECCA: I felt the anger with my mother. I know I'm angry with her. I even feel angry with her because she's not around for me to tell her.

DR. WADE: When she was alive did you confront her?

REBECCA: I screamed and yelled at her.

DR. WADE: Why?

REBECCA: Because she can't give me what I want.

DR. WADE: Which is? Tell her.

REBECCA (talking to chair): I want you to fix everything, Mommy. Come back and sit there and let me yell and scream at you. I want to have a baby.

DR. WADE: If you could have a baby, what would that mean for you?

REBECCA: That's all I've ever wanted.

DR. WADE: Did you want to have a boy or a girl?

REBECCA: A girl.

DR. WADE: I wonder why?

REBECCA (crying): I don't know.

DR. WADE: Wouldn't it be wonderful. Then you'd really have Daddy's approval, in a way you couldn't get it just by being Rebecca. Girls were obviously what your father wanted. His father had treasured his daughters. Maybe with you there's that little girl who believes she'd finally get Daddy's approval in a way she's never gotten it before, no matter how successful she has become. Okay, it's time to say goodbye to Mom, for a while, and ask Daddy to take her place. Talk to him, Rebecca, tell him how you feel.

REBECCA (in a hoarse monotone): Daddy, I want you to go down to the kitchen and get a butcher knife and slash your wife's throat, because that's what she really needs.

DR. WADE: Why?

REBECCA: Because she's a whore and a cunt.

DR. WADE: What is there about her?

REBECCA: She's so ignorant.

DR. WADE: Tell him, tell Daddy why you're so very, very angry.

REBECCA: Ruth is sick. He married a sick woman.

DR. WADE: No. Tell him the real reason.

(Rebecca sobs.)

DR. WADE (after a long pause): Isn't it because he loves her the way you wish he'd loved you?

REBECCA (through sobs): Yes, yes.

DR. WADE: She doesn't have to perform. She doesn't have to be a success. She doesn't have to know how to have an intellectual conversation with him. He loves her unconditionally.

REBECCA (rocking in pain, her hands over her face): Yes!

DR. WADE: He even showers her with the gifts he was unwilling to . . .

REBECCA (in a petulant child's voice): No! He hates her!

DR. WADE: But what does he give her?

REBECCA (screaming): Every goddamn thing she wants.

DR. WADE: That's right.

REBECCA (sobbing): I've tried. I tried to step in and help him but that fucking cunt married him and I . . . (begins crying, choking)

DR. WADE (her arms around Rebecca): It's alright, Rebecca. You're so hurt. You're in so much pain . . . This woman . . .

REBECCA: She has always been in the picture. For twenty-five years she was there. Then she sat at my mother's bedside and waited for her to die. As soon as the doctor said my mother was going to die, Ruth left her husband and waited. Three weeks after my mother died she moved in with Daddy.

DR. WADE: So she's not going to score any points with you in the field of honor, but the biggest hurt and greatest insult to Rebecca is what?

REBECCA: She married him.

DR. WADE (rubbing Rebecca's shoulders, loosening them up, patting her back forcefully. Rebecca begins coughing as she sobs): I'm doing this body work intentionally, Rebecca. You're coughing because you're releasing some of your anger. Your body is just tortured as you talk about your stepmother.

REBECCA (between coughs): She's not my mother!

DR. WADE: Keep breathing, Rebecca. We're going to get through this. There's no way through this torment but to walk through it. You'll know when to stop. You'll feel a sense of completion.

REBECCA (looking up, palms raised, face drained of color): I just feel so lost. I don't want to care about this. I want my own life.

DR. WADE: So you feel there's no way to heal or ever complete this business from the past.

REBECCA: There isn't.

DR. WADE: You think you're stuck forever, is that it?

REBECCA: Yes.

DR. WADE: Do you feel the same way about your marriage?

REBECCA: Yes.

DR. WADE: That's no coincidence. Right now they're one and the same, your marriage, your past. And whether you leave one another this day, whether you live alone, or with new mates or whether you continue this exquisite game . . . you and Frank will always be stuck until some of this is resolved. I know you can't continue like this, not even one more day.

Rebecca, dear, you're so afraid of confronting your feelings about your parents that you've appointed stand-ins. You can safely be furious with Frank and Ruth. It keeps you at arm's length from how you really feel about your father. When it comes to Ruth, it doesn't make a bit of difference how you feel about her. But it does with Frank.

Look, we're going to try something different. Rebecca, sit back in your chair, close your eyes. Go on, lean back. You're such a tiny thing when you sit back you can't even put your feet on the floor. Palms up, please. Okay, I want you to turn on your inner vision so I can move you to a deeper level. I want you to visualize those stars up there where you're going. Look at them glowing against a dark sky. With your eyes remaining closed, focus on the brightest star in the dark sky. Can you see it, Rebecca?

REBECCA (in a whisper): Yes.

DR. WADE: Good, because it's getting brighter and brighter.

REBECCA: Yes, yes.

DR. WADE: Brighter and bigger as you breathe along with it, taking in that cleansing air. Now, Rebecca, bring the light down, down, further still. It's in the center of your inner vision, getting larger, warmer, comforting, and we're breathing as it glows and becomes the size of a basketball. It touches your head and begins flowing down. Keep breathing as we take some time to feel the light and its comforting warmth flow down over your head, bathing your shoulders with light as you keep breathing, deeply.

(Rebecca's face relaxes; she breathes gently.)

DR. WADE: This light is a gift we all have. Many of us are unaware of it. Some call it intuition. Some call it God. Let us, for the time, call it your higher power. It has comforted you for the moment and will put you in touch with some important answers. Let's begin. Ask your higher power to tell you or show you what it is that's keeping you stuck. You have no control over this. You are powerless and must trust your higher power. As you ask, keep breathing, deeply, in and out. Go ahead, ask for guidance. What do you hear?

REBECCA: I don't know.

DR. WADE: That's right, you do not know. But your higher power does. Ask what it is that you don't want to lose.

REBECCA: I have nothing to lose.

DR. WADE: Your intuition is strong. It's glowing, Rebecca. It has given you knowledge in the past and is offering it now. It says, the reason you're stuck is . . .

REBECCA: I can't hear anything.

DR. WADE: You can, but you're afraid to repeat it. I'll say it for you. You don't want to let go of the fantasy that your father will . . .

REBECCA: one day . . . (she begins coughing repeatedly, choking)

DR. WADE: The words are choking you, cutting off your air supply. Ask your intuition what you can do to let go of this fantasy that your father will love you enough, so you can get unstuck? What can you do?

REBECCA: Die.

DR. WADE: That was your intellect talking. But I do find it fascinating that you'd choose death rather than give up this fantasy.

Your higher power wants you to live. Ask what you can do to help yourself.

REBECCA: Kill myself.

DR. WADE. The intellect again. Rebecca, you don't want that, believe me. Suicides are messy and quite expensive. So why don't we consider killing off the fantasy about your father rather than killing Rebecca.

REBECCA: I would prefer that.

DR. WADE: Of course you would. So, let's go back. You're doing wonderfully with this intuition work. Your intellect is so highly developed that it's difficult to get around it, but you will. Now ask yourself, ask your intuition, how to get rid of this fantasy so you can see your husband.

REBECCA: I don't see how.

DR. WADE: Trust your higher power, because believe me, you do have the answer. Uncross your ankles, please. Now, tell your intellect to be quiet for now. Just go down to a deeper place. Say, I want to be free more than I want to keep this fantasy.

REBECCA (after a long pause): I don't want this pain. I don't want to give it to my son.

DR. WADE: Yes, yes, Rebecca. If Kevin must be the reason you let go of this fantasy, if you don't think you're worth the fight, then you've found your answer. You can do it for him. Tell your higher power. Say yes, I want to heal for Kevin.

REBECCA: What do I have to do to heal, what?

DR. WADE (standing and picking up an armful of cushions): Keep your eyes closed, Rebecca. I'm going to place something in your lap. (Piles pillows onto her lap.) This one is your mother and what she did to you. This is your father and what he did. This is Ruth. I can barely see you. But don't worry, even with all this, you're still able to be a success. You're doing fine, aren't you?

REBECCA: No.

DR. WADE: But you can haul that baggage around with you the rest of your dear, sweet life. You're just as strong as your mother was and grandmother.

REBECCA: Yes, I am.

DR. WADE: Yes, but how do you feel?

REBECCA: Like shit.

DR. WADE: Yes, and when your husband tries to have a relationship with you he can't get very close, can he? Especially because he's got his own pile of luggage in his lap. And you've both got your son on top of it all. So now, ask your intuition, what can you do?

REBECCA (voice muffled, weeping): I'm buried. I want to get rid of it. (yelling) I want to hand it back.

DR. WADE: Yes, Rebecca. There's your answer. Give it all back to them. Be my guest.

(Rebecca stands suddenly and, holding onto the pillows, she moves toward the two empty chairs and places the pillows carefully on them.)

DR. WADE: Yes, put them in the chairs where they belong and tell them how you feel.

REBECCA (trembling, standing over the chairs): Take your craziness, I don't want it. I won't keep it. I won't. (She begins coughing, bends over coughing.)

DR. WADE (rubbing Rebecca's back): Yes, yes, cough it up. You've given the pain back. You've been holding it in for so long it's been choking you. This coughing fit is no coincidence. Look at the chairs. Can you tell them what you just gave them?

REBECCA (gesturing toward the crumpled tissue in her fist): I wish I knew what was in all this.

DR. WADE: All you really need to know is that you're not going to let it cripple you and your family anymore.

REBECCA: I feel I have the strength to fight it, but how can I just say goodbye to all the anger?

DR. WADE (picking up the pillows): Do you want it back?

REBECCA: No, I don't want it, but what if it keeps coming back?

DR. WADE: It will, for a while, but you can keep rejecting it, releasing it. In time you'll be free. Tell yourself that you've let it go, that you're rid of that, never-to-be-satisfied need to make Daddy love and approve of you. It's such old baggage, it's been passed along so many generations that it's too heavy to carry anymore.

(Rebecca looks at the chairs and begins crying again.)

DR. WADE: Any chance of asking Frank for help?

REBECCA: No!

DR. WADE: So why stay with him? You're telling me it is torture.

REBECCA: I don't know.

DR. WADE: Ask your higher power. You know it's there now, ask.

REBECCA (closes her eyes for a few seconds, then opens them slowly, with a wry smile): I like intractable battles.

DR. WADE: Let your intuition talk. Go back to it.

REBECCA (closes her eyes, and after a momentary pause, she speaks in a rush): If I beat Frank I can beat my father. I want to hurt him.

DR. WADE: Would you like to do something about all of this?

REBECCA (opening her eyes): Yes, I would. I want it to end.

DR. WADE: Then let's begin by looking at your complementary piece of the puzzle. Sit back for a minute. You've got to be exhausted. Frank, will you please come forward. (Frank and Rebecca change chairs; Dr. Wade continues talking.) These next few minutes may well determine whether you and Frank can stay together. I'm less invested in that than in you two leaving this all behind and living on a healthier basis. Okay, I'm expecting a lot from you Frank. (They all laugh.) You guys are incredible. One of your biggest problems is you're so doggone smart.

FRANK: My mind has been running with all this. I can't turn it off.

DR. WADE (points to one of two chairs): Frank, my intuition tells me it will be easier to put your mother in that chair. She's there, isn't she?

FRANK (voice suddenly lowered): Yes.

DR. WADE: Is your father next to her?

FRANK: Yes, but move the chairs apart. It doesn't make any sense for the two of them to be together.

(Dr. Wade moves the chairs apart.)

FRANK: Now, that chair, turn it over on its side, put the legs up in the air. (He shouts at the chair that has been turned over.) How would you like to get it doggie style, Mom? That's what you deserve.

DR. WADE: Is it your mother? Your rage has sexual overtones, doesn't it?

FRANK: Yes, I'd like to kick her.

DR. WADE: She can't feel it, so go ahead.

FRANK: I don't want to hurt my foot, she's not worth it.

DR. WADE: Tell her why she's not worth it.

FRANK (to Dr. Wade): It's just a certain economy. (sneering at the chair) You never gave me anything. Why should you get anything? You're always right, and what I got from that is, I've got to be right, too.

DR. WADE: Frank, I noticed when you speak to her that you're all hunched over. Are you afraid of something? It's as if you've closed up on your pain. (She begins tapping his chest.) Let's get some air in here, breathe.

FRANK: This is going to take some courage.

DR. WADE: You've got courage. You're a courageous man. A lot of people wouldn't have come this far.

FRANK: I need to protect myself or she'll get me.

DR. WADE: You think you need to protect yourself, but do you really need to? You're a pretty big guy. Is she still big and scary to you?

FRANK (shaking his head, fear in his eyes): Yeah.

DR. WADE: Powerful enough to shame you, humiliate you, to have people laughing at you?

(Frank nods his head yes, while still watching the chair.)

DR. WADE: Then stand up in your chair, please. (He stands up, towering over the other objects in the room.) There now, she's down there on her side. Do you feel a little bit more powerful?

FRANK: No.

DR. WADE: What do you need to do to take your power back, so you can stop acting and feeling like a little boy who can only be in his marriage if he's oppositional and passive-aggressive? Frank, you've only had two models of manhood. The first was your father, an alcoholic disaster who drifted through life, the second is your illustrious father-in-law, who didn't know how to be a loyal father or husband. You wouldn't want to be like him either, would you?

FRANK: I wish he'd been my father.

DR. WADE: Of course you do. But then, who could blame you? He had to seem a hell of a lot better than your father, the failure. Her father was at least a brilliant success. Yes. But you don't want to love the way your father-in-law does. So what do you want? Try holding your hands up high, freeing your chest, letting the air in when you talk.

FRANK (sagging): I want . . .

DR. WADE: Please keep your hands up. I'm asking you to do this so you don't shut down. Open your heart and find the answer. Listen for the words. What can you do to release yourself from the fear and rage that binds you to your mother and has you living it out daily with your wife?

FRANK: I want to take care of myself.

DR. WADE: How would you do that?

FRANK: Take pride in myself. Stop trying to fail.

DR. WADE: How can you possibly believe in yourself if you think you're loathsome?

FRANK: I am loathsome. I fool almost everyone.

DR. WADE: Don't you see, that's part of that trap that you've put yourself in. You think of yourself as your mother's victim. She tantalized you sexually, awakened forbidden longings that you could never satisfy. So, you've convinced yourself that she's to be feared, and you act out the "poor me" scam. It's the look-at-what-they've-done-to-me scam. The you-won't-have-sex-with-me scam, the I'm-going-to-be-brutal-and-keep-you-from-hurting-me scam. You're really angry with your mother, but also angry with yourself because your own budding sexuality betrayed you. You wanted your mother. A lot of those scams came straight from your dad. And with exquisite care you found Rebecca and asked her to play your mother. She as much as said, 'Fine, if you'll be my dad.' Frank, I was wrong, you don't belong up there. Why don't you get down for a while. Let's dismiss your real mother from the room and ask her understudy to play her part. My intent is not to hurt you, but it's important to show you two just what you've been doing. Come on over here (gesturing toward Rebecca). You little Genghis Khan, you. Frank, would you, for a moment, stretch out on the floor. After all, that's where you've been in this relationship. That's where victims usually find themselves. Go ahead, you mean mommy, you. Torture him. Humiliate him. Tantalize him, but he can't have you.

REBECCA (standing over him): What should I say?

DR. WADE: You tell me. You've used your words as weapons all these years.

FRANK (snarling viciously at Rebecca): Why don't you repeat what you said to me this morning?

REBECCA (venomously): I want you to stop making me make up for what your mother didn't give you. I want you to grow up. Be a man. Be powerful, be a success. And stop being violent. I don't want you to hurt me, anymore. I don't want you to yell at me. (Tears run down her face.) I don't want you to tell me I'm crazy (begins crying) and (holding her head back howling) and I don't ever want you to say again that I'm a barren bitch.

DR. WADE: You're on Frank, the next line is yours. You two have really got this going. What do you say back? You know your lines better than anyone.

FRANK (to Rebecca in a childlike voice): I want you to stop belittling me. I want you to understand me. I want you to show some interest in me. I want you to love me.

DR. WADE: Frank, why don't you add, poor me.

FRANK (weakly): What do you mean?

DR. WADE: At the end of your sentences, say, poor me, because that's what you really mean.

FRANK: Poor me.

DR. WADE: No, Frank. You know how to play this role. Say, poor me, you never give me what I want.

FRANK (looking up at Rebecca, sadly): You don't know what it's like when you never believe in me.

DR. WADE (softly): Frank, dear, I bet you feel helpless and pathetic. If only she'd love you, support you, connect with you, have sex. What then?

FRANK: I don't get it.

DR. WADE: No, you can't get it from down there. Just as it's impossible for Rebecca to let you in close if she's holding all that baggage, it's hard to have a grown-up relationship when Rebecca is up here, and you're (with emphasis) down there.

FRANK: What if I got up?

DR. WADE: What if you did?

(Frank rises, while Rebecca steps back, forcefully.)

DR. WADE: Rebecca, you looked like a terrified girl when he stood up.

REBECCA: I felt scared.

DR. WADE: Yes, you're terrified of men, you believe they cause pain, and that's one reason you keep your foot on his back. You saw what Victor did to your mother with his rage and you aren't taking any chances, are you? With your looks, your money, your success, you could have had any number of men. But he's the one who would play victim so you could get back at Daddy. Rebecca, I can feel your heart. It's pounding so hard. Keep breathing. What are you afraid of right now?

REBECCA: That he'll hurt me.

DR. WADE: Like . . .

REBECCA: Daddy.

DR. WADE: But Daddy isn't here. We sent him away. I want you two to try something. Rebecca, can you look at Frank and just be here with him? I'm going to get behind you and hold you up, if necessary. I give you my word. I won't let him hurt you. Frank has frightened you, hurt you, and so you have confused him with Daddy. But if you can, allow yourself to be with Frank. I want you two to look at one another. Turn the dial. Click. New channel, new faces. Stop seeing Daddy and Mommy. Take deep breaths, you two. Frank, try and let yourself be seen. Open your arms, Frank. Throw back those shoulders, Frank, and take a deep breath. Now, if you will, please, take her hand. You're safe, Rebecca. Now look at her. There's no one between the two of you. Keep breathing and allow the connection to take place. Frank, I'd like to introduce you to your wife, Rebecca. Rebecca, this is Frank. Now, Rebecca, this guy in front of you, who is he?

REBECCA: Frank.

DR. WADE: What color are his eyes?

REBECCA: Blue, blue, but I only know that from memory. I can't really see him without my glasses.

DR. WADE: Rebecca, you can see if you step in closer.

REBECCA: Yes, it's true. Up close I can. Your eyes, they're so intense.

DR. WADE: Beautiful, aren't they?

REBECCA: I'd forgotten about his eyes.

DR. WADE: Frank, what comes up for you when you begin to see your wife.

FRANK: I see so much unhappiness, a wall.

DR. WADE: Well, you're so much taller than she is you may actually be looking at a wall. Rebecca, will you stand on this step stool if Frank and I support you? (To Frank:) You wouldn't let her tip over, would you?

REBECCA (seethingly, to Frank): I don't trust you.

FRANK: Do you think I would let you fall?

REBECCA (angrily): No, you'd push me.

DR. WADE: You're both so busy with all the old childhood, mistrusting patterns. I asked you only to be in this moment, but neither of you have been able to do it for more than a few seconds. I don't want to make it hard for you, so let's say, for sixty seconds you're not in the past, you're not your parents, you're Rebecca and Frank in this moment.

(Frank begins laughing.)

DR. WADE: What's going on?

FRANK: It's not such a big deal. (He looks kindly into Rebecca's face.)

REBECCA (to Frank): We used to have a lot of fun together, didn't we?

FRANK (softly): Um, hm, we did.

REBECCA: When I really see you I remember your eyes.

FRANK: I'm looking at your mouth, your lovely, lovely mouth.

REBECCA: My mouth?

FRANK: Your lips, really. It was always your mouth I wanted.

REBECCA: You never told me that.

FRANK: It never occurred to me. (Whispering, as if in bed.) But you know, right after I met you I was telling a friend about you. Randy, you know him, from D.C. Well, he asked me to describe you and I told him about your luscious . . . enticing . . . mouth. (They gaze at one another for a while.)

DR. WADE (after a minute has passed, softly): The therapist I trained under was the founder of family therapy, Virginia Satir. She used to call moments like this (playfully switches to German accent) "Vit whom am I having the pleasure?" You are not projecting right now, you're just being with one another.

FRANK (still in the intimate whisper to Rebecca): I told him how stunning you were, you still are.

REBECCA (quickly): I'm not.

FRANK: You've never looked more beautiful. I don't always think of you as beautiful. Sometimes my anger gets in the way and I . . .

DR. WADE: Forget all that anger and be together. Rebecca, he's right. Your face is glowing. You're remarkably beautiful right now. Why are you smiling?

REBECCA: It's nice to feel like this. It's been so long.

FRANK (taking a deep breath): It has been a long time.

REBECCA (eyes narrowing): I'm not a tower of strength for you.

DR. WADE: Oh, are we going to start that again? Rebecca, it's almost as if you stopped breathing when you said that. I thought I'd have to get you a respirator.

REBECCA: I have asthma.

DR. WADE: Asthma is exacerbated by emotions. Let's try and move back to where you were. Before, when Frank was telling you you were beautiful. How did it feel?

REBECCA (laughing, and turning back to Frank): I felt the way I did that time we were in that little cottage on the beach, remember? I fell in love with you, with your eyes.

FRANK: Yeah, everything seemed to be going right that night.

DR. WADE: Do you want to make it right again?

FRANK: I want this person I see here.

DR. WADE: Then you're going to have to stop making her Mommy Dearest. You're going to have to stop setting her up to be the gatekeeper to your own private purgatory.

REBECCA: Frank, I felt as if I had to be angry.

FRANK: I like this better. Maybe a little of this could go a long way.

DR. WADE: As adults we have choices. You can choose to be with this lovely woman, and Rebecca, you can choose your husband. (The stool on which Rebecca is standing begins to tip over, but Frank catches her in his arms.)

DR. WADE: Was that okay when he was trying to keep you from falling?

REBECCA: Yes. (laughing) You sure you're not going to push me over?

FRANK (smiling softly, still gazing into her eyes, his hands about her waist): Umhummmm.

REBECCA (murmuring): Your arms are so big, so strong.

DR. WADE: Rebecca, you could balance a lot better if you leaned a bit on him. When you're mutually supported it's a lot safer for you both . . . Okay, so what do you feel you want to do now?

FRANK: Amazingly enough, not have sex.

REBECCA (giggling): Good, good, I like that idea.

DR. WADE: That's true. Right now, sex is just another of the ways you two have been beating each other over the head. So Rebecca, what do you want to do?

(Rebecca giggles, throws her head back, laughs loudly, and pins her elbows to her sides.)

DR. WADE: What's going on here, you two? Oh, you're tickling each other. I love it.

REBECCA (to Frank, still giggling): You'd better stop. You know what happens when I get tickled.

FRANK: No, I don't. What?

REBECCA (still laughing): I kick. You mean I've never kicked you?

FRANK (smiling): No. You've thrown things at me, a lamp, a book but never . . .

DR. WADE: So Rebecca, what do you think?

REBECCA: I prefer my husband.

DR. WADE: I'm glad to hear that. You look wonderful together, so different from when you walked into this office. Rebecca, Frank, let me give you a piece of advice. Every time you begin to feel mean or critical, excuse yourselves from the room. Go find a quiet spot, take a pillow, and whack it, shout at it, let the pain come out. But stop demanding that you play one another's parents or the roles will destroy you.

REBECCA: I don't always know when I'm going to say something mean.

DR. WADE: Because you've got such a backlog of anger. For a while you both need to do some release work on your own. Hit the pillows, curse at them if necessary, but don't take it out on one another. I learned something very heartening about you two, that you have the ability to be together, to be lighthearted and playful, which surprised me. Do you still want to get divorced?

REBECCA: That's how I felt when I first came in.

DR. WADE: Tell Frank what you'd like to do now.

REBECCA (gazing intently into his eyes): I want to go home.

FRANK (to her, just as intently): I want to keep feeling close.

REBECCA (whispering): Me too.

DR. WADE: I wish I had a mirror so you could see yourselves.

REBECCA: I really like you Frank and I love your mind.

DR. WADE: I have a lot of suggestions I'm going to give you about how to move on from here. But I think you've got a full plate in front of you for now. The only thing I'd ask you to do before we talk again is that you take a strip of paper to remind you of that intuitive message you got today, Rebecca. Write down: "We decided to remain married and be joyful together." Put the note in your family Bible and just leave it there. Maybe years from now your son will find it and know that you've kept your promise. What a rich legacy for him. (As they rise to leave, Frank helps her tenderly into her coat. They say a few more words to Dr. Wade, then leave. Soft laughter can be heard as they walk down the hall.)

DR. WADE'S FOLLOW-UP NOTES

Recommendations to the Kinkaids: That he begin attending Alcoholics Anonymous and Al-Anon meetings, given his drinking, marijuana use, and the fact that Frank's father died of alcoholism. Rebecca, as the wife of an alcoholic, is a prime candidate for Al-Anon, the twelve-step support program for family members of alcoholics. I find it also works well for family members affected by other kinds of addictions.

Another critical issue that needed to be addressed was Frank's physical violence. Every couple needs fundamental ground rules that certain behaviors are not to be permitted, and physical violence is one of them. Aside from the fact that it can be dangerous and potentially mortal, it destroys the safety of a relationship.

For this issue I've recommended that Frank seek the support of Men Against Violence and remove himself from any situation in which he feels he may erupt into violence.

Also, this couple needs to literally "lighten up." I've recommended that they wear lighter colors, keep flowers in their home, play soothing music, and date one another—weekly—to restore some of the love and joy in their relationship.

Ongoing therapy and marital counseling are certainly in order, but a less intellectually-driven therapy might help them to heal some of the deep emotional wounds. Therapists trained in humanistic, Gestalt, psychodrama, or another more active form of therapy, would be best for them. Their tendency has been to overintellectualize and analyze their issues but never move on to actual change.

MAKING CHANGES

STEP 3 ♥ We made a decision to turn our will and our relationships over to the care of God, as we understand God.

This is the final step in surrendering. Steps 1 through 3 are really leading us to the point of being willing to ask for help, of giving up self-will and opening up to the possibility of a higher will. One way I view this step is as a taking off of the blinders that block us from seeing other than our own point of view. One of the biggest problems for most couples, as with Rebecca and Frank, is that gaining any sense of perspective or higher view is beyond their reach once they're locked into their battle stations. This step opens the way for disarmament.

I've repeatedly seen something akin to a mysterious force take hold in people's lives when they surrender. Suddenly they're able to see or understand their partner's feelings, their own feelings, to reach out in ways that only a short while before had seemed impossible. That's what you witnessed in the Kinkaids' therapy. When Rebecca could stop focusing on Frank, get centered, and talk to her higher self, this couple had a deeply moving breakthrough.

Step 3 is the step most couples return to when they hit a snag in their relationship. It requests intervention by a higher power and acknowledges a positive desire for an improved marriage.

♥ EXERCISE ♥

Learning to use Step 3.

This part of the process is for you whether you have a partner who chooses to participate in this process or not. There are two ways to use this step. First sit quietly and repeat the step three times. As you repeat it allow yourself to feel an increasingly deep sense of letting go. You might envision letting go of the problems in your relationship as if you were releasing your end of the rope in a tug-of-war and quietly allowing it to drop. A tug-of-war ceases to exist if one person lets go.

Creating your own ritual allows you to put Step 3 into practice. If you have a family, this is very important to do together, because it's one of the best ways to build a positive bond. This ritual can give you the opportunity to acknowledge the existence of a higher power (nature, or God) as we understand God to be. There are few hard and fast rules in creating a ritual. It can be practiced in any number of ways, as long as it's done regularly and in a heartfelt manner.

Some people take a walk in the park or woods; others sit on a beach and are affected by the power and majesty of the waves; some like to hold hands around the breakfast table and say a prayer; others make sandwiches on Sunday evenings for the poor.

You'll meet one couple who observes Shabbat on Friday nights, another attends an Episcopal parish church every Sunday morning. Whatever your spiritual path, your ritual will help you turn aside self-will and encourage a recognition of another power in your life.

If you have children, a family ritual produces a different kind of legacy, one that your children can draw strength from and remember in a loving, comforting way.

♥

Rewriting family scripts out of the family patterns you identified in Chapter 2, certain key themes will emerge, similar to those identified by Frank and Rebecca. In Rebecca's family, hers were: Love equals pain, men can't be counted on, and men will betray you. Frank's were: Men are a disappointment to women, men are lethal, and women are cold and withholding. These themes represent decisions that children make unconsciously when exposed to family patterns. These decisions create the magical "Pygmalian Effect." In other words: "This is what I believe relationships are and therefore that's what they are." M. Scott Peck, in *The Road Less Traveled,* put it this way: "A woman who believes men can't be trusted will never meet a man she can trust." These themes usually surface when an intimate bond is formed.

Identify your themes. Write them on a separate page in your notebook, leaving a few lines beneath each theme. You're going to transform these negative, damaging beliefs into positive, healthy beliefs. For example, we take "men always disappoint me," and turn it into, "I, Rebecca, am married to a loving husband who faithfully supports me and cares for me. He is not my father."

A theme like Frank's can be changed from "Women are cold and withholding" to "My wife is a loving, caring woman. She is not my mother." Strange though it may seem, no matter what your partner is doing, you can't afford to accept anything but this positive theme for him or her. The alternative is to continue in the cycle of despair and pessimism that has haunted you throughout your relationships and to continue setting your partner up to keep playing out the old role of your parents.

This theme is the basis for a new family script.

───────────── ♥ EXERCISE ♥ ─────────────

Exchanging new scripts with your partner.

Write a brief scene, including setting and dialogue, that portrays your new theme. Write the dialogues in the form of affirmations. For example, Rebecca could say to Frank, "I'm so glad I can count on you and I'm proud of you." And Frank could say, "Rebecca you're the kind of woman I've always wanted to marry, loving, warm, and accepting."

Like all affirmations, repeat these ten times, to yourself—as often as possible—especially just before sleep.

Now it's time to have fun. If you are working through this process with a mate, you might invite him or her to take part in this with you. Ask her to play the part you've written for her and later you can trade off and act out what she's written. Plan to continue playing these new roles in real life.

Daily affirmations provide practice in staying with your new role. For example: I am a loving supportive mate (if that is the role your mate is asking you to play). Say it to yourself as often as possible, especially at bedtime.

♥ | *Love saver:*
  | **Kiss your mate hello and goodbye each day.**

And now let's meet our next couple.

5 REOCCURRING THEMES

It looks as if Monica Bonadonna has captured the sun from the long, quiet strip of Southern California beachfront that stretches outside her door and has stored the light in her hair. A long, blonde lock of hair slips over her eyes as she works noiselessly opening a can of tuna. For a while there are only the outdoor sounds of gulls' cries and ringing wind chimes, then a shouted interruption.

"He took my truck." It is Stacey, the Bonadonnas' six-year-old daughter, racing into the kitchen through swinging doors. The child is dressed in a pink-flowered bathing suit and matching thongs and is followed by four-year-old Michael, who wears sand-encrusted Osh Kosh overalls. He hugs a toy dump truck and yells, "I did not take her truck."

"Darn it!" Monica sticks an index finger in her mouth realizing the distraction has cost her a few drops of blood. Before she can settle the dispute the doors swing open again, this time releasing a medium-tall, dark-haired, slender man in tennis whites.

"Daddy, isn't that my truck?"

"Is not!"

"Thank God you're back," Monica says to her husband.

"I had the greatest game," Jimmy says, ignoring the debate

75

and Monica's entreaty. "Remember Parsons, that stiff from the bank? I beat his pants . . ."

Monica holds a hand out inches before his face, like a traffic guard at the school crossing. "Not now, please," she says, coolly.

The irritation in her voice has silenced the children. They seem to know what will come next. Jimmy slams his racket on the counter. "Just forget it then, you bitch! You're the one who encouraged me to go in the first damned place."

He's gone back through the doors, and the children exchange blows over who will get the tennis racket their dad has left behind.

Later, Monica talked about the scene. "His anger comes on just like that, in sudden outbursts. When it boils over, it lacks self-control. Why couldn't he have just saved that conversation about tennis for later, when it wasn't so crazy? He's the most important person in my life, but he certainly doesn't treat me the way I'd like to be treated. Verbal abuse is not one of my methods for getting what I want accomplished. When he rants and raves like that, I just get cool toward him and turn away."

"He usually helps a lot with the kids and does the dishes," she continued. "I plan the meals, do the shopping. I do a lot, and probably don't let him do enough. I'm stuck in the same routines from when I was home all day with the kids. I'm tired. I'd like to be less fully charged, less uptight. I am always trying to run things, always ahead of Jimmy instead of standing aside and letting him make the effort. So we wind up competing."

That afternoon Jimmy was asked to trace their relationship from its inception up to and including their present-day problems. He said:

"Monica and I met about two years after my divorce, when a mutual friend set us up for a tennis date. I found her then, and still do, physically very appealing. She is probably one of the most beautiful women I've ever seen. I also like and love her a lot."

"The problem is that we never have a chance to talk," he continued. "All our obligations have forced us to sacrifice our personal commitment to one another. You like to walk away from a sexual situation feeling you've had great sex. Well, with Monica, I don't feel I've been given good ear."

"I feel hurt by not being listened to and being unable to discuss my dreams. I tell Monica, 'Don't ignore me. Don't insult me by not listening.' I need her to give me eye-and-ear contact. I don't care if she calls me an S.O.B. when I'm done. Because we can't talk, we have a habit of not resolving things. She'll give me the cold shoulder for a while, then we'll start talking again. But you know what? All these unfinished conversations, they're appendages. The words, the thoughts, the dreams have to go somewhere. If you ask me to sublimate them they'll manifest. I can't swallow them. They might give me an ulcer. So what do I do? If I put them in my pants they'll stick out there, too."

♥

They are the Bonadonnas of Manhattan Beach, California. He is thirty-three, she, twenty-nine, and they have been married seven years, most of them good, they say. But recently problems have erupted. It may have something to do with Monica returning to her job last September, as a kindergarten teacher, after a one-year leave of absence.

Bills had forced their hands. Taxes had gone up, again, as well as other expenses, and they couldn't make do any longer without her paycheck. Jimmy sells medical equipment and his income varies from month to month. The extra salary has come in handy. But the new schedule gives Monica less time for Jimmy. Between the housework, the kids, and the job, Monica said she has precious little time even for herself.

Their recent problems may have been brought on by her schedule change, or perhaps they were simply inevitable. They said that their argument after his tennis match is typical of their squabbles, that they just "fight over little things."

That may be so. It may also be that since relationships have a way of bringing old problems into painful focus, there are far deeper issues than the "little things" they say they argue over. Their communication styles are certainly typical of many of my clients. One partner blows up and the other responds with a chilly silence.

Monica was correct when she called her husband's profanity abusive. His response is akin to hitting her with his fist. Any verbal exchange that is overtly intended to wound and demean is abusive. Name calling and profanity are well past acceptable limits.

In addition, Jimmy's enthusiasm about his game led him to some pretty inconsiderate behavior. When he burst into the kitchen and tried to distract his wife, who was knee-deep in children, he was like a third youngster fighting for her attention. In his excitement he was unable to understand that, at that moment, Monica needed him. If he had, he might have asked her what he could do to help and saved his victory speech for later.

One clue that can help us understand Monica may be that she says it's difficult for her to let Jimmy share the work load. She encouraged him to go out, insisted on trying to handle the children and lunch herself, and yet when he walked into the kitchen, she was annoyed that he did not understand how harried she was. It stands to reason that she'd be tired. After a year's leave, she has returned to a full-time job and has adjusted her home schedule only minimally.

None of that really justifies her exasperating method of silencing him. Holding one's hand up in the air in a military fashion may be an effective way to stop a moving vehicle, but it seems a bit insulting when directed at the "most important person" in her life. Simple words such as "Honey, right now I could really use your help" might have diffused the issue. She had a need to control the situation, even if it meant she treated her husband insultingly.

The truth is, both Jimmy and Monica sound hostile and controlling. That leaves us wondering why two loving and intelligent adults did not simply tell each other what they needed.

The answers will become clearer as we take a look at their family histories and their childhoods.

CAST OF CHARACTERS

Jimmy's family

Paternal grandparents: ARTHUR
ROSA

Maternal grandparents: MARIK
VAYTA

Jimmy's mother: LYDIA
     father: VINCENT

Monica's family

Paternal grandparents: HENRY
KATHRYN

Maternal grandparents: CHESTER
SARAH

Monica's mother: PATRICIA
     father: EDWARD

Family Themes: In Jimmy's family the men believe they were misunderstood by women and that they would never really be able to find a place where they "fit in," even home.

In Monica's family the women believe that they have to take care of themselves because men can't be counted on.

Let's begin by meeting Jimmy's paternal grandparents:

ARTHUR: born in 1900 in the southern Italian city of Caliabria
ROSA: born in 1900 in Caliabria

Jimmy's paternal grandparents, Arthur and Rosa, married in Italy and immigrated to Cleveland, Ohio, where Arthur worked as a fire engineer for the railroad, a job perceived by other immigrants in their ethnic neighborhood as relatively dangerous and requiring some skill. It won him respect on the streets. His wife, Rosa, who Jimmy said "called the shots" in her household, would eventually have eight children, all of whom attended Catholic schools and learned their parents strong work ethic. Food was king in this home, and the meals Rosa served were feasts. The tempting array of food didn't make sitting through family meals any easier, though. Rosa and Arthur had such a fiery relationship that dinner with them was like sitting in the middle of a boxing ring.

Still, they managed well financially, enough so that at one point they were able to move from their modest home in a predominately working-class neighborhood to a larger house in a white-collar section of town. A tragedy marred the cheer of the family's upward mobility when the oldest son was killed, at nine years old, in a cooking accident. Boiling hot sauce was spilled on him. One of the children, who may have been particularly frustrated at not being able to save his big brother, is the next character in our drama. He would grow up to be a fireman, and of course, Jimmy's father:

VINCENT: born in 1923 in Cleveland, the fourth Bonadonna child

Vincent was the first in his family to go to college. He hoped eventually to earn a medical degree, but after two years as an undergraduate, his plans were thwarted by World War II. When Vincent was discharged from the Army he accepted a job as a fireman, where he rose to the position of captain. Vincent was proud of his uniform and badge. It earned him the same type of respect his father had enjoyed back in their old Italian neighborhood. At home Vincent made bittersweet jokes about not becoming a doctor. On a few occasions, when he was with Jimmy, Vincent pointed to a well-known doctor and said, "See that guy over there? I went to school with him and he used to steal my homework."

Vincent became an outcast in his family when he married a woman from a Polish family. This woman, who would eventually become Jimmy's mother, points the way toward Jimmy's maternal family history. Let's begin with his grandparents:

MARIK: born in 1900 in Poland
VAYTA: born in 1900, also in Poland

Vayta and Marik were married in Poland and came to Cleveland together, where Marik worked in a factory. They had six children. Vayta was quiet, serene, and pleasant. As for Marik, even in his eighties he remained diligent about his domestic chores. The emphasis in this family was to make a good effort no matter what the task. Early on in their marriage Marik and Vayta purchased the small home in a Polish neighborhood where they lived for forty years.

There was also a tragedy in this family. One of the children, who had Down's Syndrome, was killed in a freak accident. He tripped over a curb on a city street and suffered what looked like a broken leg. After being taken to a hospital he died of medical complications. His death was a great loss for the youngest and favorite daughter:

LYDIA: born circa 1928 in Cleveland, youngest of six children

When she was twenty-one, Jimmy's mother joined the Women's Army Corps. She and Vincent met at a USO party, married in 1948, and began a life together in Cleveland. It would be twelve years before Lydia gave birth to their only child, a son:

JIMMY: born in 1959 in Cleveland

Even after they were finally "blessed" with a son, Lydia and Vincent's marriage was stormy. There was little emotional support from either family, who resented that the two had married outside their ethnic boundaries. When Lydia complained to her mother about her husband's bad temper, she was generally dismissed with a statement reflecting their cultural prejudices. She'd tell Lydia, "You made your bed when you married an Italian, now lay in it."

Vincent and Lydia had different ideas about how to live life. Vincent liked having guests over often, especially for the holidays, serving fine Italian foods and showing off his comfortable house. Lydia, who was quiet and introspective, preferred keeping to herself or visiting family. When Vincent worked on Sundays, she spent the day with her parents.

Lydia and Vincent and little Jimmy did spend a lot of time together attending the weddings and funerals of their many relatives. They also ate out often at Italian seafood restaurants, another of Vincent's ways of demonstrating a particular level of success.

He enjoyed his image among other Italians as a good role model. If someone became difficult in public he was quick to flash his badge. When he walked the streets of the Italian neighborhoods, on his way to a local bar for a brew and good conversation, he'd shout greetings to the guys on the corner. He was shrewd and knew the "right" people. When it was a question of who you knew or needed to know, people called Vincent. He usually worked a second job, sometimes moving furniture for friends who had a moving company.

Vincent, Jimmy's father, died in 1985. The year before, while working as a fire fighter, he'd been on a burning rooftop and breathed in noxious air. Although he survived a long hospitalization in critical care, his health continued to go downhill. He was in his yard fixing a lawn mower when he keeled over and died. Jimmy was left with conflicting feelings about both parents.

JIMMY'S CHILDHOOD AND LIFE AS A SINGLE ADULT

In an ethnic, predominately Catholic family, it was a stigma in the sixties to be an only child. Jimmy's aunts and uncles on both sides had lots of kids, but his cousins were older, and that made him feel even more estranged in his family. He was teased by kids in his Cleveland neighborhood because of his fancy clothes. As Lydia's only child, Jimmy was given her undiluted attention. This meant even his play outfits included a wardrobe of shirts she starched and pressed so carefully that, according to Jimmy, "If a corporate president had met me, he would have asked for the name of the person who pressed my shirts so he could get his done there, too. That's how well they were done." Jimmy recalled frequent clashes between his parents. "My mother was quiet and tended to hold things in. My father's approach was to let whatever was bothering him out, to insult and hold a grudge. He ranted and raved and my mother was just nonreactive. About five or six times during my childhood my parents didn't speak to each other for months. Once, when I was about twelve, they stopped speaking for thirteen months. My mother just clammed up. They'd communicate through me. He'd say, Tell your mother such and such for me."

They seemed to save all their love and affection for their son. Jimmy said his father only spanked him once, when he was seven years old. Even then, Jimmy said, "I looked up into his face and saw it was really hurting him as much as me. He really loved me. Every morning before he went to work, until I was nine or ten, he kissed me. When he talked about his childhood he'd say, 'You're gonna have what I never had.' He'd played with balls that had no covers, and had old broken toys. When I was five or six he took on an extra job so he could earn twenty-five dollars to buy me a bicycle."

"I was terrified about my father's job when I was a kid," Jimmy continued. "My mother would say, 'Let's watch the news and see if there have been any fires.' I was always relieved at the end of the newscast not to have seen my father."

Jimmy said he didn't have a lot of one-on-one time with his father and not simply because of his heavy work load. The few times they were alone together, when they went fishing, Vincent invited Jimmy's older cousin along. "My father didn't have the patience to show me how to bait my hook, so my cousin showed me," said Jimmy. "My dad talked mostly to my cousin. I didn't feel a part of the outing."

That was pretty typical of the communication between Jimmy and his father. "He seemed a little uncomfortable talking to me. There was jealousy between him and my mother about me. My father was afraid I'd be a mama's boy. My mother didn't want me to be a young Vincent. I was always a good kid. I'd hear my father's friends say, 'Your kid is fabulous, he has the manners of a gentleman.' My father would say, 'I don't want him to know it, he'll get a big head.' He seemed to want me to get in trouble.

"When I was sixteen, he said, 'Why don't you go get laid or get into some kind of trouble?' He was afraid I might be a little light in the loafers. Maybe he wanted to live through me vicariously. He expected a lot of me and set very high goals. It was always, 'Let's do better.' The compliments were far and few between. The agenda that they set for me was always reaching, reaching, reaching. When I needed advice about future plans, my father's question to me usually was, 'Are you better off doing this?'"

Jimmy was very close to his mother. "We spent lots of time alone together and she hung on my every word. When the other kids were out playing ball in the alley, I was in the house with my mother, reading the Sears catalogue and pointing to a picture, saying, 'If I bought this doghouse I could build, add onto it, and expand it.'

Jimmy said he never felt a sense of belonging in his home. "I wasn't able to decide where to put this or that in my room. It didn't feel like mine. It seemed I was always in the way, always causing trouble, like when I overhauled the lawn mower so I could figure out how to put it back together. At Christmas I could never help with lights because they felt I would break them."

That sense of not belonging was compounded when Jimmy was sixteen and he and his parents were out riding in the car through an affluent and beautiful neighborhood. "We passed a house and they said, 'What do you think of this place?' I shrugged and said, 'I don't know, it's fine, I guess.' My father said, 'Well, we just bought it.' Just like that. They never consulted me," Jimmy recalled, "never asked me how I felt about moving, or even tried to prepare me for the fact that we would move. We just moved."

The year before high school graduation most of the other students in Jimmy's class were visiting different campuses. But Jimmy's parents weren't speaking, and they were unable to discuss his future. "I wanted to go to college, so I took the path of least resistance. I came out here to California, to a local junior college. One of my mother's sisters lived in Pasadena." But he didn't seem to fit into his new school either. "Socially, I felt displaced in college," he said. "I didn't have many friends. I wasn't secure enough. Sometimes I'd show up at a bar and smile at somebody and that's all I knew that I could do."

One night, during the Christmas vacation of 1979, he went to a bar and a beautiful young woman walked up to Jimmy and spoke. He was flattered that someone had approached him and considered him worthy of talking to. Before the evening was over he was infatuated with this young woman, whose name he couldn't pronounce. It was Cayenne, like the pepper, and she was a social worker home for the weekend. They dated for six months and Jimmy decided to propose. "I thought, 'She's smarter than I am. If she feels good about this relationship, I should too.'"

Cayenne's family and their Episcopal minister arranged a wedding at their home. They were upper middle class and lived in a wealthy white-collar suburb. Since tradition dictated a few meetings between both sets of parents, they tried to arrange a time together for their folks. But that didn't happen. "Of course my parents weren't speaking to each other," said Jimmy. His mother had dinner alone with Cayenne's parents.

One year after the wedding, Jimmy and Cayenne found an old ramshackle house in Manhattan Beach and signed a mortgage. "It was a big commitment, the house was in terrible shape. It had been an old rooming house, and there was so much work to do." Their life seemed to be progressing smoothly, "We had very few arguments and got along fine," said Jimmy. "One day though, I came home and found a note she'd left saying, 'I can't bring myself to be committed to the relationship.' That was it; she was gone."

After Cayenne filed for divorce, Jimmy heard from her once more, but in error. She told him she dialed him by mistake, that she had been trying to reach someone else. He invited her out for a drink. "It was one of the strangest situations I've been in," said Jimmy. "I kept looking at her thinking, 'I know you. Didn't we spend some time together once?' I felt as if I'd never been married to her."

He learned later that Cayenne had taken up with her old boyfriend, whom she'd met again while still living with Jimmy. Cayenne had hired this man to do some carpentry work on the house. "She married him within a year of our divorce," said Jimmy. "I knew who he was. When Cayenne and I were married, she had talked about him. There had been something about me that reminded her of him. I had only been a holding pattern."

Jimmy, distraught over the divorce, consulted a therapist. "He helped me to understand that I am one helluva guy, intelligent, creative, passionate, all those wonderful traits. All of a sudden I learned that I'm a reasonably valuable being."

♥

Despite his ability to list some of his attributes, it's impossible not to notice Jimmy's low self-esteem. It practically leaps off these pages. His low self-esteem is not surprising. It is one of the most prevalent diseases of our time. I generally use the term dis-ease to describe this trait, because it negatively affects every aspect of an individual's life, especially love relationships. I think Jimmy wants his wife to make him feel valued, but that is an impossible job. No one else can fill that void for him. Even if Monica had begun dropping everything to give him the "good ear" he said he wanted, it would have altered their relationship only slightly, and not necessarily for the better. He would be unable to believe any-thing she said or did that was contrary to his deep-seated convic-tion that he is not worth listening to.

Jimmy's low self-esteem probably didn't begin in his generation of the Bonadonnas. In the past, when survival needs were so pressing, most parents simply did not have time to address a child's emotional needs, nor their own for that matter. As we refer to Jimmy's family background we can feel certain that meeting emotional needs was not a priority.

The immigrant saga in America has become so interwoven with our history that we tend to romanticize it. The truth is that for immigrant families, who often came to America with little more than the clothes on their backs, it was a period fraught with physical hardships and emotional losses.

To understand how this affected Jimmy, let's concentrate on the Italian wing of Jimmy's family, for it is them we know most about. Just as his Polish grandparents had, the Bonadonnas also left behind many loved ones, including extended family members—their support system, that is, anyone to whom they might have turned for solace, comfort, and strength. Even more difficult, in their new land there was little time to talk about their despair. They were in a frenzy to survive. That meant finding a home and a job, mastering a new language and customs, and overriding the inevitable ethnically-based hostility that greeted each new group of immigrants. The idea of soothing a persistent sense of alienation would have been considered an expensive and unnecessary luxury.

Like so many immigrants, the Bonadonnas probably dealt with their homesickness stoically—meaning they did not deal with it at all. They rolled up their proverbial sleeves, began forging better lives for themselves financially, and impoverished themselves emotionally in the process of submerging their feelings.

Their distress undoubtedly resurfaced, though, in their stormy marriage and in their child-rearing. We're told Jimmy's grandparents' dining room table was like a boxing ring. Well, we will never know how much of this was built into their personalities and how much of it was due to frustration. We do know that they must have felt deeply conflicted. Their new lives offered hope of material contentment in the midst of emotional isolation. They eventually handed their inner confusion, and their anger, down to their offspring.

Of course, this does not mean that every immigrant and child felt emotionally dislocated. To some extent, the individual's response is dependent on personality. But like so many immigrants, they must have been saddened to arrive in their new land and discover America's ethnic hostility, especially toward the darker skinned, Southern Italians. Their discontent would have been compounded when the oldest son was killed. This was tragic enough for the parents, and perhaps overwhelming for young Vincent, who lost his big brother.

Later, as an adult, Jimmy's father would undergo another emotional separation. His parents and siblings distanced themselves from him when he married Lydia, an outsider. While he was still viewed with pride by his family, his marriage denied him the position of "honored" son. His parents turned to a son-in-law to mediate family disputes and Vincent felt angry and insulted about this.

With Vincent's macho demeanor, he probably handled it the way he did all his deepest disappointments—with caustic wit. Do you remember Vincent's oft-repeated joke at the sight of the neighborhood doctor? This man must have been a stabbing reminder of Vincent's failure to attend medical school. He knew he was smart enough; it had simply been a bad break for him. He wouldn't have considered it manly to speak of this nagging pain, so he relied on gallows humor. While a good sense of humor is always healthy and welcome, it's unfortunate that Vincent used his to mask his feelings. Sound familiar? It's the same trait we heard in Jimmy's description of his marriage. Like his father, he has learned to keep us laughing . . . so we won't hear his pain.

There is a definite trait from Vincent and Lydia's marriage that echoes in Jimmy's marriage today. There is surely some connection between Vincent's outbursts at Lydia, and the angry, swearing Jimmy we met in tennis whites.

You might wonder what has made Jimmy so angry. After all, we're told his parents showed him a great deal of affection and love. Well, perhaps Jimmy's childhood story best makes the point that love and even good intentions are not enough.

You've probably heard the expression "feeling homesick at home." This was certainly a resounding theme in the story of Jimmy's life. A home is supposed to offer a child restoration, strength, and love. Jimmy's was a bloodless civil war. Vincent's explosions were followed by months of Lydia's hostile silences.

Jimmy was not simply left on the sidelines as a casual observer, he was a wounded noncombatant. Vincent's mode of attack was inferring that his son was not manly enough, that he was a mama's boy, and that he could never do anything well enough. Jimmy reacted by distancing himself the only way he could. He shut down and began to function on a purely intellectual level.

Even worse, his parents unwittingly continued this familial sense of alienation. His father took him on a fishing trip but, ignoring Jimmy, talked to someone else. Jimmy wanted to help out with chores, but he was told he was in the way. His parents kept moving up to bigger and fancier homes because, I'm sure, they wanted to give their son the best life they could. And yet, as if he did not exist, they bought a house without even telling sixteen-year-old Jimmy they were considering a move.

It is not surprising then that Jimmy first married Cayenne, the only woman ever to initiate a conversation with him in a bar.

One of the few things they had in common seems to be that they both had a low opinion of Jimmy. He said Cayenne only married him because he reminded her of an old flame. How insulting. After a year of marriage, in which time Jimmy said there were almost no arguments, Cayenne had such little regard for him that she ended the marriage with a ten-word note: "I can't bring myself to be committed to the relationship."

When Jimmy did talk to Cayenne again, she admitted she had called in error, telling him in effect that he was not even worth a phone call, that he was a wrong number. He took the insult on the chin and agreed to meet her for drinks. Only then was he able to see what she had tried telling him by her sudden departure, that they were strangers.

It is as if Jimmy's inheritance from his grandparents was a sense of disconnectedness. There is a part of him that realizes it. He cried when he discussed his Polish grandparents with Brenda Richardson, saying he was shocked by his tears, that they had come out of the blue, but that he was moved when recalling the warm and loving marriage they'd shared. I don't think that was actually the reason for his tears.

I believe it saddened him to look back to the start of their lives in America, because it tapped into his own rage. Make no mistake, this quiet and well-dressed youth was bristling with hostility toward his parents. This is especially evident in his hostile fantasies of Vincent's death by fire, which he interpreted as fear that he would learn of his father's death on television.

Still, children usually choose one parent to mold themselves after, whether they intend to or not, and it is often the parent they assume controls the home. Jimmy adopted Vincent's reactionary, abusive style. Then he searched for someone who responded to his outbursts just like his mother had to Vincent's, with vengeful silence. For what could be more painful or more familiar to Jimmy than a mate who shuts down in the face of his rage. He got what he did not know he wanted. "I don't care if [Monica] calls me a S.O.B.," he said earlier. And he meant it. Nothing could make him more desperate than being treated as if he were not there.

I do not want to sound as if I am blaming all of Jimmy's

woes on his parents. They loved him and gave him the financial advantages they never had, as well as the drive to succeed, love of family, a refined intelligence, a sense of humor, and a stable life-style that helped him win the woman he loves.

There were just some things they did not know how to give him because they had never experienced them in their own families and could not make the emotional leap for themselves. So they offered Jimmy their love as well as their pain, and it added up to the message that "love hurts."

He was introduced to Monica and he thought her beautiful. But, as we learned in our earlier chapters, there's always something more, some undercurrent that must have attracted them, made them aptly suited for one another. Perhaps we can find out what that certain something is by taking a look at Monica's family history.

MAKING CHANGES

STEP 4 ♥ We made a fearless and searching moral inventory of ourselves.

This step provides the key to effective conflict resolution, which is what the Bonadonnas need right now. Resolving a conflict necessitates both people looking at what they did to create the conflict and taking responsibility for changing the behaviors and words they've contributed to the problem. Most battles seem insolvable because each partner tries to prove he is right and his partner is wrong. Both lose in the end because they simply beat one another down. Monica and Jimmy both express a considerable amount of hostility that needs to be released and sorted out. Who are they *really* angry with?

──────────── ♥ EXERCISES ♥ ────────────

(First do your relaxation and breathing exercises.)

1. Taking inventory: List all your resentments toward your past lovers, then in your second list, your present mate, if you have

one. (Again, this helps you discover the hidden patterns that keep tripping you up in your current relationship.) Then list your resentments toward your parents, being sure to include stepparents and foster parents.

Make a list of all your past lovers' positive traits and your present mate's positive traits. Then add what you learned or gained from each of these people (inner lessons and outer lessons).

Make a list of all your negative traits, include your fears, secrets you haven't shared with your mate, and ways in which you manipulate or attempt to control your mate. Also your character flaws, those parts of you that consistently create more difficulties in your life and relationships. (These may include flaws such as being critical, tardy, overspending, speaking harshly, etc.)

Make a list of all the positive traits and abilities you bring to your present relationship.

Save these lists until after reading the next chapter.

2. Conflict Resolution Skills: Rather than exploding on your partner in a vicious or physical way, this exercise provides a safe alternative to releasing anger without doing any damage.

When you feel yourself beginning to feel so angry that you're about to explode (which you will now recognize as a family pattern or as one of your personality traits from having taken your inventory) stop and do the following exercise:

First, get a pillow or tennis racket or rolled-up towel or newspaper. Raise both arms over your head and bend your knees. Open your mouth so you can exhale, as you bring your arms down and strike a chair or bed or another pillow. Direct whatever feelings you're experiencing at an inanimate object rather than your partner.

If you're in a location where this proves impractical, excuse yourself and go to a rest room. Stare into a toilet, if necessary, and hurl your angry words into that. The idea is to release your anger in the safest way possible.

Also, if like the Kinkaids and the Bonadonnas, you feel you have a backlog of anger, do these exercises regularly. Be sure that you make sounds, don't hold back. The combination releasing the anger and looking at your part in the upset clears the way for healthy communication, which is the next step in conflict resolution. We'll get to that in the next chapter.

Affirmations:
(Repeat 10 times; critical at bedtime.)

1. I am a success; I will persist until I succeed.
2. I have poise and balance and self-control.

♥ *Love saver:*
Make new ground rules. Don't go to bed angry or argue in your bedroom.

6 SAYING THE RIGHT WORDS

It's important if we are to understand the Bonadonnas as a couple in the 1990s also to take a look at Monica's family. We were able to discover only the barest facts about her paternal grandparents. They were

Monica's grandparents:

HENRY: born in Delaware in 1890
KATHRYN: born in Boston in 1905

Henry was a descendant of Civil War (Union) veterans, and was the president of a Rhode Island bank that failed during the Depression. He headed to Portland, Oregon, to begin a new line of work. Unfortunately, his wife, Kathryn, died early in life, leaving Henry with their three young sons, who remember their father as a quiet and pleasant man. One of these boys was

Monica's father:
EDWARD: born in Portland in 1930

Although Edward suffered from the early loss of his mother, his father did remarry a woman who was kind and loving toward the boys. She was considered very "forward" thinking and raised a neighbor's daughter who was a lesbian. Edward, Monica's father, eventually attended the nearby private Reed College, where he met his future wife. That leaves us to explore Monica's richly detailed maternal background. Monica's grandparents were:

CHESTER: born circa 1900 in Seattle, Washington
SARAH: born in 1900 in Tacoma, Washington

Chester, Monica's maternal grandfather, was the son of prosperous Irish Catholic restaurateurs. As an adult, he became the head of a major bank in Seattle. He and his wife, Sarah, would have seven children. The youngest had Down's Syndrome. Chester and Sarah raised their children in a morally conservative Roman Catholic atmosphere, but there were also many luxuries. There was a large house, servants, and expansive acreage. Chester worked long hours at his bank and taught at a local university.

Despite his wealth, he was self-effacing. Once, while crossing a street, he was hit by a car and left for dead. Eventually, he was carried into a city hospital, where he waited for hours to be seen by doctors. Although in a critical state, he never alluded to his social standing nor did he try to "pull strings" to get better care. When a member of the staff recognized Chester from the society pages and tried to convince him to transfer to a private hospital, he insisted on staying where he was and being served in the same manner as less fortunate patients. He soon recuperated.

Chester allowed himself only one great indulgence, his daughter, which brings us to the next generation. She would eventually be Monica's mother:

PATRICIA: born in 1930 in Seattle, Washington

♥

As Chester's favorite child, Patricia was pampered and even given the freedom to be a tomboy. She has warm and loving memories of riding her pony on the family property and of reaching up to pick red, crisp apples from the trees, some of which she would later offer her father. Theirs was a strong father and daughter bond that remained for the rest of Chester's life. Before his death he showed Patricia where he'd left his will and business papers and asked her to look out for her Down's Syndrome brother.

Patricia was so close to her father it caused a schism between her and her mother. Sarah had always been cold and ungenerous toward her, and after her husband named Patricia the executor of his estate, the hostility grew. Even after Monica's grandmother was elderly and living in a nursing home, she showed no appreciation for her daughter's weekly visits. There was no love lost on either side. Patricia felt relieved when her mother died.

Patricia's mother had fought her on virtually every major decision regarding her life. She had not wanted Patricia to attend college, and gave in only after Patricia and her father applied pressure, and then only on the condition that their chauffeur would go to pick up Patricia on weekends and bring her home.

Patricia, who was tall, blonde, thin, and fashionable, fell in love with Edward, a soft-spoken fellow student and he returned her love, quickly proposing marriage. They married after graduation but were separated by the Korean War.

Monica's grandmother had resisted Patricia's marriage, on the grounds that a good Catholic woman had no business marrying a Protestant. Circumstances dictated that she live with her mother in Edward's absence, but when he returned stateside, Patricia was more than happy to move out of her mother's house. So, she and Edward bought a large house in Seattle. He accepted work as a junior executive and the two settled in for a long honeymoon. It would be several years before they began their family of three girls and an equal number of boys. Their marriage seemed perfect. Patricia and Edward got along well and seldom argued.

Her only disappointment was Edward's income. The daughter of a rich man, she'd never even considered asking her fiancé how much money he earned. In fact, she'd never really thought about the price of anything she'd wanted. She had married Edward assuming he could provide the same luxurious life her father had. But Edward was an executive at a small firm, and although his salary might have seemed ample for many families at that time, with their six children and Patricia's expensive tastes, the money only stretched so far.

Patricia wanted to shop at the finest stores, eat out often, and frequent the theater. This she did, using the inheritance left to her by her father. Edward, who hated conflict, let Patricia do exactly as she wanted. For the next several years, she spent her inheritance on any of the "extras" she desired. Edward asked her only to pay for clothing the children, while he handled everything else.

By the mid-seventies, though, her inheritance was exhausted. Patricia began working part-time as a teacher of fashion and design. She seemed to resent working out of the house, but there was no choice, they needed the money. She was skilled in drafting and had a flair for sophisticated fashion. Her designs were well received at the school.

And what of Edward? Well, he began repeating a very familiar pattern in Patricia's family. Of all the children, Edward seemed to favor their firstborn, a little blonde girl, who was named:

MONICA: born in 1963 in Seattle, Washington

Let's hear what Monica has to say about her childhood.

MONICA'S CHILDHOOD AND LIFE AS A SINGLE ADULT

"I grew up in a very happy household and I was a real tomboy," recalled Monica. "We had a big old house with lots of trees surrounding it and the house had lots of porches and a big attic. We were usually outside climbing those trees, or on a rainy day we'd dress up as women. My mother had tons of clothing. We were also into cowboys and indians. I was always the chief. We helped with the little garden outside the kitchen and grew radishes, carrots, corn, beans, and rhubarb—enough to feed the whole family."

Monica said the house always seemed to be full of kids and pets, including two dogs, pet mice, fish, turtles, and William

Shakespeare, their pet guinea pig. Her folks frequently entertained at home, with the children serving as waiters and wait-
resses. Liquor was offered during these parties but neither
Edward nor Patricia drank. Edward was afraid of alcohol. He
had two brothers who had developed alcoholism.

"When my mother was angry with my father she tried not to
let it show," said Patricia. "They didn't fight in front of us. When
she was angry, she would clam up on my father. They slept in
separate beds, but I think they continued to have a love life. When
I was a teenager, I came home from a date one night and found
my mother and father in the same single bed. My father jumped
up and was rushing around getting his clothes back on."

Edward and Patricia were strict as parents and didn't allow
any "outbursts" or shows of disrespect; that meant no disagreeing
with them. They didn't believe in making a big fuss over the way
a person looked. "I was never taught that there was any value to
being pretty. My parents certainly didn't say I was pretty. They
didn't compliment me or encourage me," said Monica. "They
didn't seem to think I needed it."

Monica did feel burdened with housework though. "I did the
laundry, cleaning, dishes, and general upkeep on the house. I was
pretty level-headed, was very religious, and was active in our
family's Episcopal church," she added.

There was just one nagging issue for Patricia. "I was very
close to my father," Monica said. "I went to the grocery store
with him each week, did the dishes with him, did almost everything with him, even playing catch after dinner and accom-
panying him to baseball games. I don't think my father excluded
the other children, but he did make a lot of time for me. My
oldest brother is homosexual, and right from the beginning my
father didn't know how to handle him."

Just as in Patricia's childhood, all this attention from the father toward his oldest daughter affected the mother-daughter relationship. "My mother and I were never close, never had
heartfelt, warm talks," said Monica. "When I was a teenager I
was tall and gawky. I desperately needed her help, but I really
had no guidance. I also gave the impression I didn't want any

help. I looked just like my mother, with the same height and the same coloring. Everyone told me how lucky I was to have such a beautiful mother."

Clothing turned out to be a major source of conflict between Monica and her mother. As you'll recall, Patricia was the parent designated to buy the children's clothes, but Monica felt cheated in that department. "She bought herself exquisite things," said Monica. "She made us some beautiful clothes. But mostly, we got hand-me-downs or cheap things she picked up. I was terribly embarrassed about my clothing, and I was allowed no hand in what I could buy."

Monica recalled the Christmas of 1973, when she turned ten. "I opened a box from my mother that had a green corduroy robe in it that she had sewn for me. It was so ugly. I can't say it enough. There was nothing in the least attractive about it. I wouldn't have given it to a stranger to wear. When I saw it, I couldn't help myself. I made a face to show how disgusted I was and my father slapped me. That was the only time he has ever struck me. I was shocked. It was a terrible Christmas day, but it was not the last bad one. Now that I'm an adult, I've learned to open gifts from my mother after Christmas. They're always so disappointing and insulting. One year she sent me a mildewed plastic Christmas tablecloth. It still had the damp smell from their basement in it. My sister and I still talk to one another about how selfish my mother is."

By the tenth grade Monica's active social life had ended. She had attended the same private school for a decade, but her parents could not afford to continue sending all their children to the school. They could only fit tuition for two of the kids into their budget, and they felt one brother, who had dyslexia, and the sister, with a physical impairment, needed the private school education more than she. Monica was sent to a public school.

"None of my friends were there and I entered the year the public schools were trying to do away with academically segregated classrooms. All of us of the same age were thrown in together. It was a real shock for me to be around kids who had discipline problems or who had a hard time learning. And not feeling pretty and having unattractive clothes didn't help either."

"The worst part of the picture was that I needed glasses," continued Monica. "But my parents felt I didn't. Finally, the school called home and said I couldn't see, so I got glasses. There I was, skinny and tall, these god-awful clothes, glasses, and braces, too. What a sight."

By her junior year, life had improved. A girl had moved next door who became Monica's best friend. Monica became a cheerleader and got involved in athletics. "Even today, though, my mother makes references about how I upset her life and how I was impossible during that period," said Monica. "I think I just needed somebody."

After high school graduation, Monica went away to a Catholic women's college ("because my parents didn't want me to attend a Catholic college, of course"). One Christmas, when she came home for the holiday, her mother found a packet of birth control pills in Monica's suitcase. "She didn't speak to me for two days. My father told me to tell my mother that I was a virgin but that I was using them to regulate my period. I refused to lie. I later told her that she'd had no business at all going through my suitcase."

After graduating from college, she took off for Iran, to join an international volunteer program. That's where she met her first husband, another American volunteer. When they returned to the States they settled in Los Angeles, where her husband began attending medical school and Monica started work on her master's degree. But life didn't progress smoothly. Her husband proved to be an alcoholic and was cold toward her. "He never told me he loved me, never even told me I looked nice. He couldn't have an erection, and he said terrible things to me when we argued. His language was abusive," said Monica.

Her response? "I had an affair," said Monica. "When I told my husband about it, he ended our marriage. I think I told him because I knew that it was the only way I could get out of the marriage. I would never have ended it on my own."

When she met Jimmy, two years later, it took Monica a while to fall in love with him. But she liked him for so many reasons. "There was his intelligence, his sense of humor, his thoughtfulness, his compliments, and seemingly unappeasable sex drive.

He seemed to be the exact opposite of my first husband," Monica said.

Today, she's not so sure.

♥

I'd almost be willing to wager that if Monica were to walk out on Jimmy today, the odds are highly in favor of her finding another man who is very similar to Jimmy and her first husband.

Fortunately, though, Monica isn't looking elsewhere for a mate. She's interested in improving her union with Jimmy. To do that, we need to shine some light on her family history, because it could be dangerously deceptive. There is so much that is good and comfortable that we could almost be lulled into believing that it was as "happy" as Monica described it.

First let's turn to Edward's background. We know Monica's father lost his mother as a very young boy, and that must have been a profound experience for him. To a small child, attachment to mother means survival. As an adult, Edward, with a deep fear of losing another woman he loved, may have been a weak father. It was vital to him to keep Patricia content.

On the other side of Monica's family tree, there is Patricia, and the disconcerting relationship she had with her beloved father, Chester. What a pair they must have made. Chester, who'd been left for dead on a street corner, was too modest a man to even demand proper medical attention for himself. Yet he loved his eldest daughter so much that he gave her what he could not give himself: the best that money could buy. It purchased a lot, and in some ways, Patricia appears to have had a perfect life. In childhood there were ponies that trotted her about fields laced with blossoming apple trees, and as a young woman she received the education she demanded.

But as we have seen, she paid dearly for being Daddy's favorite. It cost her her mother's love. Her mother sent Patricia a mixed message, that "love hurts." That's a refrain that will be heard again and again in this story. As it plays we are left wondering, If Patricia was never loved by her mother, what kind of parent could Patricia be to Monica?

We know the answer to that. Patricia's family theme is played again in her own household and, again, it is almost drowned out by the happy memories. All the ingredients were certainly in place. There was a large house, a thriving vegetable garden, lots of children and pets. Overseeing it all there was even a beautiful mother and a handsome father.

It all sounds so perfect that as an adult, Monica might easily dismiss any unhappy memories and assume her present difficulties have nothing to do with her past. That would be a mistake. You have only to look at Monica's and her mother's childhoods to see convincing evidence of history repeating itself in the most cutting fashion.

Patricia, then Monica, were both tomboys who adored their fathers and qualified as "daddy's girls." Understandably, their mothers resented the special affection their husbands gave their daughters.

The closeness that Monica and her father shared indicates something was amiss in her parents' marriage. A child can only come "between" parents if there is a lot of distance there to begin with. It is impossible to say with certainty just what caused that rift in Patricia and Edward's marriage, but we are told Patricia was extremely narcissistic, that she was unhappy with her husband's low-wattage earning power, and it may well be that her own self-loathing—caused by a loveless relationship with her mother—would have made her as difficult a spouse as she was a parent.

Edward, having lost his mother, may not have known how to be truly intimate with his wife. Consequently, Edward elbowed his way emotionally into a relationship that was comfortable for him, but hurtful for the two women he loved best. Both Monica and Patricia got mixed messages from Edward. He was close to Monica, but often failed to protect her from her mother. He gave in to his wife, but gave his daughter the lavish love and attention Patricia must have craved.

At one point, when he discovered the birth control pills, he even tried to coerce Monica into lying with him to appease his wife. Oh, how frightened and small he must have seemed to his daughter that day. In fact, it may have been a turning point in the way she viewed her father. Years before that, however, Monica probably interpreted his failure to defend her as proof of her worthlessness, that her mother was actually right.

Patricia dealt with it her own way. We have heard that she loved fashionable clothing. In fact, she had so many clothes that during the interviews Monica said she and her siblings used to laughingly refer to Patricia's bulging closets as the garment district. And boy, could she put the right looks together. She had such a sense of style she was able to bring in sorely needed cash by teaching fashion design.

Yet in the same area where she excelled, she deprived her daughter. But it would have been a hard case to prove. That Christmas morning when Monica dared to make a face after unwrapping her homely robe, her father slapped her. How ungrateful Monica must have appeared to him, and how enveloped in shame she must have felt.

Not getting pretty clothing sounds like a weak complaint . . . at first. But when you allow that her mother was a clotheshorse, was considered beautiful, and that many daughters, especially gawky teenagers, long to look like their mothers, you can understand how this bizarre punishment worked.

This is no Cinderella story. Monica was not starved or dressed in rags. No one could accuse Patricia of that. She even sewed some of her daughter's clothes herself. What a show of love. Her punishment of Monica was quietly hurtful. The child was simply not allowed to look good, which translates into not allowed to feel good about herself.

It is a tradition that has been carried on. Recently, when I met Monica, I was struck by how she hid her finely chiseled face behind glasses and her lithe figure beneath dark baggy clothing. It was like watching the lead character in a made-for-television movie. You felt certain that at any moment she was going to whip off the glasses, burn the clothing, and revel in the way she looks. She's positively striking under this "disguise."

Not that it is necessary for everyone to emphasize good looks. But this attempt to disguise her own loveliness is in keeping with what I know about Monica. Not only did being fashionable mean a great deal to her as a teenager, but today she apparently cares about aesthetic detail in other areas of her life. Her home is elegantly styled, and even her daughter's dolls wear Victorian heirlooms handed down from Patricia's mother. And the simplest meals that Monica prepares are presented with an almost magazinelike flare.

Though her husband, whom she loves, urges her to put on makeup and to buy herself some pretty clothes, she will not. When I asked her why she made such an effort to downplay her looks, Monica said, "I never want to be like my mother." Despite the many years that have passed, Monica is unable to see that she could not be more unlike Patricia. She is a caring, loving, generous, affectionate mother who would rather spend time making Christmas cookies with her children than attending a Broadway play.

To top it all off, Monica suffers from survivor's guilt. One brother was dyslexic, at a time when people were not understanding about learning disabilities. A sister, with a congenital defect, limped. Then there was her homosexual brother who was forced to deal with his differences in our acutely homophobic society, and during the sixties, no less. How he must have suffered. In fact, I later learned that he'd attempted suicide.

From Monica's subconscious vantage point, it looked as if she too deserved to suffer in some way.

Embarking upon a search, she went all the way to Iran before she found just the "right" partner: an alcoholic who could not show her love, could not compliment her, could not even make love to her. In one blow, she perpetuated her mother's emotional distance and coldness, replicated her unconsummated love affair with Daddy, and suffered like her siblings. She didn't feel worthy enough to end her first marriage on her own, so she orchestrated a way for her husband to bail out.

Then came Jimmy. He seemed so different. He loved her looks, told her so, and was Johnny-on-the-spot in bed. There was also all that hidden emotional inheritance between them. Consider it. Both their mothers had been favorite daughters and had had a Down's Syndrome sibling. What's more, their parents had married "outsiders" and their mothers responded in similar fashions when angered, by simply shutting down. They had both had one parent who'd been jealous of the special relationship that they'd had with the other parent, and most importantly, they had been raised to read the same words in the family scripts: that love hurts. Once again, the roots of their family trees make them seem predestined for one another.

Monica married, feeling she was safe from hurt at last, as did Jimmy, who must have thought his sense of alienation would be put to rest. The first time Jimmy lashed out, blowing up over something seemingly small, Monica must have regarded it with horror. She surely failed to realize that with faultless emotional radar she and Jimmy had found a place where they could finally feel at home.

Looking injured, Monica must have responded predictably. She clammed up. And the more prolonged her silence, the angrier it made Jimmy. Their unhealed wounds brought to the fore, they were like a psychic duo positioning themselves to move to an old and haunting melody.

But these two want more for themselves, for their children. Let us see what can be done to dispel their old themes.

MAKING CHANGES

STEP 5 ♥ **We admitted to God, to ourselves, and to our partners the exact nature of our wrongs.**

For many this is the most challenging step of all. To admit shortcomings to another. Not just anybody, but the person who by now knows which buttons to push. As difficult as it may be to employ this step, it can give you a new sense of power and freedom. "Speak the truth and the truth shall set you free."

Anything we feel we must hide creates a sense of shame, which produces guilt. Guilt always creates anger and resentment that has to come out somewhere.

If there are wrongs you know will wound your mate share

them with someone who will keep your confidence. You can free yourself without damaging your partner.

─────────── ♥ EXERCISES ♥ ───────────

Start with breathing, relaxing, and visualizing light. I hope you've been practicing so that this is easier and more effective for you now.

1. Take out the lists you've written and line them up next to one another. Mark any resentments and character flaws that appear on more than one list. Do you see a pattern emerging? Most likely, the things you resent your parents for also appear on your list of character flaws. Perhaps your common pattern shows up as a 180-degree shift from your parents' behavior. But this is polarized and not any healthier. John Bradshaw, in his PBS program on dysfunctional families, says, "180 degrees from sick is still sick."

2. Now assess what you learned from your past loves, your mate, and your parents. What have they given you that has served you well in your life? Don't forget the most basic and most important gift from parents, the gift of life.

   Before completing this step, that is, admitting the nature of your wrongs, ask him or her to limit the response to thanking you for having the courage to share this.

3. Read these lists to your mate and share with your mate your discoveries—overlapping patterns, traits, etc. Take responsibility for the ways you have hurt your mate and notice how you learned those hurtful ways.

4. Then it is your partner's turn. After listening, remember to simply say "thank you for having the courage to share this."

Affirmations:

1. I am a success; I will persist until I succeed.
2. I speak the truth and the truth frees me to bring forth the best in myself.

♥

Love saver:
Spend three minutes gazing into one another's eyes, without talking.

EMOTIONAL INCEST

I worked with Jimmy and Monica on a Saturday morning in a hotel conference room a few miles from their home. We had only four hours together because they had their children to get back to and I had another couple in another city to see.

I was aiming for one brief but transforming moment, when a window of understanding would open and allow them to see into their relationship in a new way, so they could make different choices in their behavior.

Jimmy and Monica had met me at the local airport. There we were, three strangers en route to a sharing of intimacies. I was delighted to meet them. Brenda Richardson, who was not with us, had described them perfectly—her fine-boned face swathed in hair, his dark and athletic looks. But reading notes about someone is one thing, seeing the Bonadonnas together was something entirely different. Two people bound together seem to create a third personality. I found the Bonadonnas intense, curious, and charming. I'm sure you will also enjoy knowing them.

(The Bonadonnas sit facing Dr. Wade.)

DR. WADE: Monica, the first issue I want to concentrate on is a dangerous need you seem to have. How does it feel to hear that? I believe you've been programmed for a certain amount of abuse.

MONICA (softly): I would accept that.

DR. WADE: I'm not suggesting your mother wasn't a good person, but she trained you in that pattern.

JIMMY: That's pretty abusive.

DR. WADE: Well, in fact Jimmy, that's what you do also when you lose your temper with Monica. One of the things I want to work with today is how you can manage your anger in a way that will work better. But Monica, his rage works well for you. That way you get to meet your quota of shame. First, though, let's talk about how you feel when your husband is angry.

MONICA: I think, "Oh no, I'm doing this again, falling into a trap. I feel helpless."

DR. WADE: Yes, listen to your description. You could be talking about a defenseless animal caught in a trap. But, in fact, you're a strong, competent, independent woman. When I walked off that plane I knew you the minute I spotted you, with all your strength and beauty. So what do you see as the nature of the paradox? Why do you feel you need this abuse?

MONICA: I don't know what goes through my mind. I feel awful, helpless. I withdraw, then I feel kind of cold and wait for the time to pass so I can overcome it.

DR. WADE: Have you ever said to Jimmy, "Hey, this is abusive and I won't take that."

MONICA: No, I just clam up.

JIMMY: And that makes it worse for me.

DR. WADE: Oh, I know, Jimmy, your mother was the clam-up champion, one time for thirteen months, right? And your mother would clam up, too, right Monica?

MONICA: Yes.

DR. WADE: So, one of the first things we can do to break that is to have you practice, right here. I want you to turn and look at Jimmy, and I'd like you to say in whatever way you can, "It's not okay. That's abusive and I won't accept it."

MONICA (she pauses a while, then raises her voice at Jimmy): Now, don't give me that look, raising your eyebrow. You may not yell at me anymore. I don't deserve that.

JIMMY (looking embarrassed): I'm sorry.

DR. WADE: Now Monica, this may sound peculiar, but I really believe you set him up to be angry and to be the "acter outer," and to dump a lot of the rage—because it isn't okay with you to express your rage and anger. You still see yourself as that good little girl.

MONICA: So I make him angry for me?

DR. WADE: Yes, think of it. You have to be seething. You were subjected to the most bizarre abuse. It was really quite vicious. With your mother's exquisite clothing she drew a distinction between herself and her importance, and your lack of it. So where did you put that anger?

MONICA: Well, there was some rebellion. I didn't go out and wreck cars or anything.

DR. WADE: What did you do?

MONICA: I dated the wrong boys. That's normal.

DR. WADE: And what was your experience with them?

MONICA: More abuse.

DR. WADE: That's right. Do you see the pattern here? What you did was take the anger you felt toward your mom and your dad, because he didn't stand up for you, and you found people to abuse you. So the trick here is to integrate a more loving version of yourself and to pass back to Mom, pass back to Dad, some of that rage. Because each time you trigger Jimmy, he can act out all his anger, and you get to be abused and have your anger expressed.

JIMMY: I'm carrying on the tradition.

DR. WADE: Yes, this is a marriage made in heaven. You can act this all out together. Jimmy, how does it make you feel to have me talking to Monica about this abuse.

JIMMY: It appears I'm part of an equation.

MONICA: He has said I set him up.

JIMMY: Yes, in a very clever way. It takes a lot to set me off. The best trigger is when Monica just closes down. That sets me off. For me that's like lighting a bomb. I need to be heard.

DR. WADE: But why does it bother you?

JIMMY: It lights up rejection.

DR. WADE: Take this back one generation.

JIMMY: Yeah, I think it's the reason my father didn't spend a lot of time at home. His idea of leisure was going back to the old neighborhood. He probably couldn't stand my mother's firm grip of control on the house. I see that coming up with me.

DR. WADE: This is a complex picture, but it's like a big puzzle, so let's see if we can start fitting some of the pieces together. Jimmy, you can see that Monica sets you off, but do you see your part in it? You allow her to do it. She could put the bait out and you could say "No thanks." But you hop right on it.

MONICA: He gets frustrated with the job or something that has nothing to do with me, but he'll use it as an opportunity to complain about how I don't meet his needs. Let's say he's been away all day and he pictures me as being more than I am, more beautiful, more ready for him, more intellectual, more worldly, and he comes home and I'm tired from work. I'm just this ragged mess and I'm trying to cook dinner and one of the kids is crying. I feel he has this need to let it all out and I happen to be there, and he turns things I have nothing to do with into my fault.

DR. WADE: Jimmy, is that right?

JIMMY: Yes, I think I get very angry. I probably do have unfair expectations of her.

DR. WADE: Where did you learn that?

JIMMY: My father was always pushing me to do better, work harder, reach for more. He was never giving, never accepted me, nothing I did was ever good enough, so I suppose that's why I push Monica.

MONICA: When he comes in I won't let him go along with his high expectations. I may defend his boss or not agree, but one way or the other I don't say, "Sorry, I can't talk about it now." I try to keep myself busy and listen with one ear while he talks about his problem.

DR. WADE: Jimmy, how was your mother about listening to your dreams?

JIMMY: She hung onto my every utterance.

DR. WADE: I know that, and why do you think she did?

JIMMY: Because she was a homemaker and she was there.

DR. WADE: And most importantly . . .

JIMMY: I was all she had.

DR. WADE: That's right. You were her husband, everything Vincent was not. One of the things you told us when you were interviewed was how crushed she was when you moved out.

JIMMY: That's right.

MONICA: I never knew that. Really?

DR. WADE: Jimmy, you're not going to like what this is called, but we have a name for this. It's emotional incest. That's when a child is made to fulfill an adult's needs, needs the adult should be fulfilling with another adult. That's why your father felt so angry, so jealous of you, despite his love for you. And to some extent, Monica, you were in a similar situation. There was a certain lack of continuity in your parents' marriage. I read this part over and over trying to make sense of it. It was an odd piece of the puzzle. Your parents loved each other, but in some sense your mother wasn't going to really let anybody be close to her.

MONICA: I know.

DR. WADE: So your dad took you all these places and did all the things he couldn't with his wife.

JIMMY: That's part of our emotional dynamic that matches up then. We dovetail in that way.

DR. WADE: Yes, you both learned how to be in inappropriate relationships.

JIMMY: We went in this together hoping to have a party, but we brought the wrong dishes. The next step is, how do we face each other and do it properly?

DR. WADE: You give back some of the anger.

JIMMY: I don't remember having one argument with my mother when I was growing up.

DR. WADE: What do you suppose your reaction was when you realized that this was not appropriate, that you really should not have been sitting in your father's place?

JIMMY: Guilt?

DR. WADE: Yes, but guilt always has another companion, anger. You had to wear the pressed clothes and be the little man with all the manners, sitting in the house with your mom. She made you what she needed you to be. While what you wanted . . .

JIMMY: Was to be her son, to go out and play and have a good time.

DR. WADE: And there was that longing for your father's acceptance.

JIMMY: That's the thread that goes through my life. I'd kill for it.

MONICA: But why did Jimmy pick me, someone who was the furthest point away from accepting him? I'm so different than he is, and so cool.

DR. WADE: That's right. You guys are cooking with gas, as they say. Why do you think he picked you, Monica?

MONICA (after a long pause, then sadly): I was virtually unattainable.

DR. WADE: That's right, and . . .

JIMMY: All I know is hard work and reaching for the sky, asking myself, Why not? You fit that description, Monica, and because you were different from me, so . . .

MONICA: I was therefore better.

JIMMY (with a mournful sigh): Yeah.

DR. WADE: You guys are doing great. Now what's the next piece of the puzzle?

JIMMY: I don't know.

DR. WADE: All you know about a love relationship is that you have to work to get the love and try even harder to get the approval.

JIMMY: My life was bittersweet. There was comfort and solace on one hand, and on the other, I was never good enough.

DR. WADE: What did you learn watching your parents interact, about what a husband and wife were like in a love relationship?

JIMMY: Probably nothing, because I didn't get a ticket for that game. What I saw was a nonevent. I didn't see interaction. I saw conflict and tension.

DR. WADE: And what else, you're close.

JIMMY: The distancing, the shutting down.

DR. WADE: That's the missing piece.

JIMMY: But what about in Monica's family, where there were strong interpersonal relationships?

DR. WADE: That was a child's view of the marriage. Remember, that, in truth, it would have been hard to be close to her mother.

MONICA: That's okay with my father because he's so independent. He was able to cope.

DR. WADE: Do you realize who you're really talking about?

MONICA: No.

DR. WADE: Yourself. You were telling yourself that it was okay, that you could cope with her because you're so independent, so strong. But you were in a lot of pain.

MONICA: I think that's right.

DR. WADE: So, what if we do a little work here to symbolically pass back some of this to your parents. I'm going to pull these two empty chairs in front of you. Monica, the fancy one is your mother, okay? Now Monica, I want you to talk to them, tell them how you felt.

MONICA (She is quiet for a while, as if struggling within. Her words come out slowly, then in a rush.): Mom, I felt like I was not human, was not important in your life. There was never any room for me. You'd tell me what I had to do and I would cooperate with you. I was afraid of you. And Dad, you always backed her, no matter what. I needed you to be there for me. I needed someone on my side. We got very close a couple of times, but you always backed down.

DR. WADE: Tell him some more. Don't let him off the hook anymore.

MONICA: I needed you to help me reach Mom. You understood me better than she did. Instead of giving me an out when she found my birth control pills, you told me to lie, to say I wasn't just using them prophylactically, that I was still a virgin, and that I intended to be a virgin, just like she was when you married. You could have said to her, "Look, she's obviously sexually active and she's doing the right thing. She doesn't want to get hurt and pregnant." But you wanted me to go and lie for you. (with her voice raised) I am not going to do it. (turning toward chair representing her mother) I went to you and I said, "Yes, I'm using the pills and be glad that I'm not getting pregnant because the last thing you want me to do is marry that good-for-nothing."

DR. WADE: It's hard for you to use the word "anger." Could you just say, I felt really angry with you?

MONICA: I felt angry with you both.

DR. WADE: Yes, that's right.

MONICA: Mom, you let me sign up for the American Field Service. It was so competitive, and when I found out they were going to pick me to go to France, you said, "No." I said, "Then why did you let me go through all that stuff?" And you said, "I didn't think you'd get this far." I had to appear in front of all those respected people in the community and tell them I couldn't accept. I remember their faces. I remember what I was wearing.

DR. WADE: What?

MONICA: A gray dress, red shoes, and a crisp red ribbon in my hair. I am so pissed, Mom! I could just strangle you! (She sobs.)

DR. WADE: What could Jimmy do right now that would help you? He feels for you, too.

MONICA (Crying softly): I felt so powerless.

DR. WADE: It was good for you to get that out, because you won't use it to beat yourself up with it anymore. Monica, I hadn't heard of that story. It wasn't in the notes.

MONICA: No, it was just so painful . . .

DR. WADE: Is there anything you could use from Jimmy?

MONICA: I don't know.

DR. WADE: Do you ever tell him when you are feeling pain? Do you ever ask him to just hold your hand, to comfort you?

MONICA: I've tried to, but I can't.

DR. WADE: I'm going to give you a chair over here, Jimmy, so you can sit closer, for as long as she needs you. What was that like for you, Jimmy? Can you hold her hand and tell her how you feel?

JIMMY (Holding her in his arms as she cries): I feel a sense of satisfaction. I feel valuable. My wife has a need and she needs me.

DR. WADE: But you see, we are all children in a sense, too. That little girl inside this grown-up, competent woman was badly hurt. Monica, it's good for you to share your feelings with Jimmy. That pain you've been keeping inside is what you get him to act out. So you beat yourself up with him, instead of telling him how hurt you are from all these crazy and bizarre things that were done to you.

MONICA: It still hurts to this day, and I can't tell them.

DR. WADE: That's okay. Telling it here will help. You're sharing it with the person that you need to be with. Now, Monica, I noticed that you just pulled away. Tell me what was going on.

MONICA: I was thinking that I can't let anyone share my pain.

DR. WADE: What are you really afraid of if you should share your feelings and allow Jimmy to be close to you?

MONICA: That he'll see the real me.

DR. WADE: And the real you is what?

MONICA: Needy.

DR. WADE: Yes, you don't want anyone to know there is someone inside who is hurting. Tell him what your needs are that you've been afraid to show him, that you are desperately afraid to acknowledge.

MONICA: I don't know.

DR. WADE: Oh, yes you do. I won't let you off that easily.

MONICA: I don't want him to know that I need love, affection. Because if I do I'm not me, I'm not whole. I'm weak.

DR. WADE: And if you let yourself be "weak" with him, what will he do?

MONICA: Hurt me.

DR. WADE: So the last thing on earth that you're ever going to do is give Jimmy the opportunity to hurt you the way your mother hurt you.

MONICA: That's right. That's the parallel.

DR. WADE: But don't you see, you'll never gain a thing by being counterdependent, which is what you are?

MONICA: Counterdependent?

DR. WADE: That means you have so many needs that you can't possibly let anyone know. Some people, like your mother, whine and think, "Me, me, me." You could never be that way. But you are good at playing the game. You want the battles. So why don't you just look at your husband and say to him right now what you would like to do by changing the pattern. Tell him how he can reach you before you get those walls up again.

MONICA: I need not to be your mother. I need to be your wife. I need you, I need your comfort, your love. (They stand in an embrace. She tucks her head into his shoulder.)

DR. WADE: How does that feel for a change, Jimmy?

JIMMY: Wonderful, sincere.

DR. WADE: Is it very frightening for you, Monica? Tell him what it feels like.

MONICA: I'm frightened that I need you. No one else in the world can give me what you do.

DR. WADE: Isn't that why you married him?

MONICA: I want to keep this marriage, and I'm asking you for that. (They are both crying now, embracing, comforting one another.)

DR. WADE: Isn't it interesting that you are able to unload some pain and anger, and that you are able to connect with Jimmy in a way perhaps that you couldn't with anyone else.

MONICA and JIMMY: Yes.

DR. WADE: Your parents have been very much in the way of you two, and unless you can do the exercises and put the anger where it belongs, you two will continue hurting one another.

Okay, before we turn to Jimmy, Monica, tell him what you've learned about yourself today.

MONICA: When I'm getting into a situation when it looks like I'm provoking you, I'm really begging you to look at a bigger issue that I'm angry about. I need you to help me move the garbage out of our way, look at me, and ask me what I really need. I'm not trying to put you down.

DR. WADE: So, Jimmy, what you are going to have to do is be a bit of a wizard, now that you are on to her game of counterdependency. A lot of strong, beautiful women who play this game just really want to be loved.

MONICA: So the more I want to be loved, the harder I disagree.

DR. WADE: Then you get angry with him for not meeting your needs. Yes, good for you, Monica. Nice work. Okay, Jimmy, your turn.

JIMMY: Now what?

DR. WADE: I'm just going to set these chairs up to represent your mother and father. To get on with your marriage, you need to divorce your mother. You can still be her son, but you already have the wife you want. Now, relax and see if you can allow the flow of feelings in your body. It has been a long time for you. Jimmy, I want you to tell your mother something.

JIMMY: We didn't have any harsh times.

MONICA: Are you kidding? You're furious with her every time she just comes to the house. You can feel the tension.

DR. WADE: Take this pillow and I want you to beat the chair with it. Say, "I don't want to be your husband." (He swipes at the chair playfully.)

DR. WADE: Come on, Jimmy. Talk to her the way you would to Monica. Try bending your knees, loosen your body up, and just let the words come out. (He begins pounding, harder and harder.)

DR. WADE: I can't hear you.

JIMMY: I'm not your husband. I'm myself. I'm not your husband. I don't want to be there for you like that. (He continues pounding for a few seconds, then drops the pillow and crosses the room to Monica.)

DR. WADE: Okay, Jimmy, so can you talk to old Dad and tell him what you need to say?

JIMMY: Dad, I am very upset with you. You never understood me. There could have been more. You gave me no direction. I had to grow up on my own. Your work ethic was just a little too difficult.

MONICA: You were the greatest son anyone could have had.

JIMMY: Yeah, but he didn't know that or didn't bother to tell me. It's upsetting.

DR. WADE: Upset, is that some kind of code word?

JIMMY: It was halfhearted. I am angry, but I can't do this so well.

DR. WADE: Tell him what you feel about his halfhearted efforts at loving you.

JIMMY: I tried so hard. We could have had so much. We could have been dangerous.

MONICA (She crosses the room and holds Jimmy. They are crying together, holding onto one another. Monica looks up and cups Jimmy's face in her hands.): You know what, Jimmy? When we're cooking we can be dangerous together.

JIMMY: We do have a lot of strength. We're better together than we are apart, aren't we?

MONICA: When we get going no one can touch what we can accomplish, nobody we know.

DR. WADE: Yes, and now that we've got the pieces together you can see what the puzzle says because you've just connected in a new way, with words, with feelings. I can feel your strength. You are far better together than apart.

MAKING CHANGES

STEP 6 ♥ We are entirely ready to have God remove all our defects of character.

Deciding to let go of the old, entrenched negative behaviors, that's what this step suggests to me. This strengthens anew the idea that we are each responsible for our own shortcomings. We must look inside if we want real change in our love lives. Jimmy and Monica are now aware of their character defects, the need to control, his vicious temper and her self-neglect. Now they must make a decision that they are truly ready to surrender these defects, these useless but troublesome burdens.

Ask yourself, am I ready and willing to change?

———————————— ♥ EXERCISES ♥ ————————————

1. Spend three minutes breathing, relaxing, and visualizing the soothing light washing down around and through you.

2. I recommended that the Bonadonnas plan for regular time to talk together, free of distractions. A weekly date is perfect for this, as long as it includes some real fun. This couple time forms a foundation for any two who want to keep their love full of zing and closeness. Please implement this time with your mate and never let go of it. Set one weeknight aside and stick to it. If you can't avoid being apart on your "date night," do a makeup night to compensate.

I have also encouraged Monica to attend Al-Anon meetings to work on her control issues. Although liquor is not a problem in their household, Al-Anon is an excellent twelve-step program for teaching people how to "let go" and stop trying to control loved ones.

Jimmy should attend a male peer-counseling group. He needs to have supportive and gratifying relationships with other men.

3. I have given them each cognitive work in the form of personal affirmations. For Jimmy: "The more I love myself, the more I have to give." Monica: "I am a worthy and deserving person. I enjoy taking care of myself."

4. Recommended Bibliotherapy:

   ➤ Monica should read *Codependent No More* by Melody Beattie. This book addresses the issues of control and the inability to meet one's needs.

   ➤ Jimmy should read *Making Contact* by Virginia Satir, for details on changing communication styles.

   ➤ They should both read *I Deserve Love* by Sondra Ray, because they both have self-esteem issues.

♥ | *Love saver:*
   | **Make love with the lights on and your eyes open.**

Now let's meet our next couple.

8 DEPENDENCY AND CODEPENDENCY

The beauty of the Kenyan countryside must seem light years away as Bernard Ogot makes his way across the littered yard of a housing project in Atlanta, Georgia.

"Hey, Mr. Ogot," a young girl calls in greeting.

As a district housing supervisor, Bernard Ogot has become a familiar face at the projects. He smiles as the girl passes, then waits until she is out of earshot before he begins speaking again. He speaks in an educated British accent as he tries to make sense out of what has happened to his marriage.

"This is very difficult," he says, wiping his face with a damp hankie, "this talk of our personal concerns. But Constance and I have agreed, you see. It is quite necessary that we seek intervention." He pauses in the middle of a field glittering with broken glass and rests a foot on a cement block as he searches for words. His hands close, then open, his fingers poised as if before an altar rail. Sweat lines cross his white short-sleeved shirt. With the humidity at 100 percent and temperatures in the upper nineties, it is an authentic Southern depression.

"All I want," he begins, "is for Constance to accept me the way I am. I think I'm a very caring man, very trustworthy. I don't run around with other women. I arrive home evenings in a timely manner. I work hard for my income, but I don't stop after work and drink or even keep liquor in the house. I might get drunk if we go to a party, but then I let her drive us home. I just want her to show appreciation for me, tell me I look good when I'm wearing a new suit, to recognize my efforts."

He walks toward his Chevy Malibu, and once in, holds his face over the air-conditioning vent. Warm air rushes out. By the time the car is fully cool, he is pulling into the driveway of his modest brick home. He looks spent from the heat and the talk, but his words continue.

"Romance is the whole issue for me," he continues. "I want romantic love, but that doesn't exist for Constance. Sometimes I must entice her to say certain things I want to hear. I need, a slight bit, to be mothered by her. There's something missing in our marriage which I need but am not getting . . ."

Eyes downward, he continues, as if forcing the words out. "At the end of the day I would like to embrace and kiss my wife. I'd like sweet talk, shows of concern about my work. But most of the time we don't even talk. She's the same with friends, with the children. With me, she's a hindrance in the area of socialization. On the job I have many friends, but we've distanced ourselves from other Kenyans. She wants to have me home, alone, and at the same time she doesn't want me. We're alone in a room. If I want company I must pick up a book, a newspaper. She does what she does—sews, cleans, watches television. But for the two of us there's nothing. Even when she's angry she does not verbalize what she's thinking. If I suggest she's angry, she becomes very sensitive. She denies me, suppresses me."

He opens the door to a house where only the voice of a popular television talk-show host can be heard. Their three teenage children will be back later, he says. He and Constance have arranged time for the start of these interviews. He gestures toward the interior of his home. Though the house was of course built in America, it feels foreign inside. The furnishings are spare, the floors polished and cleanly swept, and except for a small piece of Kenyan craft, the walls are white, without decoration.

From the kitchen, the television is clicked off, and then Constance moves forward. She is a timid looking woman standing in the living room doorway—trying to smile. She wears a draping floor-length outfit, of African print, with a matching headwrap. Constance is forty-two, eleven years younger than Bernard, and at least two inches taller. They are both reed slender.

Bernard excuses himself. He must return to work, he explains, but will be back "in time." He rushes off, into the heat, as if relieved of some difficult chore.

Constance begins by sharing photographs of their children. There is James, seventeen, Stephanie, fourteen, and Roberta, eight. "I taught her to read at three," Constance says, then looks embarrassed, as if caught at bragging.

As the interview begins, Constance sits with her hands underneath her legs, looking resolute, like a soldier, even when the subject turns to love.

"Do I love him, now?" she repeats. "Well, yesterday I thought, I'm a lucky person. I was watching Oprah Winfrey and the show was about how women can be so hurt when they meet the wrong men. Some men are so brutal they beat their women, wind up killing them. Bernard is tender. He's a good father, and reliable. I would miss him if he went away. But the only fear I really have, if Bernard were to leave, is the financial part. I'm not well-educated enough to support the kids.

"To be honest, there are times when he touches me and it's embarrassing, in front of the kids. He touches me in . . . in . . . places I don't like. I've enjoyed sex a few time with him but not often. It's hard for me. I've told him I don't know why. I don't often have an orgasm. I have only a very few times in my life, and only with Bernard. I don't think the sexual attraction is gone, but if it has, it's his fault. Has he told you he's a drinker? Well, it turns me off completely.

"I enjoy sex if I'm in a good mood, and then we have sex about three times a week. Bernard spends a lot of time with foreplay. He asks me what parts I want him to touch on me. We talk about my fantasies. We have oral sex. I don't do that for him. I do it because I like it. Most of the time I'm too uptight for anything.

"I do love Bernard, but it's hard to show it because I never learned. Even my kids, they come to me when they need a hug, I don't go to them for it. We're not brought up that way in Kenya. There, hugging is a greeting, not for love. You could see the affection in the eyes. As a child, I never saw adults kiss. That is something for these Western countries, and that's where I first saw this kind of outward affection. When you live in America, it's easy to begin to expect the same things you see others getting.

"I enjoy being around other Kenyans here, but I had to cut out all those Kenyans who dropped by for drinks. They were always expecting beer in the house. They seem to have control over Bernard. It seemed he could forget all about us and his energy was put into them. He would begin drinking with them, and I'd say, 'I think you've had enough.' He'd repeat what I said very loudly, let everybody know, so that I'd cool it. Everybody would turn on me and say, 'Come on, let him have another one, don't be so rough on him.' I had to start defending myself. I'd talk back very loudly, embarrassing him. I had to. Then I cut him off from these people.

"He says I interfere with his life, that he wants to enjoy life. That has been a big problem. For a long time, I didn't consider Bernard an alcoholic. Two or three times a week, he drinks one or two beers and falls asleep, or sometimes will start an argument, which I don't like. I put much of my energy toward his problem. Sometimes, if liquor has been in the house, I pour it down the sink. I grew up without a father, and I don't want that for my children.

"When he cut down on his drinking four years ago, I said, let's go to a dance class, put your energy into something instead of drinking. But what he really enjoys is going out alone, coming home drunk. I said, either we both go or we both stay. Nobody goes out alone. So we stay home. Since I've said this he doesn't like to go out as a family. I make plans, but then he doesn't seem interested in being with us."

♥

As I read the Ogots' discussion of their marriage, I was reminded of a training session almost two decades ago with Virginia Satir, a woman who was my mentor and who is considered by many to be the founder of family therapy. During that session, we novice therapists were shown a film that had been produced in Germany, of a couple talking about their marital conflicts. Although we were able to see them, most of us couldn't understand their words, for they spoke in German. Fortunately, the audio portion of the film included the voice of a translator. The effect was mesmerizing. More than anything, as I sat there watching this couple from a continent away, I realized just how universal problems are in love relationships. But for their language, the couple could have been from any country.

Constance and Bernard's comments underscore that point. He wants romance, reassurance. She wants him to quit his compulsive behavior, stop making her family's future precarious. They are from Kenya, a country with customs radically different from ours, but the Ogots' values in love are familiar. They remind us that across the continents couples struggle with the elusive experience of intimacy.

Constance and Bernard also seem universal in their inability to sort through their motives and identify their feelings. One thing is clear to us, that despite any addictions Bernard may have, Constance is depressed and controlling. She said it was necessary to cut off his friendships because other Kenyans encourage him to drink. In a working marriage that is not for her to decide. When someone obsessively tries to control others, that is called codependency. Constance is so worried about her husband's ties to alcohol that she has become addicted to keeping him away from it and that addiction zaps any energy or enthusiasm she might have had.

With that in mind, it is of particular interest that Constance cites Bernard's drinking as the reason for her sexual coolness. Could that simply be an excuse? She mentioned that she seldom initiates physical contact even with her children. She says it's cultural. That may be so, but my guess is that her dislike of physical intimacy is an important clue about her past. We are left wondering what historical events could have forced Constance to shut down physically as well as emotionally.

As for Bernard, he admits he gets too inebriated at parties to drive himself home. As his story progresses, the question of whether or not he is suffering from alcoholism will be answered. We will also be searching for clues to why he needs to be mothered by his wife. He says he puts sweet words in her mouth and asks her to repeat them to him. In the end he's left with the feeling that something is still amiss. We shall learn how and when these feelings first arose, as we look into their family histories.

Bernard's family

(Virtually nothing is known about either of the Ogots' grandparents.)

Bernard's father:	CHARLES
mother:	MARY
brother:	ADAM
Constance's father:	DANIEL
mother:	EDNA

Family Themes: In Constance's family the women believe that men will abandon you. In Bernard's family they believe women will turn on you.

As so little family history has survived the Ogots' migration to the United States, we'll move directly to Bernard's parents:

CHARLES: born in 1915 in the Kenyan countryside twenty miles from Machakos
MARY: born in 1916 in a village near Machakos

Bernard's parents, Charles and Mary, were of the Christian faith but practiced polygamy. In addition to Mary, Charles had two other wives and respective sets of children. They lived in different hamlets only a few miles away, and there was frequent communication and visits between the families.

Mary was considered the head of Charles's "first" family, because they married in church, while the other wives were what some might call, common-law. Charles would spend Monday through Thursday nights with Mary, at their home near the city, and weekends, he went to his families in the country. Having more than one wife was a sign of a man's prosperity.

Charles was a salesman for a private company, then he became a clerk for the city and also invested in property. He and Mary had eight children and she pushed him to get ahead financially. Although she hated the idea, Mary gave in to Charles's desire for a polygamous life.

The birth of Mary's first two children raised her to a special position in their village. The first son was one of our two main characters.

BERNARD: born 1940
ADAM: also born in 1940

Both the boys looked just like their father and exactly like one another. Although Bernard was older, with only seven months between them, the boys grew at the same rate. Mary even dressed them identically. They looked so much like twins that a religious significance was attached to their births. They were viewed as a blessing, answers to prayers of fertility. It was as if Mary and Charles's family had been especially chosen by God to raise these special boys, who seemed destined to excel in life. Mary delayed Bernard's entrance in school for a year so they could attend together. Once enrolled, few of their classmates could tell them apart.

At the end of the work day the boys would race to the bottom of the hill to meet their father as he returned from work and to push his bike uphill for him. It was a simple show of respect and, at the same time, allowed them to bask in their pride of Charles. On the way up they'd meet other villagers who would hail him, for he was well known and greatly admired. Best of all for the boys, Charles would sometimes allow them to ride his bike, rather than walk it. In the evening, as the journey uphill began, Charles would sometimes throw his arms around his boys and give them dual hugs.

Charles was viewed as an especially liberal father. He'd attended a nearby college for a few years to study education and had read about the dangers of corporal punishment. He forbade Mary to beat their children.

As for his relationship with his wife, their domestic life was not as peaceful as it seemed outwardly. When the boys were sixteen, an event occurred in their household that they would not learn about for decades. Mary became pregnant by another man and left home for a few months until she gave birth. During this time, Charles brought home one of his "country" wives to run the family. Meanwhile, Mary gave birth to a daughter, who she brought back home eventually and passed off as a "guest." It wasn't until this guest was dying of a chronic disease, years later, that the truth was revealed to the rest of the family. The girl's biological father spoke up and claimed her as his own. Mary explained to her astonished family that she'd been lonely because Charles was so seldom home, and she'd thus felt driven to another man. She admitted that she'd been unhappy in her marriage and that she saw herself as a victim of a man married to more than one wife.

BERNARD TELLS OF HIS CHILDHOOD

"Although it was typical in my country for a man to practice polygamy, I began to believe this was degrading, wrong. I look back and I don't know how families worked it out. Perhaps they didn't. But as a young boy, it all seemed quite natural. Although my father was a good parent, he had these several homes he had to go to so I don't feel he really knew me."

Bernard became an avid soccer player, and eventually made the national team. In the classroom, though, he said, "I only played stupid." His brother, Adam, however, did quite well. "He was a brilliant chap," said Bernard. "I was very jealous of him and we used to fight violently. I used to think of killing him so I could separate us for good. My strongest hate for my brother occurred because my mother emphasized his success. She'd say, 'Adam is smart, he's going to make it in this world.' She would say I was stupid. 'You're not going to make it,' she told me.

'Soccer players don't make it. If you're good at sports you'll wind up working as a bricklayer.'"

Like most children, Bernard did not contest his mother's line of reasoning and, believing he was stupid, began to hate himself. "All through those years I prayed to God, asking, 'How can I turn this around?'"

One of the worst experiences of Bernard's life occurred when he was a child of six and was caught stealing. It happened during the summer, when he was visiting an aunt's home. "Our society is so interwoven that it's as if children don't belong to one family," said Bernard. "They might stay at this aunt's house one summer, at another's the next."

A boy who lived near the aunt Bernard was visiting that summer had been given a Waterman fountain pen. It was a prized gift in their small African village, where usually only grown men possessed sophisticated writing instruments. Bernard thought this boy's pen beautiful and watched to see where the boy placed it at bedtime. Then he stole it.

The next morning the boy's father came to where Bernard was staying and questioned him. "I started crying," said Bernard, "and gave it back, of course, but my aunt beat me and said she would tell my parents. News of the crime went round my village, for word of mouth travels like lightning in these areas. What I had done was an anathema. My parents seemed understanding, but for years, repeatedly, my mother would bring that up. She'd say, 'Of course I can't trust you. You were caught stealing.' I'd beg her, 'Please, can't you forget that?' She could not."

The story of Bernard's theft dogged him for years. Neighbors considered him a thief and stupid. By the time he was thirteen, he was so fed up with Kenyan society that he decided to spend a few months visiting a boy he'd met from Uganda. This was highly unusual. People in his neighborhood traveled so seldom that the idea of going to another country and living among strangers was almost shocking. When he told his mother he wanted to go she laughed at him and said they didn't have the money for him to travel. But his father intervened, saying he understood the boy's need to leave. Charles gave his son train fare and spending money.

Bernard stayed away for a few months, and when he returned,

"I was hailed as a hero," said Bernard. "As the first child from the area to have an adventure, I was considerd quite brave. The tide changed then for me. Certain flaws in my reputation remained, but my father seized the opportunity and offered me a chance to collect rental money from tenants. It was a public declaration of his trust in me."

By the next year the boys were old enough to show interest in girls. Adam, always the victor in their young lives, was tremendously popular. "He had good looks," Bernard explained. "Yes, we look alike, but the women went for him. I think he got them because of his academic successes."

After graduation the boys were selected by the World Council of Churches for a scholarship to attend a theological seminary in Greece. "I was nineteen years old and frightened," said Bernard. "I didn't want to go, but competition in our country to attend the local universities was very stiff. It depended on corruption and social standing. I knew I had to accept the scholarship offer. My grades were poor. I was taken along with Adam only because the committee didn't want to separate us."

Their new school was a religious institution, somewhat like a monastery, and was academically rigorous. Bernard and Adam took as many as sixteen courses in one year. "It wasn't just difficult for us," said Bernard, "but for everyone there. It didn't take long for Adam to move out ahead of the pack. By that next semester he'd made the dean's list by learning the language immediately and typing his papers out in Greek."

They were in the same classes, but Bernard fell behind. In their junior year they had to give a sermon in Greek. The professor, who heard their sermons on different days, said Adam had given an impressive speech, and that he had mastered the intricacies of grammar. Adam was awarded the top grade, a nine. "The European college system is different from in America," said Bernard. "Here if we fail, no one else knows. In Greece, when the results of our sermons came in, we were all in the dining room. The professor read aloud the names of those who had passed and those who had failed. Adam had done tremendously. When it was announced that I had failed, I laughed it off, saying, 'It's okay I'll pass it in the summer,' but I was quite humiliated."

Bernard was determined to change the downward spiral of his life. Realizing there was still a slim chance for him to get into an American university for graduate study, he invested all his efforts in his class work. By the end of the year, in fact, when the grades were announced, Bernard had nothing to be ashamed of. He still remembers the dean's schoolwide announcement. "Adam received 9, 8, 9, 10," said Bernard. "I got 9, 10, 10, 10."

That next February Bernard received word that he had been accepted to Emory University in Atlanta. "They turned Adam down," Bernard said. "I received a full scholarship. My involvement in sports had helped me. Athletes were seen as being more well rounded."

Adam was accepted at a smaller college, but he became disillusioned. This was the first time he had not fared better than Bernard. Although Bernard insisted that they could still hope to work on their doctoral degrees together, Adam insisted on returning to Kenya. Today he's a minister. "I send money back home to him," concluded Bernard.

It would take another twelve years, in which time Bernard completed his master's degree, married, and divorced, before he would meet Constance during a visit home to Kenya.

♥

Before we can bring them shoulder to shoulder, however, it is important to understand just how Bernard's childhood may have affected him as an adult. Although it lacks obvious trauma, it certainly was emotionally taxing. We are led to believe that his mother had high expectations for him to live up to. But did she really? We do know that she entered her sons into a high-stakes race as if they were horses. The winner would get Mother's love, the loser, her disapproval and scorn.

What she meted out to Bernard was so hurtful that despite his great intelligence he became an underachiever at school. When a bright child begins doing poorly in school it is like a red flag, a call of distress. Bernard felt angry and depressed and his academic performance reflected that. I'm certain he had come to believe his mother's repeated epitaph of "you're stupid."

The truth is, his mother did not turn against him because he brought home poor grades. Mother love doesn't work that way. She was obviously furious with his father (witness her affair), and projected that anger onto Bernard. Why him? Well, it's not surprising that she looked to her oldest son to dump her anger. They looked just like her husband and he took great pride in them. But though the boys looked like twins, it's obvious their personalities differed. Bernard, as he fully demonstrated in his junior year of college, was a fighter. Just consider how he refused to simply accept the villagers' scorn without trying to reestablish his reputation. His never-say-die attitude, which ultimately made him a winner professionally, may have served him poorly in his mother's household.

Since a child's survival depends on his parents, a youngster usually views his parents as unassailable, all-powerful beings. Rather than focusing his rage on his mother, Bernard looked to Adam. Bernard said he wanted to kill him. It's true that Bernard did want to kill someone, but it was not his brother. It was his mother. He retaliated in the most effective way he could. He dropped out of the race and gave up in school.

This doesn't mean he stopped longing for her love. His need for it surfaces throughout the discussion of his relationship with Constance and what he needed from her to feel good. As a child, this need drove him to steal that pen. When a child steals, especially in a society where theft is such a taboo, it, too, is a cry for help. The theft represents an attempt to fill a sense of emptiness.

Bernard's father did not rebuke him, and does appear to have been an important ally in his life. But he was there so seldom, Bernard could not count on him to buffer his mother's assaults. He finally left home for a while. He did not leave to find adventure, but to escape the sense of shame he felt. Fortunately, when Bernard returned, his father began to show his trust in him by allowing him to collect the rent money.

I don't want to exonerate his father completely, though. When one parent stands back good-naturedly, while the other parent is abusive, he or she is equally as guilty as the abuser. Charles was wise enough to rise through the ranks of his society to become a respected neighbor, and to understand that corporal punishment damages a child. It's too bad neither he nor his wife comprehended the destructive effects of verbal beatings.

Once in Greece, Bernard's first years at college were only replays of the humiliation he had known as a boy. It must have been disturbing for any of the students to hear their failures announced; probably exceedingly so for Bernard, who was locked in a bittersweet rivalry with his brother, Adam.

The incident convinced Bernard of a need for change, and change he did with stunning success. His determination to turn his academic failure into victory must be acknowledged. But as great as it may have been, it could not undo any of the hurt and humiliation he'd suffered as a child.

Fifteen years later he was introduced to Constance, and even if he had known every detail of her past, he would have still loved her. For as you will learn there are troublesome issues in her past that make this couple seem a perfectly matched pair.

CONSTANCE'S CHILDHOOD

Constance's parents:

EDNA: born in 1930 in Nairobi, Kenya
DANIEL: born in 1930 in Nairobi, Kenya

A tragedy occurred six years into Edna and Daniel's marriage. Daniel was a heavy drinker and he paid the price for it with his health. At only twenty-seven years old he died from kidney failure and Edna was left with their four children. Even worse, some members of Daniel's family took their grief out on Edna. They were very superstitious and felt she was to blame for her young husband's death. They'd overheard her complaints in the past about his heavy drinking and how it interfered with their ability to run a local fruit business. They claimed Edna had cursed him and wished him ill.

The finger-pointing campaign began during Daniel's funeral. Some of his cousins said Edna deserved to be pushed into the grave alongside the deceased as punishment for her evil doings, and that her children should be taken away from her. Boldly, Edna's mother rose and stood before the crowd, defending her daughter. She warned anyone who would listen that to get to her daughter they'd have to go through her first. This woman was respected in the community and the angry crowd backed off. The fearless mother took Edna and her children to her home to plan a course of action.

While they were there, some of Daniel's relatives crept into Edna's home and stole everything—blankets, plates, even the food from her cabinets. Even so, Edna borrowing strength from her mother, could not be easily bowed. Taking her youngest daughter with her, she headed for the nearby city of Nairobi, where she hoped to find work. She had been trained as a registered nurse. She vowed to return to the area one day, and reclaim her other children, whom she left in the care of her mother.

The three children remained with the grandmother for a year. But she fell ill and could not continue caring for all of them. She kept two of the children, and sent one away. This was the oldest child and one of our two main characters in this drama.

CONSTANCE: born in 1950 in Kitui, Kenya

Constance was seven years old when she found herself among strangers. Recently, when asked about this time in her life, she said, "It was very hard for me. I couldn't ask my grandmother not to send me. There was no way for my mother to support me. I went to my uncle's home."

Constance said she did not cry when she left her beloved grandmother and her brothers and sisters. "I was hard-hearted. Before that, at my father's funeral, as I was getting out of the car, a relative had spanked me for not crying. Even then I did not cry."

The uncle with whom she was sent to live was an accountant who worked in the city and who was away most of the week. Constance was therefore left with his wife and her four cousins. "My aunt had a bad temper," said Constance. "Scolding was a way of life there. If you were sent to get firewood you got scolded for not getting the best sticks. When I was eight, I can remember striking a match to light a lantern. In those days our lamps had wicks in them. My aunt scolded me. She said I should have gone into the kitchen and lit the lantern from a fire in the stove, rather than wasting matches. She said, 'Your mother doesn't buy anything here, not food, not matches, not even your clothes, so don't waste what we have.' That hurt me. I thought my mother had been contributing food and money for my care. I felt like a visitor, never at home there."

Her uncle and aunt owned a plantation where they grew casabas and corn. The children were expected to work hard. They'd rise at six, work in the fields for one hour, walk home from the fields, bathe, and have tea and breakfast before school. When the aunt prepared a meal, she saved most of the food for Sam, her biological son who was five years older than Constance. Sometimes Constance left home hungry, but there were fields on the way to school where she could pick passion fruit and sugar cane and eat them along the way.

For about two years, from the time Constance was eight, James, a fourteen-year-old boy who lived at the aunt's home, and her cousin Sam sexually molested her. Until this interview, Constance had never shared this story with anyone except Bernard, who had advised her that it was best not to talk about it.

"It's a secret I've kept," she said. "James started it first. He did it playfully, pretending to be my friend. He seemed to know what he was doing, but since I was eight, I didn't really. After James had started I think he and Sam began colluding, for they both began sneaking into my room at night."

James eventually went away to school and Constance began fighting off Sam's advances. But Sam forced himself on her, raping her when he pleased. "I couldn't struggle or scream because I was afraid the others would hear," said Constance. "There were no walls between the rooms." Sam eventually stopped abusing her when she continued fighting him off.

Another childhood incident that has remained painfully buried in Constance's past occurred when she was eleven. A neighbor had come to visit them with her children. When they left, Constance escorted them home. Her aunt went along, too, but left earlier than her young charges. When Constance realized her aunt was gone, she raced back home. She and the other children were expected to feed the pigs and had forgotten. The aunt said the children would be punished by not being fed themselves. The children hid in the bushes until dinner was over and the aunt began searching for them. When she found the children she made them strip, walk out into the garden, and bathe outside like animals, where everyone in the neighborhood could see them. "It was humiliating," said Constance, "walking around with no clothes on."

Constance did not fare well in elementary school. "When I went to visit my mother on holiday and brought my report card home, she became concerned about my grades. She moved me home with her when I was fourteen, because by then she'd found a job as a nurse and was living comfortably. The next year my mother's brother helped her build a two-bedroom house, and we were all reunited again. It was a good feeling. She showed us love and it seemed, although it wasn't actually true, that we could get everything we wanted. My mother did seem to love my sister, the youngest one, Ann, the most."

Slowly it dawned on Constance, as she watched her mother and Ann together, that no matter how difficult her mother's financial situation had been in the past, she had always managed to take Ann with her. Constance became jealous of the closeness between them, especially when her mother compared Constance with Ann. "Whenever I got bad grades, she brought up the comparison. I wanted to do well in school, but I used to think so much about what had happened to us when we were young," said Constance.

Even with a tutor, Constance's grades failed to improve. At fifteen she was sent to a convent. "I was sad to go, but I knew I couldn't cry or complain. Children who attended boarding school did better in college."

After high school graduation Constance spent two years training in a local hospital for a degree in nursing. Although friendless and dateless in high school, she found love in college. She admired one young man in particular because he was so different from her. "He was very popular and I fell in love with him," Constance said. "We had sex, but I can't say I enjoyed it. I did it so I could keep him."

She paid a harsh price for the affair. At nineteen she discovered she was pregnant, and though she kept it a secret until she was eight months along, her mother finally discovered the truth. "She wanted me to have an abortion, but it was too late," said Constance. "She took me to the hospital and had a friend who was a nurse induce labor."

Once the baby, a girl, was born, her mother took over. She named the baby, and then gave it away. "She didn't want anyone to know about it, not even the baby's father," said Constance. "The birth was to remain a secret. I got to hold the baby for three days, but then I had to go home alone."

A few months later, Constance made some diapers and a few hand-sewn gifts and took them to the baby. Her mother learned of this and forbade Constance to go back. "It was very upsetting," said Constance. "After I moved to this country, one night I went to bed but couldn't sleep. I began thinking about the child. She's a woman now, with her own child. I started crying and told Bernard about her. He told me that when he was a young man, he'd had a baby out of wedlock, too. I was so angry that he hadn't told me. But then I realized I'd done the same thing to him. I don't know where my baby's father is. I would have liked to have married him. Right now I feel angry for what my mother did. I know she did what she felt was best. But I wish at least she had let me tell him."

♥

Constance's story of her childhood is fraught with losses: her father, her mother, her grandmother, her siblings, her first child, even her own life. For although she thinks, talks, and moves about in her roles as wife, mother, and employee, there is but a flicker of emotional life remaining in her. She numbed herself long ago.

We should begin our discussion of who she is in relation to her father, since her anger started with him. How could she not feel nagging resentment toward the person whose death left her vulnerable to all of the abuse and humiliation she later suffered. I can imagine the thought often crossing her mind, "If my father were still alive things would be different."

When a child's parent dies, they lose not only the emotional attachment but a primal sense of security. Even if in reality, the father was lacking in some way, or emotionally distant, that does not lessen the blow. In fact, the child imbues the missing parent with idealized qualities and imagines he would magically make things better if he reappeared.

Everyone Constance trusted or looked to for solace in her childhood let her down, including her mother, who left her with abusive relatives. Constance might say she understands all the reasons her mother had to leave her as an innocent young child, barely school age, but in truth she knows her abandonment by her mother cannot be so easily dismissed.

Even if it had meant Constance's mother had had to spend occasional weekends driving or hitchhiking to visit each of her children and talk to them about their lives and how they were faring, it could have made all the difference for Constance. Her mother can offer no acceptable excuses for her neglect.

It isn't difficult to point to the time in Constance's life when emotions ceased to exist. She said she was so "hard-hearted" at her father's funeral that a relative beat her for not crying. What she really was was broken-hearted. The tears would not come because she had shut down to protect herself from more pain. She could feel nothing, not anger, and surely not sadness. It was not just that her father had died. Her relatives had accused her mother of murder, robbed her family, cast them into the street, and left them to starve.

Then, as if her mother had chosen which of her daughters would live and which would die, she chose Constance's sister, Ann, and sent Constance away. Certainly Constance wondered, "Why Ann and not me? What is there bad about me that would make me undesirable to my own mother?"

Away from home this eight-year-old was repeatedly fondled and raped. Victims of sexual molestation usually believe that they are the ones at fault. A child has a deep sense that this act is wrong and dirty and is usually silenced by her attacker. Further confusion occurs if the child's genitals are stimulated in a way that might trigger some pleasurable feelings. The child confuses sexual pleasure with guilt and scalding shame.

The rapes were tragic enough. Add to that the sadistic punishment by her aunt forcing her to walk outside nude, at the age of eleven, when a child is just entering puberty and feeling painfully self-conscious. This cemented her conviction that her body was a repulsive object and a source of humiliation.

Having spent her formative years with a debilitating sense of neglect and suffering, she finally went home. Her mother was able to provide material comforts, but still, in comparing Constance's failures to her sister's achievements she continued to deliver the message that Constance was not as valuable as Ann, and that she was simply not good enough. Then, after only one year, she was sent away to school, yet another loss for this poor child.

Not surprisingly, in college, she used her sexuality only to keep a boy she loved from leaving, not for pleasure. She was incapable of experiencing physical satisfaction. The special connection and warmth that lovemaking should offer was beyond Constance's frozen sensibilities.

We know the result of that joyless sexual union. This time there was no dark bedroom, no giggling boys with sweaty hands, but that induced labor was another rape. Her baby was forced from her, then given away.

The miracle in this is that Constance survived at all. She is a striking example of courage and strength. Proof of her determination to prevail came when she met Bernard and tried to open her heart to him.

Not surprisingly, Bernard and Constance have very different stories to tell about their early life together. I believe it's important to hear them both, because it helps us understand more about what bound them together and how that strains their marriage today. First, we'll hear from Bernard, who opens with their first meeting, during his trip home to Kenya, almost two decades ago:

"When I met Constance, marriage was not the issue. Her mother, a widow with four children, was looking for a husband for her daughters. This is a reserved, conservative family, respected, something like the Kennedys. People knew them there.

They are highly esteemed. One of the brothers is a councilman in the Kenyan commission. The mother talked nicely. My good friend who had traveled overseas with me introduced me to the mother and then to Constance, no strings attached."

In Kenya, when a countryman comes from abroad, he's considered a resource, someone to get applications and help finding scholarships. Bernard offered to help the mother in any way possible, and suggested that perhaps he could get Constance out of the country and into the United States.

Unbeknownst to his Kenyan family and friends, Bernard was in the midst of a difficult transition. He had taught for eleven years at an historically black college that had just reduced the number of faculty in his department. Bernard was one of the instructors who had lost a job and was feeling frustrated. He'd enrolled at Duke University in North Carolina, and was accepted for work on his second master's degree. "I had taken the trip back home to see my family, but I had no intention of getting married," said Bernard. "My previous experience in marriage had not been good. I had wed an American woman and it ended in a divorce in the late sixties."

Then the friend who'd introduced him to the young nurse suggested that she'd make a good wife. "I still had other ideas. But by then I'd developed an interest in her," said Bernard. "I stayed in the country a week longer than I'd planned, getting to know Constance a bit, then went straight to school that September."

Back in the States Bernard missed Constance and wrote to her, inviting her to join him. "I suspected she was fighting the age differences," he said, "and I worried there might be an encroaching man, self-invited. She's not the kind of woman to fool around with a lot of men."

Six months later Constance gave in to the pressure. But soon after her arrival in the States, Bernard's hopes began to dim. Living with Constance, coming to know her ways, was for him, he said, "like seeing grapes sour on the vine. My financial picture had been misunderstood, and I had to fight her shyness. She was very detached. In our culture women don't challenge a man's view. Because of that and her personality, she was not helping me make decisions, wasn't talking. I'd look up and say to her, 'Why don't you say something?'"

He finished his master's degree in 1974 but couldn't find a professional position right away. He accepted a job as a clerk in a luggage store, where he was employed for three years. "The people I worked with kept saying things like, 'I thought you went to a big university? So why are you working here?' These things would hurt me. Afterwards, if someone would ask me, I'd go out and have a drink. Constance detests drinking.

"My drinking is an ongoing issue. I spent a night in jail for it. I realized the change had to come from within me. I was drinking heavily and it had to do with my job dissatisfaction. But since then I've changed, and she has been amazed."

♥

It was of course natural that Bernard longed for romance and companionship. You'll recall, though, that he was introduced to Constance shortly after the humiliation of being laid off from his job. His newly adopted country, at this juncture in his life, was more a symbol to him of his failed desires. Even worse, the extreme racism of the States made his homeland seem all the more sweet. So he had a big job planned for Constance. He saw her as capable of wiping out all his loneliness, sense of rejection, and failure.

Imagine his frustration when she arrived. He had pictured someone who could offer him love and warmth. Instead he got criticism and more rejection. He described it as "like seeing grapes wither on the vine." It is a chilling image, but, as I said earlier, it's a familiar pattern in relationships. In the beginning of our passion, we invest our mate with extraordinary powers: someone who can make us feel loved, smart, happy, secure. The list could go on ad infinitum. To us, the person looks like someone who can do the impossible, namely give us what our parents couldn't. When we realize he or she cannot, our disappointment and anger is all the greater. We have been duped . . . by ourselves.

Right from the start Bernard's drinking became an issue in their relationship. Bernard offers us a classic excuse. He blames his drinking on external circumstances, in this case, his inability to find a good job. This is called denial. Sometime in your life you may have heard these kinds of excuses from someone you love. It is symptomatic behavior for alcoholics and drug addicts, who comprise fourteen percent of our population. That number alone, however, does not adequately indicate the magnitude of the problem. There's a good chance that you're in love with someone who is something like Bernard. Try substituting another word for alcoholism and see if it fits. This person may be destroying a relationship because he works too much or smokes too much or eats too much or controls or spends or saves or cleans or talks about religion too much. (This is another of those almost endless lists.) The point is that the obsession can always be blamed on something else, just as Bernard points to a job he doesn't like.

It is true that Bernard had good reason to feel disappointed over his job status. After all, he'd just invested twenty-five thousand dollars in graduate school, but his drinking had little to do with disappointment. Alcoholism is a genetically transmitted disease that includes emotional and psychological patterns of dysfunction. It can't be merely explained away. Meanwhile, there was his bride eyeing his failures closely, thinking how very different he had seemed when she met him. Let's listen as she talks about those early days.

"I met Bernard when I was twenty-four. Perhaps my mother had said something to her sister about finding somebody for me, I don't know. My aunt and uncle invited me out to lunch, and when I arrived, Bernard was there. I recognized him as being one of two brothers who looked just alike. I didn't know which one he was.

"After lunch, my aunt asked me what I thought of him. I really had no feelings for him. The age difference contributed to my lack of interest. I'd dreamed of having a man my own age, but I was impressed with Bernard. He was introduced as a teacher at a great university in America. I assumed he was well off financially."

Once Bernard returned to the States, Constance began receiving love letters from him and offers of his assistance in helping her move to America. Her mother would read the letters and insist that Constance write back to him. "I didn't say anything about love when I wrote," said Constance. "I'd tell him about progress in getting my visa and news from home. I went along with my mother because in our country we quiet things, like feelings. We don't say everything. Now I say whatever I want. Then, I did what my mother wanted. What the elders say in my country, even if it's an elder sister, you have to go along with. I felt I would learn to love him."

Constance arrived in the States during the winter. It was a difficult time for her. Bernard, broke after spending his savings on graduate school, could only give her forty dollars for a coat, a sweater, and a pair of slacks. "The financial problems were big," Constance said. "We had no money. He hadn't explained that he had been terminated from his job. The only money he was getting was one hundred dollars a month from a pension. We lived in a bedroom in a boarding house and shared a kitchen and a bathroom with other men. I spent a lot of the time in my room alone. I was angry about being misled."

She soon discovered that Bernard drank, and often. "We had become engaged, but I stopped the wedding the first time. I never knew when he was going to come home. This continued for about six months. He got a part-time job that January, and we had a little more money. I'd give him bus fare and he'd walk instead and use the money for beer."

♥

So, because Bernard was too insecure to have presented a true picture of himself, he set the stage for a marriage of ongoing distrust. Constance fit right in as the leading lady, for she had learned her lines about men early in life: that they could not be trusted, and that they'd leave you and betray you in the most hurtful ways. Somewhere, in the back of Constance's psyche, she must have realized their emotional dynamics matched perfectly. This woman whose father drank himself to death, with uncanny precision had found a man who also drinks. Unconsciously she tried to re-create a major turning point in her life, hoping this time she could make it better, that her father would stop drinking and not abandon her. What else could she do? This was her script, and her mother's script . . .

She must have entertained some hope that her new life would be better, yet she placed herself squarely in the middle of her biggest fear and crossed the oceans and joined hands with Bernard.

Once she was there, Bernard said he began noticing her coolness, her quiet misery. I think a man of his great intelligence might have noticed it long before, during those early meetings, had he wanted to. But he was probably overcome by something she exuded that was especially familiar. Did he sense that she too was a less loved sibling? That she had been humiliated in childhood? Or that, like his mother, she also mourned for an unclaimed child? To paraphrase a verse from the Old Testament, "Her ways were as of old." Constance must have seemed as familiar as home cooking.

He had taken his lingering impressions of her back to the States, savored them, then sent her a one-way ticket from Nairobi. Once arrived, she told him she could not trust him and that he was a great disappointment. He felt the old shame rising around his collar. Should he send her back to Kenya? Absolutely not. He paused for a minute, inhaled the aroma of familiar foods, and set the wedding date.

Now that they are married and their hidden dynamics have kicked in, let's see what can be done to bring about a transformation in their relationship.

MAKING CHANGES

STEP 7 ♥ **We humbly asked God to remove our shortcomings.**

Having made the decision in Step 6 that we are truly ready to change, to surrender our character defects, we can now ask for help. Praying for help to change, to become a better person, adds octane to our progress. Bernard must pray for sobriety. There is an A.A. story in which, when a speaker asked to see the hands of those who had slipped (returned to drinking) since joining the program, every hand in the room went up. Then the speaker asked to see the hands of those who had a slip on a day they had asked God to keep them sober, *no* hands went up.

Bernard has the motivation to change, he loves Constance, but he needs the kind of power evoked through spiritual surrender, and prayer. Constance meanwhile could use prayer power to keep her focus on herself and her own life and needs and to end her attempts to control Bernard.

Ask to have your shortcomings removed in whatever way you choose to pray. The Indian spiritual leader Sai Baba says, "You must ask God for what you want in words; a mother may know that a child needs nourishment but she only gives food when the child says he's hungry."

♥ EXERCISES ♥

1. Breathe, relax, visualize light—determine once again to persist until you succeed.

2. In that relaxed, uplifted state of mind, picture yourself as the kind of mate you want to be, see yourself with the positive characteristics you desire. For example, rather than being critical or controlling, picture yourself as patient and accepting. See yourself living your life, not your partner's.

3. Affirm: I am a worthy and deserving person. I love and respect myself and I love and respect my beloved.

4. Bibliotherapy: Both Bernard and Constance should read *Live Your Dreams* by Les Brown or listen to audiotapes by this popular motivational speaker. He has a reputation for turning lives around.

♥ Love saver:
Read romantic poetry to one another.
Practice in advance.

9   THE TIE THAT BINDS

On the day I came face-to-face with the Ogots I was unsure of what to expect from Constance. Brenda Richardson had said that during the many hours she questioned Constance in the quiet of her living room, Constance never let her guard down. She was polite but stern and wary, very wary.

Brenda had worried that she just wasn't getting through to Constance, that unless she could get her to open up and do more than recite the facts about her past, the value of her future session with me would be jeopardized.

Brenda is someone who believes fully in the power of her intuition. So as she sat there with Constance, letting the late afternoon sun slip from the room, she searched her heart for the question, the one that would open Constance's floodgates. Then suddenly the question came to her, but she hesitated. She said it was the first time in her twenty years as a journalist that she'd actually feared asking a question.

"Constance," she began slowly. "Who was it?"

Constance's head shot up. She eyed Brenda and asked suspiciously, "What do you mean?"

"Who was it that touched you when you were a little girl," Brenda asked, and added. "It was someone who wasn't supposed to touch you."

Brenda later said that as her words came out even she didn't know how she had guessed Constance's secret with such absolute certainty. But as you've already learned, she was correct.

Constance began twisting her wedding band and answered. "It was my cousin," she said, "from the time I was eight years old."

Then the real interview began. Later, when Brenda had had a chance to think about what had occurred, she said her intuition had told her to stop treating Constance like Mrs. Ogot-the-staid-African-lady and, instead, to speak to her woman to woman.

"Once I did that," Brenda said, "the conversation was no longer between reporter and subject. I sensed that few other experiences could wound a woman so deeply that she'd close her entire body down around her secret. I'd mistakenly judged her as shy. What she was was a woman filled with guilt."

When I met the Ogots I prayed for Constance to take the next step toward healing and allow the experience to touch her heart.

CONSTANCE: Dr. Wade, I have a question I want your help with.

DR. WADE: Of course.

CONSTANCE: It's about the child I had before I married. My mother took the child away from me and forbade me to see her. Now she has become a woman, married, and had a child of her own. She has written that she and her daughter would like to come and visit us. My children don't know about her. They don't know they have a sister and a niece.

DR. WADE: I'm sure this has been eating away at you.

CONSTANCE (nodding vigorously): It has.

DR. WADE: I think this could bring about a healing for you to welcome her and her child here.

CONSTANCE: Yes, but my other children don't know about them.

DR. WADE: Intuitively, your children already know. Families have this kind of psychic connection. They sense that you've been unhappy and that you've sheltered a secret.

CONSTANCE: My oldest daughter gets very upset whenever anyone else comes into the family. I don't know how she would take it.

BERNARD: Yes, she's very fiery.

CONSTANCE: I'm worried.

DR. WADE: Do you feel guilty about this other child?

CONSTANCE: Now that you mention it, I suppose I do.

DR. WADE: Anger and guilt go hand in hand. Are you aware of your anger?

CONSTANCE: I sense it sometimes.

DR. WADE: If you were to express your anger, who would you need to talk to right now?

CONSTANCE: Him. (She points at Bernard.) And my children.

DR. WADE: I don't think so.

CONSTANCE: My mother?

DR. WADE: I think you knew that from the start. (She places an empty chair in front of Constance.) Go ahead, tell her.

CONSTANCE (sits silently and looks sad): I'm angry with you. You took part of me away. At least I wanted my child to know me as her mother. I feel cheated, angry, and left out. It hurts so badly that sometimes I put the anger toward my children for no reason at all.

DR. WADE: What do you feel right now?

CONSTANCE: Guilt.

DR. WADE (gesturing toward the chair): Tell her about the guilt.

CONSTANCE: I feel guilty about my children. I don't know what they'll think of me.

DR. WADE: Constance, when are you going to let yourself off the hook? You did the best you could. Bernard, will you tell Constance how you feel about it?

BERNARD: I want you to know that there's nothing wrong that you've done by bringing this child into the world. I feel they are our daughter and our grandchild, we must help them grow. They need us and that's the most important thing we can do for them now.

DR. WADE: How does that feel, Constance?

CONSTANCE: Good.

DR. WADE: What were you afraid he might say?

CONSTANCE: Before I told him, I was afraid he would leave me.

DR. WADE: Bernard, will you leave her?

BERNARD: No, of course not.

DR. WADE: Tell her.

BERNARD: I want to reassure you that I won't leave you.

DR. WADE: Why?

BERNARD (turning to Constance): Because I love you.

CONSTANCE (barely audible): I love you too.

DR. WADE: You were barely able to respond. Is it hard for you to tell him?

CONSTANCE: Not as hard as it used to be. We've been working on it.

DR. WADE: Good. But what makes it hard?

CONSTANCE: Through the years I guess I've been afraid of rejection and being let down.

DR. WADE: Tell him.

CONSTANCE: It was not so much my problem as his. Because of his drinking. He promises not to drink and then he does it again. It makes me feel like I'm suffocating, like I can't breathe.

DR. WADE: Tell him directly please. I notice you two have some trouble talking directly to one another.

CONSTANCE: When you make promises you don't keep it hurts me inside and I just can't face you when it builds up. I keep it inside and don't say anything.

DR. WADE: What do you do with the anger? It never just sits there.

CONSTANCE: I try to get him one way or the other.

DR. WADE: How?

CONSTANCE: I use sex as the weapon.

BERNARD: Yes, yes.

CONSTANCE: I try to stay away from him.

DR. WADE: That's what a lot of women do.

CONSTANCE: So he gets angry and that makes me feel good because then at least he feels the way I do.

BERNARD (in his most rational tones): I tried to make you understand that time I went on a binge. I wasn't happy with what I was doing. I couldn't get a good job after graduate school. Things were not very easy. I tried to make you understand this several times. I only drink occasionally now. Why can't I convince you?

DR. WADE: Are you two aware that you're talking on completely different levels? She's talking about how she feels in here (pointing to the chest). You're speaking from your head, saying "Why don't you understand?" This has nothing to do with reason for her. This is raw emotion, hurt, and anger. You are not going to get her to reason away these feelings.

BERNARD: Okay. Constance, I think that . . .

DR. WADE: I'm sorry Bernard, I have to interrupt again. You just started with "I think." Now I now you have a beautifully developed intellect, with all of these degrees. But when your wife says to you, "I'm hurting," all that education is not going to help. You might want to respond to her with something that is also emotional.

BERNARD: I've tried to explain to you. (Constance begins to giggle.)

DR. WADE: Again, please.

BERNARD: I understand your feelings.

DR. WADE: Good start. Now put your hand over your heart. Try to sense what it must feel like to be suffocated. Constance, try to stay with him. He's trying hard to reach out to you.

BERNARD: Constance, I'm really trying to understand and come to your side. I have feelings, too.

DR. WADE: Tell her about them.

BERNARD: When we have arguments and you deny me having sex with you, I feel left out. I want to know why.

DR. WADE: No questions now, Bernard. Tell her how you feel and where you feel it.

BERNARD (with sudden, almost convulsive force, his arms sweep the length of his body): I feel it all over my whole body.

DR. WADE: Excellent.

BERNARD: I feel my whole body is empty. The emptiness is so great that I feel lost. (He gestures in despair.) I need you and I wonder why you do this to me.

CONSTANCE (to Dr. Wade): I want to hurt him. I want him to know how I hurt.

DR. WADE: What's it like when you hear that you've hurt him?

CONSTANCE: It makes me feel good.

DR. WADE: Tell him, then, that you're glad you've hurt him.

CONSTANCE (with embarrassment): I'm glad.

DR. WADE: Okay, you two have achieved your goal. He hurt you. You've hurt him. Is that what you want?

CONSTANCE and BERNARD: No.

DR. WADE: Then what do you want?

CONSTANCE: To be close.

BERNARD: But when I try to talk to you in bed you turn your back.

CONSTANCE (to Dr. Wade): He doesn't want to talk at the right time. He wants to play with the children when I want to talk.

DR. WADE: You want to control when he talks, when he drinks, when he has sex, when he plays with his children. So, is it working?

CONSTANCE: It's not.

DR. WADE: What is happening in your marriage?

CONSTANCE: It's falling apart.

DR. WADE: I want to go back to your childhood to help you understand what this need to control is all about. Let's go back. What most stands out for you in your memories?

CONSTANCE: My father died and his family treated us so badly. They left us with only the clothes on our backs. Not even a blanket or pans to cook in. (She is animated and clearly angry now.) My mother had to give us away to relatives because she couldn't take care of us. I don't have any anger toward her. She did the best she could.

DR. WADE: You know, if I walked over there and broke your foot accidentally, you might understand that I didn't mean to. But would your foot hurt any less?

CONSTANCE: As a mother, I sympathize with her.

DR. WADE: As a mother, would you send your children away?

CONSTANCE: I could never do it. One reason I try to control Bernard is because I lost my father. I don't want Bernard to die. If it weren't for the children I would have left him because of the drinking.

BERNARD: I feel very bad about what you're saying. You're saying that since we have the children you'll stay. Without the children you would go your way. It makes me feel like you don't care for me.

CONSTANCE: I do care, but it seems that you don't appreciate my caring.

DR. WADE: You two are stuck here, so let's shift gears. One of your problems is your sex life, so maybe we can kill two birds with one stone. Constance, when your cousin started molesting you, you were eight years old. Would you be willing to go back to that painful time so we can heal it?

CONSTANCE: I guess so.

DR. WADE: Have you shared this with Bernard?

CONSTANCE: Not details.

DR. WADE: Why not?

CONSTANCE: It's embarrassing. (after a long pause) It's shameful.

DR. WADE: That's the word. But who does the shame really belong to? Who committed the shameful act?

CONSTANCE: Him, Sam, and James, too.

DR. WADE: Then why were you reluctant to tell Bernard about this?

CONSTANCE: I just wanted him to understand that it wasn't my fault and that I did not initiate any of it.

DR. WADE (turning toward Bernard with a smile on her face): Of course, you suspected all along that she initiated this?

BERNARD: No, of course not. Constance, I want you to understand that I know it was not your fault. You should not be shameful of it. (He has reached for her hand and grasped it.)

DR. WADE: Talk to your cousins about this, Constance. These chairs are them.

CONSTANCE (slowly, in a child's voice): What you did to me was wrong. You took advantage of me and it makes me angry.

BERNARD: Do you forgive them?

DR. WADE: Nope, no forgiveness yet. Constance, tell him about your anger.

CONSTANCE: It makes me so upset, I just don't have the words. (She presses her chest.)

DR. WADE: You keep pressing your chest, what's in there?

CONSTANCE: A lot of the resentment and anger. It makes me feel that somebody is pressing down on my chest.

DR. WADE: Don't give up, Constance. I know this is frightening, but you've got Bernard with you now, there's no way through this but to wrestle with those memories.

CONSTANCE: I don't know what to do.

DR. WADE: What impulse comes to you?

CONSTANCE (with sudden anger): A punch in their faces would do.

DR. WADE (applauding): Very good. (She puts pillows in chairs.) Go on, give it back to them.

CONSTANCE (punching with all her strength): I hate you, I hate you! I hate you! How dare you! An apology would help. But I'll never forgive you.

DR. WADE: You were an innocent child. Your daughter is the same age now that you were then. What would you do if someone did this to your daughter?

CONSTANCE (vehemently): I'd kill him! (She lifts the pillows, shaking them, and slaps them together, then stands over them threateningly.)

DR. WADE: Anything else before we put these fellows away?

CONSTANCE (a short pause): One more time. I'll attack them. (She punches the pillows with vigor. Everyone laughs, Constance is almost joyful.)

BERNARD: We're going back home for a visit.

CONSTANCE: I would like to know, if I come face to face with Dan, what should I do? Should I let bygones be bygones or what?

DR. WADE: What do you want to do?

CONSTANCE: I will feel satisfied if I say something, but I will be more hurt if he denies it.

DR. WADE: Of course he'll deny it. They always do when confronted. Do you know that some studies report as many as one in four women have been sexually abused? The abusers almost always deny it. (gesturing toward the chair) Tell him that you know the truth and that you don't care what he says.

CONSTANCE: I know what you did to me and it was wrong. You may keep it inside you the rest of your life, but I'm not going to live with the lie anymore. I'm not ashamed anymore.

DR. WADE: Bernard, you'll be together, so you can back her up. What would you say to Sam? Tell him.

BERNARD (almost growling): That devil! I don't want to say anything to him. (He turns suddenly, brandishes his fist, and talks to the chair.) I'll punch you in the face. And you'd better not go around trying to molest other children, because if you do that's bad news for you. (After a pause, he and Constance laugh heartily, and as he sits, they reach for one another.)

CONSTANCE (softly, to Bernard): That made me feel good, like you're on my side.

DR. WADE: Why did you doubt he would be?

CONSTANCE: I think all these things inside me made me not trust men. (She gestures toward Bernard and pulls away from him.)

DR. WADE: Oh, I get it. That must be "men" sitting next to you?

CONSTANCE: No.

DR. WADE: Who is he? Look at him.

CONSTANCE (taking his hand): It's Bernard, my husband.

(The following excerpt begins later in the morning, midway through Dr. Wade's work with Bernard.)

DR. WADE: All right, we know that you both have your own scripts. Constance's is called, "All Men Are Disappointing," and yours is, "All Women Will Reject Me." You two could continue reading your parts for the next fifty years unless we find some way to put a stop to this. Bernard, I want you to get on the floor for a minute. And Constance, I'd like you to stand over him. Bernard, you're the poor helpless little boy who says, "screw you" to your mother. You not only won't play her game, but you're determined to disappoint her. That will teach her. Constance, you're that big, bad, controlling rejecting woman.

BERNARD: That's right, she is.

DR. WADE: Constance, while he's sitting there, take his arm and try and pull with all your might. I want you to shout at him as you try lifting him. Say, "Stop drinking. Stop hanging out with your friends. Stop disappointing me." (Constance repeats these phrases and tries pulling and lifting Bernard, but he resists and his body remains firmly anchored to the floor.)

DR. WADE: Pull harder, Constance.

(A minute passes as Constance yells and tugs without results.)

DR. WADE: Think about it. Who's in control here?

BERNARD: I am.

CONSTANCE: Absolutely.

DR. WADE: Bernard, you can have her pulling and trying to control you until the cows come home, but she can't make you do a thing. Are you still feeling sorry for yourself, Bernard? Do you want to stay in that position?

BERNARD: That's not what I want.

DR. WADE: What do you want to do?

(He grabs Constance's hand, she helps him up, and he leaps to his feet and is about to embrace Constance, but Dr. Wade intervenes, standing in between them. She turns toward Constance.)

DR. WADE: Hold on for a minute, Bernard. Please sit back on the floor. You may want to get up, but Constance likes this game too much to just give it up. Constance, in all your painful experiences you learned that you had to keep on pulling and controlling and maybe one day you could have what you wanted. But it's only going to get better if you let him stand on his own and be empowered.

CONSTANCE (clearly shaken): I want that, Bernard. I want you to take responsibility for yourself. (He gets up from the floor on his own. They remain standing, staring into one another's faces.)

DR. WADE: Good. As equals. That's the only way it can be, because you can never change another human being. And Bernard, here's the final part of the puzzle. How can you stop setting her up to reject you?

BERNARD: I can stop drinking.

DR. WADE: Can you? I don't think you can, not on your own. You've inherited a genetic disease that runs in your family. You can't just stop. You need help, but not from Constance. If she gets in this again and starts pulling, you'll do the same old things. If I told you you had diabetes and that you should care for yourself, could you?

BERNARD: Of course not.

DR. WADE: That's right, but if you join a treatment program and attend consistently, you'll have a chance. Constance, can you give him the freedom to go on his own. Can you take your hands from around his neck?

CONSTANCE: I'm going to learn.

DR. WADE: Good, there's a treatment program for you, too.

(A few minutes later, after Dr. Wade has given the Ogots a series of exercises to continue the healing process, they begin again.)

DR. WADE: Before we finish, Constance, I'd like you to tell Bernard what it takes for you to allow yourself to feel pleasure sexually. Bernard, I know you're going to want to pay close attention to this.

CONSTANCE: Sometimes it's just the way you talk. I like it when we're just sitting around and you hold my hand. (Bernard grabs for her hand and holds it.)

DR. WADE (laughing): Very good, I see you learn quickly. Constance, what does it take to get you in the mood?

CONSTANCE: It's just in my head. Like today, I feel like it.

DR. WADE: Then I'd say you two had better head home. (There is more laughter, and the session ends.)

DR. WADE'S FOLLOW-UP NOTES FOR THE OGOTS

Spiritual/Support Groups:

I think it is imperative that Bernard begin attending meetings of Alcoholics Anonymous. Should he continue drinking, his addiction will surely follow its natural course and leave him and his family open to the disastrous consequences associated with the disease.

It is equally important that Constance begin attending Al-Anon meetings so she can stop trying to control her husband's life and concentrate on her own healing.

MAKING CHANGES

STEP **8** ♥ **We made a list of all the persons we had harmed, our mates in particular, and became willing to make amends to them all.**

Making a list and making amends means taking responsibility for our actions. We cannot heal without saying, Yes, I did hurt that person and I'm willing to face my actions and make up for them. Anything we haven't cleared becomes an energy block—because it takes energy to repress guilt.

Bernard must face how much he has hurt Constance and his children with his drinking. Remember, if you hurt a child's parent, you hurt the child, because a parent is less effective when they are suffering. There will be others on his list also.

Most importantly, Constance must make amends to the daughter she was forced to give up. Here the wound was unintentional, but she can show responsibility by being willing to do what she can for her daughter from now on.

Write your list. Ask yourself if you are willing to face those on your list and attempt to correct your mistakes..

––––––––––––––––– ♥ EXERCISES ♥ –––––––––––––––––

1. Breathe, relax, see the light brighter than ever before, flowing from the top of your head down through every cell in your body.
2. Visualize clearer than ever your relationship as you want it to be. The clearer the image the clearer the result.
3. Like the Bonadonnas, it's important that this couple plan some time alone, make dates, and, if possible, a vacation without the children. They desperately need some warm sharing time together and some fun.
4. Both should use this daily affirmation: "I deserve to have a loving, fulfilling marriage," to counter their feelings of guilt, and of course, "I am a success and I will persist until I succeed."
5. Bibliotherapy:

   CONSTANCE: *For Yourself* by Lonnie Barbach. This book deals with issues of women's sexuality and offers help for healing sexually.
   BERNARD: *Healing the Shame That Binds You* by John Bradshaw. This book explains how readers can rid themselves of feelings of guilt and shame carried with them since childhood.

♥ | *Love saver:*
    Touch one another gently when you converse.

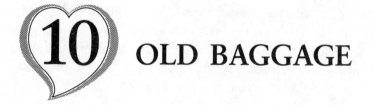

10 OLD BAGGAGE

It is Friday evening just before sundown and Roberta Levine is rushing to complete final preparations for Shabbat. She and her husband, Peter, will observe the Sabbath with Hebrew prayers, hymns, and traditional songs.

Peter, a history instructor, has been delayed by a last-minute meeting called by the dean of his department. This has forced Roberta, a medical researcher who has been under enormous pressure to complete a project, to leave work early. Their Friday evenings are of great importance to them, Roberta explains, although they don't follow all the Shabbat rules. "This is our way of making the day special. It's nice to know millions of other Jews are making similar preparations."

She slips a prayer shawl over her head of short red curls and checks her watch. There is no time to change her wide-shouldered plaid suit. She stands on tiptoe to retrieve a pair of silver candlesticks from a high shelf. They were once her grandmother's, and before that, her grandmother's grandmother's. More than one hundred years ago, these candlesticks graced Shabbat tables in tiny Russian hamlets, in rooms vastly different from this stainless steel efficiency in Boston that the Levines call home.

Roberta lights tall white candles and, as custom dictates, she covers her eyes while singing a Hebrew blessing. Her notes are clear and pure for she knows God is listening: "Baruch ata adonai. . ."

Peter enters. He is a compact man, barely Roberta's height. He shoves his glasses back on his thinning hair saying, "Shabbat shalom," as he greets his wife, wishing her a peaceful sabbath. Together they lay the linen covered card table with a platter of roasted chicken, salad, halvah and grape juice. (The Levine's seldom drink alcoholic beverages.) As they pray their voices join with a worldwide chorus welcoming the Sabbath.

The meal begun, husband and wife eat quietly, only occasionally sharing events of the day. Both Peter and Roberta are forty years old and have been together half their lives. Sometimes, it seems, there is nothing left to say.

When the dishes have been stacked in the sink, waiting, as Peter says "for one of us to give in and wash them," the Levines settle into their routine. Roberta stretches out on the bed, untangles the cords to her head phones, and with a press of the remote control, tunes into the world of television.

Peter seats himself at a tiny desk and adjusts a small lamp. There is a photo beside it. It pictures his smiling young bride, Roberta, clothed in white, walking beneath the marriage awning. She is a feminist, but on that day she changed her surname to that of her husband's. "I wanted a whole new life," she says. "I was determined to be someone new."

On this Sabbath night, eighteen years later, Peter doesn't appear to notice the photo. He has just cracked open a book of poetry that offers lush scenes of life in Latin America. Later, he will begin composing some of his own poetry. They settle in for the evening, separated by a physical distance of five and a half feet.

The Levines share a common history and religion and now a passionless love. They remain together, they say, because of inertia. But while they may have little to say to one another, when it comes to the subject of their differences they are downright loquacious.

"When we have dinner together," Peter said, "we just sit there and have nothing to say to each other. A lot of the time it's like that. It makes one wonder whether you want to be with that same person the rest of your life."

He believes their problems stem from the differences in temperament. "I think by nature I'm an optimist and life is inherently meaningful to me. And part of what makes it meaningful is creative self-expression—my own and that of others in the arts. The arts are my constant companion. That's not true for Roberta. To her the arts are peripheral and a luxury—nice if you can afford them but not at all essential. She takes a more pessimistic view that life is about suffering and you make the best compromises you can, that you don't expect self-actualization or fulfillment from your work. Her attitude is like that bumper sticker that says, "Life is a bitch and then you die."

"Roberta," he continues, "feels that my concerns are elitist and snobbish. Maybe they are, but I'm not satisfied with just doing a boring job and coming home and collapsing in front of a TV set. That's essentially what she does. She speaks of the set as being an addiction. Something in her life is so miserable she just wants to numb the pain.

"I'd like to be able to share my interests with her, read some poetry out loud, maybe. When I do, her reaction is usually annoyance or she's incredulous that I'd want to read this. Here I am reading aloud a poet who is trying to put into words his deepest feelings and she smirks. It's her way of conveying that she thinks I'm ridiculous."

ROBERTA'S VIEW OF THE MARRIAGE

"I enjoy Peter's company, when I can get it," said Roberta. "When we're out together I'm proud of him, especially when he says something brilliant. He knows so much. The big problem is, he has changed and he expects me to change in the same way. He thinks there's something wrong with me for not having the same interests. I really resent him for making me feel inadequate. I tell him that he's just going to have to accept me the way I am. But he won't. He complains when I watch television. We live in a small apartment so he can't concentrate if I have the set turned on. I've started wearing earphones when I watch television but I feel like a leashed dog when I do.

"He thinks the reason he was put on earth was to read and study poetry and that I should do everything in my life to support him to that end. He changes jobs the way some people change hats, as if he didn't have a care in the world. Even if we got along better I'd be afraid to get pregnant. If I had to stop working I'd worry about his instability. He thinks I worry too much.

"Unfortunately life isn't quite as wonderful as he'd like to think it is. I was alone last week with his father and I said, 'I don't think our marriage is going to last the year.' And his father said, 'Yes, I know, we're also concerned about him.'"

Roberta says their eighteen-year marriage began falling apart about three months ago, when Peter changed jobs again. And then there's their problem with housework. "I have to do a disproportionate amount of the cleaning," she said. "We had someone helping us before but Peter felt it was too expensive. Cleanliness is more important to me than money. Now we don't have a cleaning schedule. It's done when I break down and do it. When Peter is off he'll read or go to a museum. I have to say to him, 'Peter, clean this or clean that.' I feel like his mother."

As we've learned in previous chapters, disagreements are seldom what they appear to be in a love relationship. So let's take a closer look at the Levines' families.

Roberta's family

Maternal grandparents: HARRY
                        LIZZIE

Paternal grandparents: EDDIE
                        EMMA

Roberta's mother: SADIE
         father: JERRY

Peter's family

Maternal grandparents: SAUL
                       BETH

Paternal grandparents: RUTH
                       BENJAMIN

Peter's mother: GOLDIE
        father: AARON

Family Themes: In Roberta's family women believe life is to be endured. The theme in Peter's family is that to avoid pain, life itself must be shut out.

Let's move along by meeting the characters in Roberta's maternal history. Her grandparents are:

HARRY: born in 1908 in New York City
LIZZIE: born in Russia in 1910, immigrated with family to Boston, Massachusetts in 1918

As the youngest of ten children, Roberta's maternal grandfather led a more comfortable childhood than his older siblings. By the time he was ready for college, his parents—his father was a house painter—were financially stable enough to send him to Columbia University, where he earned a teaching degree before beginning his lifelong career as an educator.

Harry's future wife, and Roberta's maternal grandmother, Lizzie, had a far less peaceful childhood. Even late in life she retained grim memories of her family's journey, by ship, to America. During the voyage Lizzie's beloved older sister developed pneumonia. When they reached Ellis Island, the sister was put in quarantine, where she died.

Lizzie and Harry met in 1930, when she was in New York living with a cousin. They married the next year and relocated to Boston to be close to her parents. They had four children, one who was Roberta's mother:

SADIE: born in Boston in 1930

Fortunately for Sadie she did not have to endure the loss of a sibling that her mother had suffered. Sadie's beloved big sister didn't have any health problems to be concerned about. What's more, the sister was considered quite a beauty and an intellectual. The unfortunate part is that everyone, especially their mother, compared the sister to Sadie. Almost anyone would suffer in comparison to this girl and Sadie lost the competition early on. From the age of five Roberta's mother wore "beer bottle" glasses, and by ten she was considered overweight. On top of all this, she had an undiagnosed learning disability.

Despite their physical differences, the sisters got along well. But there was a lot of tension between Sadie and her mother, who voiced disappointment with Sadie's social and academic failures. When it was time for Sadie to attend college, she was forced, due to poor grades, to attend night school.

Of course, rather than criticism, Roberta's mother deserved high praise for her tenacity. In the face of her vision and learning difficulties she had to be quite determined. She eventually earned a master's degree. Instead of praise, though, her mother wore away at her, comparing her to her successful sister.

It is not surprising that Sadie had few suitors. Despite her chutzpah, which is often enough to make the dullest looking person shine from within, Sadie must have worn her low self-esteem like a mourning gown. She was probably grateful when a man did finally show some interest in her. She would be saved from what at that time was considered a fate only slightly better than death—spinsterhood. This man turned out to be Jerry, Roberta's father. Before we meet him, however, let's quickly review his family background. Rebecca's paternal history included her grandparents:

EDDIE: born in Boston in 1905
EMMA: born in 1910 in Boston

Roberta's paternal grandfather, Eddie, was a tailor who had many wealthy patrons. Eventually, he too became wealthy. He married Emma in Boston in 1926. She was a woman who lived life to its fullest. She was known for her wardrobe of fashionable fur coats, and she enjoyed long, luxurious vacations. They had two children. The oldest was Roberta's father:

JERRY: born in 1930 just outside Boston

As the only son, Roberta's father was expected to take over his father's tailoring business. He wasn't given much choice in the matter. He began helping out at the shop at an early age, took two years out for college, and then returned to his father's side. They had a tense relationship. A lot of the tension had to do with the special treatment Jerry's sister got at home. She was pampered, well educated, showered with gifts, and allowed to accompany her mother on luxurious vacations. Her parents also footed the bill for an expensive "nose job" when she wanted one.

Jerry, on the other hand, was poorly paid by his father, forced to work long hours, and had to listen to his father's frequent admonitions and scathing lectures. Sound familiar? Surely by now you've noted the connection between Roberta's father and mother. Sadie and Jerry shared a common and painful bond: They were both less-favored children. She was the bespectacled and "dim-witted" daughter, and he, the drudge in the neighborhood tailor's shop. They were raised in the shadows of their siblings and were each the object of a parent's scorn. Jerry and Sadie married in 1952.

Their marriage would last through some very difficult times. After Jerry's father retired and handed over the keys to the (now three) tailor shops, Jerry probably believed there were better times ahead for him. He would finally be able to run the business as he'd always dreamed. But his hopes were shattered as old customers and their offspring began relying less on tailors and instead shopped at some of the elegant department stores that had opened in downtown Boston.

Consider his state of mind. His father had literally written the script for Jerry during his childhood. He had spoken harshly to him, saying he'd be unable to make a go of the business on his own. Jerry fulfilled his father's prophesy. Of course he had no control over the shift in the marketplace, but Jerry, with his low self-esteem, would have discounted all this and blamed himself for the failure of the family business.

And what of his wife during all this? Well, as they struggled, with Jerry first closing one shop, and then another, and finally the last one, Sadie seldom criticized him and encouraged him to accept his fate. Her motto in life was "Don't fight back." With her own low self-esteem, she fit right into this dire scenario.

So there they were, two adults, clinging together for dear (or bitter) life, doing the best they could to raise their children, for they had two; the first was their daughter:

ROBERTA: born in 1952 in a Massachusetts suburb

"When I was a child," recalled Roberta, "I was called a cry-baby by kids and by my parents. I got Cs in class because I cried so much. By the fifth grade, my pediatrician suggested I be taken to a psychologist, but my parents decided against it. Looking back, I don't know what I was so unhappy about. My parents got along. I don't ever remember seeing my mother get really mad. When she was angry she just swallowed it. People in my household didn't talk about how they felt. They may have gotten annoyed and slammed a door or walked into another room and mumbled, but there were no confrontations."

However harsh pressure from the business world may have been, Sadie seemed determined not to repeat her mother's harmful parenting style. She was close to both her children, and Roberta remembers Sadie as a PTA leader, room mother, Girl Scout and Brownie leader, even the summer volunteer camp counselor. "She was my friend and still is, especially now," said Roberta.

Roberta has early memories of family trips together, when she and her little brother rode in the backseat, while her parents took turns driving through the spectacular New England country-side. "My father would tease me then," said Roberta, "but I don't remember being hurt by it. I felt close to him."

That closeness did not last. When Roberta became old enough to help out in the family business "Daddy began criticizing me for the smallest error."

At home, Jerry seemed lost as to how to talk to his daughter. "He'd try to make jokes, but he was so insensitive," said Roberta. When she was eleven years old there was one subject she was particularly sensitive about. "I hated going to gym and not just because I was a klutz," said Roberta. "I had to wear a gym suit and my legs were so hairy."

Jerry seemed to sense her discomfort and tried to help, but he didn't know how to go about it. "I was eleven years old, and he walked into the bathroom when I was bathing, and said, 'You should shave your legs, and use some deodorant, too.' He tried to turn it into a joke by spraying some deodorant into my face. This was typical of him."

This awkward relationship continued for years, with Jerry "joking" and teasing Roberta until she was often in tears. "He drove me crazy," Roberta said. Occasionally, according to Roberta, her mother would quietly ask Jerry to quit teasing Roberta, but not often; She wanted to avoid conflict with her husband.

School offered no relief for Roberta. Although she learned to control her tears, she was considered a social misfit, never "cool" enough for the other kids. In junior high, in the cafeteria, a prankster threw a banana peel on the floor just as Roberta happened by. "I remember every detail of that moment," Roberta said. "I had my lunch tray in my hand and I was carrying an extra dime in my fist. Kids were always asking me for change, so I never carried more. Anyway, I was passing through this crowded lunch room and slipped on the peel. It was awful having all these kids laugh at me. It was more than I could take. No one helped me up. Nobody talked to me. No one wanted to be seen with me.

"The kids used to have books they circulated called slam books, and everyone would write something about you in them. I never saw my page, but from what I heard it was not very nice. Someone wrote a poem about me making fun of my small breasts. It was just that time in my life. I don't know why some people go through this and others don't. Why some kids and not others? I was very lonely. My mother jokes with me today that during that period she liked to avoid me. She said I was depressing to be around. If she wasn't home in the afternoons when I got there she didn't have to listen to my complaints about school."

The one positive aspect of Roberta's social life was the Zionist youth group she joined when she was twelve. She met many other Jewish girls through the group, and although they didn't necessarily live in the same neighborhoods, they kept in touch for years. This also stirred Roberta's interest in the religion her parents never practiced at home. She joined a synagogue and became an active participant.

In high school her lack of popularity continued. "I was not a happy teenager, and I was thought to be too serious. I was concerned with issues such as the meaning of life." By her junior year in high school she hit upon a dangerous way to make friends. As soon as she was old enough to drive the family car, she befriended a younger group of kids who didn't have licenses, and she offered to give them rides. One of these students introduced Roberta to alcohol. She loved the sense of freedom that it helped her feel. "I began drinking pretty heavily," said Roberta.

"My parents were really naive. They had no idea about my problem. They really believed me when I said I was just driving to McDonald's. How stupid can you be to believe your teenage daughter is spending every night at a drive-in where there is no place to sit down. I think they were just so happy that I finally had friends and that I was going out, they didn't consider the price I was paying for it."

Her "friendships" didn't last long. "By the time I reached my senior year everyone was getting older and they all got their own driver's licenses, so they no longer needed me."

On New Year's Day of her senior year, after having been stood up by two different boys that weekend, Roberta, alone in the house, found a bottle of barbiturates in the bathroom cabinet. "I took about half a bottle," she said. When her parents returned home, they saw Roberta stretched across the sofa and assumed she'd fallen asleep. It was hours before they called for an ambulance.

Fortunately, Roberta survived the experience and woke up in a hospital bed. "My mother was so concerned that our neighbors would find out," said Roberta. This time, when the doctor recommended therapy, her parents agreed to it. She was in therapy for six months, but she said most of that time her therapist refused to believe that her father's teasing could be as unnerving as Roberta described it. "Finally," said Roberta, "she had my parents come in for a few of the sessions. Afterward the therapist said to me, 'I see what you mean about your father.'"

That next year Roberta began Swarthmore College in Pennsylvania and moved away from home. Once there, she became an ardent supporter of a conservative youth movement and spent her junior year in Israel, where she met Peter, who was about to embark on his master's degree. "I was really impressed with him," said Roberta. "He seemed to know so much. I also remember really laughing with him when he was telling jokes. And there was also a physical attraction. Everyone likes to feel that they're attractive. Well, when I met Peter he was positively drooling over me."

♥

If you've ever wondered what became of that girl or boy in grade school who was the recipient of the bullies' cruelest pranks, you need wonder no more. Roberta's was a classic case. She is right on target when she wonders aloud why some kids are taunted and not others. Well, the truth is that people sense how someone feels about herself and usually treat that person accordingly. These kids knew how Roberta felt. Thanks to her father's unmitigating criticism—largely due to his own hostility and rage—and her mother's failure to defend her, Roberta felt worthless. Her fellow students picked up on that and went for her jugular.

Social ineptness is an adaptive behavior, and in Roberta's family a clear theme emerged to which they molded themselves. It may have started with her great-grandparents fleeing for their lives or her grandmother's heightened sense of helplessness when her sister died. It was certainly in place by the time her parents had endured their less-favored child status. The theme was this: "When a wave hits, don't fight it, let it roll over you. We are defenseless in the face of all this."

Many people have personality styles that allow them to stand up to such a disappointing past and think, "I'm putting that behind me, taking charge of my life." Not Roberta. Not that she didn't want to, she simply didn't know how. Despite all of the love and active parenting Sadie offered, she didn't know how to give Roberta the cues she needed to survive socially in this world. Sadie had not been given any herself. Her mother had been too busy doting on her older sister and putting Sadie down.

And Roberta's father? At first it seems he tried to do what he felt his wife should be doing. But by doing something as rude as rushing into the bathroom, he only added to his daughter's misery.

Her social clumsiness cost her what teenagers most need— friendships. They need other young people to confide in, they need them for emotional support and to validate a sense of importance and acceptance. Roberta's only opportunity for even a taste of this was when she offered herself up as chauffeur. Even then she had to risk her life to do it by drinking and driving.

By the time she met her husband, who was intelligent enough to look beyond the poor self-image and see her quiet beauty and curiosity and intelligence, she must have been surprised and a little bit grateful. I'm told their first years of marriage were quite pleasant, as Peter and Roberta completed their graduate educations.

What had happened to their marriage? He complained that her unwillingness to change has caused unhappiness. His remarks reminded me of a quote that a client shared with me. "Nothing changes until something changes." Roberta's life is a constant. She isn't changing anything about her routine or her pursuits, so there can't really be inner change. Research has clearly demonstrated the importance of common interests in a marriage. Roberta may in fact need to look for new avenues of self-expression, not only to feel better about herself and her life but to benefit her relationship with Peter. This should be something that is mutually chosen, not dictated by one partner.

What's more, Peter's persistent disapproval and criticism of Roberta is likely to have a debilitating effect on her. Very few people thrive and grow under the harsh glare of a partner's criticism. Instead, it's withering and controlling. When Roberta began to hear it she had to be hurt. But without a doubt, it must have made her feel right at home, and she must have also asked herself, "What's the good of fighting it?"

With Peter introduced into this drama let's take a look at his intergenerational history so we can better understand the attraction between these two. Peter's maternal grandparents include:

SAUL: escaped from Russia
BETH: born in an area known as "Yellow Russia," between Russia and Poland

While still in Russia, Peter's maternal grandfather saw many of his fellow Jews cripple themselves permanently to become exempt from the decades-long conscription that was imposed upon Jews. Saul fled to America to escape either of these dire fates, and for a few years was even able to attend college in Philadelphia, until he was forced to drop out during the Depression. He would eventually meet his future wife, Beth, in Philadelphia, where she was employed in a cigar factory. He must have been astounded by her family history, which could easily have been made into a Hollywood movie.

Beth hailed from a brilliant Russian family, and as far back as she could remember all the men in her family had become physicians. Jews were able to attend the same universities as gentiles, do the same course work, and take the same examinations. They were not allowed to get full medical degrees. Instead, they were awarded masters of medicine rather than doctorates and were restricted to practicing in Jewish communities.

Despite the family's wealth, they so feared the random outbreaks of violence against Jewish people, that for a while they had to hide out in the countryside. None of this could deter Beth's two older sisters, who were also interested in science and medicine. They wanted to attend the university, but their father forbade it on the grounds that they were still single and therefore easily "corruptible."

The young women would not give up. They quickly wooed two of the most upstanding bachelors in the neighborhood and convinced them to marry. That done, they were given their father's consent and quickly set off for Moscow, sans husbands, where this sisterly duo studied dentistry (a profession they found more open to women). After graduation they applied for divorces and took the first ship to America they could book passage on.

They never looked back. Nor would they have to. Not long afterward, their younger sister and Peter's maternal grandmother, Beth, and the entire family would follow the sisters in 1918 as they tried to escape the uncertainty caused by the Bolshevik Revolution.

Beth was the least ambitious of the children. She found work in Pennsylvania in the cigar factory where she met Saul. He seemed to like her despite her slightly hunched back. They married when Beth was twenty-seven, then considered a fairly advanced age for a woman to marry, and quickly had three children. One of them was Peter's mother, who would inherit her aunts' love of learning:

GOLDIE: born in Philadelphia in 1927

When Goldie was seven, her father died, leaving his wife to raise their three children. Beth moved to Boston to be with her family. As a teenager Goldie spent many evenings at the home of one aunt and uncle in particular, who each Saturday night would have survivors of concentration camps as dinner guests. The young Goldie sat quietly and spellbound as she heard one after another horror-filled story of the unparalleled, genocidal destruction of the Jews.

One cousin, barely older than Goldie from Minsk, told Goldie that when the Nazis invaded, he'd climbed to the top of a tall tree that was full of large brightly colored leaves that fall day. He remained in the tree the entire day unseen by the soldiers. But he would not be left unscathed. From his high, color-filled vantage point he saw every living soul in his Jewish hamlet—men, women, children, his own sisters and brothers, cousins, uncles, aunts, grandparents, and his mother and father—rounded up, marched to a nearby lake, and shot through the heads. He could still hear their cries, the wails of the babies, the grown men who begged, the face of his grandfather, his mother's pained expression.

It was a story Peter's mother would never forget and one that influenced her life and that of her children. She swore she would bear many children as a way of negating these heinous acts. And she kept her word, although at times she must have felt torn in two. Like her aunts before her, she longed to fulfill a brilliant intellectual destiny and yet retained her determination to fulfill her biological role. Goldie graduated from Boston University, where she met her future husband.

It will be interesting to see how this ambivalence affected her parenting style, for she was Peter's mother. Before we move on to view Goldie as a wife and mother, let us first look at the paternal side of Peter's family. His grandparents are:

RUTH: born in 1900 in Boston
BENJAMIN: also born in 1900 in Boston

Both Ruth and Benjamin were from families of means. Benjamin's father had immigrated from Russia to Boston, where he had purchased several factories. Peter's grandfather, Benjamin, remembered seeing his father play poker with Diamond Jim Brady. Unfortunately for Benjamin, his mother died early in life. Following old Judaic custom, Peter's great grandfather proposed to his widowed sister-in-law and she accepted. Once remarried, the father grew cold-hearted toward his children, as if Benjamin and his sister were unhappy reminders of a former life. Benjamin worked his way through law school, and eventually met and married Ruth, Peter's grandmother.

Ruth was the daughter of a Russian accountant who had served the royal family. The new czar, Alexander III, was a rabid anti-Semite, and once he took the throne, Ruth's father, a Jew, was relieved of his duties. He and his wife sailed for the United States, where, despite their wealth, they were met by vicious anti-Semitism. So although the family had money, they moved to an overcrowded Jewish ghetto, and it was here that Peter's grandmother was born, raised, and eventually met her future husband, Benjamin, the lawyer who'd been financially scorned by his father and aunt/stepmother. Benjamin was considered a good match for Ruth, because like her, he was a member of a quickly growing Jewish "elite," educated and born in America. It turned out that Benjamin had acquired some of his father's habits. He was remembered by his family as being extremely tightfisted toward his four children, one of whom included Peter's father:

AARON: born in 1929 in Boston

Aaron remembers moving to several different houses within his Boston neighborhood, which had probably been caused in large part by his father's miserliness. There was a local law that required renters to sign a lease every two years, at which time the tenant was responsible for painting the apartment. Rather than paying for the paint and allowing his family to live a stable life, Benjamin instead insisted on moving his family every two years.

As Aaron grew up, money remained that prime issue between him and his father. When Aaron was working his way through graduate school in the 1950s, he was too poor to afford a coat to ward off the bitter winter cold. Despite misgivings, he turned to his father and asked him for the money. After all, Benjamin was an attorney, and while he wasn't wealthy, he could easily have afforded the money. Few fathers would send their only sons out into a harsh Bostonian winter without a coat, not even Benjamin. But neither was he emotionally equipped to simply hand over the fifteen or twenty dollars for the garment. Instead, Benjamin bought himself a new coat, and offered to sell his old one to his son.

Aaron was forced to accept. He had a wife and growing family to consider. He surely couldn't care for them from a hospital bed. He paid his father with the crumpled bills in his pocket and set out for his next job, the one he worked at night. But he swore he'd never be like Benjamin, never deny his children. He kept his word. Money was not a rancorous issue in Aaron's family. He gave them what he could reasonably afford.

But as we've already learned from the dramas presented earlier in this book, sheer determination is a weak competitor when pitted against old family dynamics. We'll soon learn from Peter how Aaron's past came to limit him as a father.

First, though, one more note. In graduate school Aaron began to admire the work of John Stuart Mill, who had learned to write and read in several languages as a youngster. He inspired Aaron, who in turn planned to give his own children the benefit of early childhood education. He and his equally intelligent young wife would thus begin a family with a weighty agenda. You'll recall that Goldie was bent on having lots of children. Their domestic ambitions dovetailed—a well-educated, big, and happy family. What could stop them? Well, let's hear from one of the leading characters in this drama to see how those well-intentioned principles were put into practice. Their first child was:

PETER: born in Boston in 1952

"When I was two years old my brother, Ray, was born," said Peter. "I'm told that when my mother returned from the hospital I wouldn't talk to or even look at her for two weeks." Cold-shouldering his mother didn't work. She continued bringing home infants until there were seven children in all. But not even that many seemed to satisfy her.

"My parents would argue a lot because my mother kept pushing to have more and more kids," said Peter. "It was kind of crazy. My father had to work like a mule to support us. He taught at college during the year, then summer school, and on Saturdays and Sundays he and my mother taught religion classes. All that, plus work on his doctoral dissertation." It would take Aaron fourteen years to finish his first doctoral draft, and even then the review committee continued sending it back for so many changes that it was another seven years before Aaron actually graduated.

"I grew up with the sense that my father was not quite managing," said Peter. "I wished I could carry some of his burden for him, rather than him having to carry us. I made him a card with a picture from the *Aeneid*, of Aeneas carrying his father from the burning ruins of Troy, and I copied some of the Latin phrases. My father translated it on the spot."

In one of Peter's most vivid childhood dreams he stood at the front door of the family home and viewed his father in the driveway cutting hedges with an electric trimmer. In the dream his father severed his left arm at the elbow and Peter stood there not knowing whether to run and put a tourniquet on his arm or run into the house and call emergency assistance. "I was paralyzed not knowing what to do. My father was bleeding profusely and I didn't know what to do."

As overburdened as Aaron may have been, however, he was

so deeply impressed by the philosopher John Stuart Mill that he took the time to teach Peter to read before he was three years old. "They used to buy me these little Golden Books. I'd read one page and rip it out, then another, and rip that out. I did that to one of my father's books, too, ripped it up."

Peter also began composing stories on yellow legal pads. "Looking back I realize that to command their attention I had to function on their level. In another family, perhaps, a child might have gotten attention by being cute and childish. The only way my father could relate to me was on a pedagogical level. He'd explain to me how the economy works or how food comes to our table and I would mentally slip out of the situation and think, 'He probably thinks I can't figure this out myself.' I was slightly cynical, but even now when I'm with him or my grandfather we can talk about political trends, ideas, philosophy, but never about feelings."

As a child Peter began to sense that his mother, a homemaker, was jealous of his father's work. "When he came home from work she'd want him to tell her who he'd spoken to, what he'd taught, what the students' reactions were. She was very envious of his fuller life of the mind. I know mothers who love spending hours and hours in the kitchen or who want nothing more than to be full-time parents. That was not my mother. She wanted to earn a master's degree in literature and teach at a university like my father. She spent all her free time reading books. She was not fastidious about us being neat or clean."

Their neighbors in their apartment complex took a dim view of Goldie's parenting style. "They considered her a bug-eyed radical," said Peter. At three years old he was allowed to leave the apartment on his own, carrying a stick so he could reach the elevator buttons, and he'd get adults to help him cross the streets. "The neighbors would call my mother and say, 'We saw your son a couple of blocks away.'"

Peter said he learned the word "suicide" from hearing his mother shout the word at his father when she was angry. "I'd heard her using it like some kind of threat," said Peter, "and I looked it up in the dictionary. I remember thinking that she must be psychologically disturbed in some way."

Peter also saw physical fights between his parents. "I saw them on the floor once hitting each other. My mother and I discussed this recently, and she said they were not fights between them, that my father had been beating her, but that's not my memory."

The early education was beneficial, in the beginning at least. By the time he'd finished kindergarten, Peter scored in the upper reaches of a citywide intelligence exam and was rewarded with a full scholarship to a competitive religious school. But his teachers complained he was so withdrawn he was unable to continue at an accelerated pace. The real problem, Peter said, was that they considered him to be impertinent. "It was a modern Orthodox school, but they taught me fundamentalist dogma."

In the first grade, for instance, when they were studying Noah's Ark, Peter asked the teacher how, if insects had not been included on the Ark, they'd been able to withstand the deluge. After all, the six-year-old continued, there was ample proof that many species of insect life predated Noah. "I felt that some of the stories they told us were an insult to my intelligence."

By the third grade his parents were asked to remove him from the school. "My parents were not very happy about this," said Peter. His parents consulted a therapist, one whom Peter visited regularly for six years. "They worried that I didn't go out and make friends. I seldom got along with other kids."

Throughout elementary and on through high school Peter continued getting failing grades. "My mother set up a writing table in the bathroom for me that would fold down from the wall. I'd have to work at it until my homework was done. I'd sit there and look out the window and, inevitably, nothing would get done."

By the time college rolled around Peter said he "didn't get around to applying to any of the ones I was interested in" and he instead attended a community college. After two years he transferred to a state university and, following graduation, headed for Israel to begin a master's degree at Hebrew University. While there, he met and married Roberta. He and Roberta returned to the States in 1980, and he has since held several different jobs, including computer programmer, legal clerk, and editorial assistant for a publishing house. At the time we met he had held his most recent position, as a college instructor, for nine months.

♥

One story in particular from Peter's childhood jumps out at me. The one of him as a three-year-old armed with a stick, getting on an elevator, walking out into the busy streets of Boston. It is told on the heels of a story about his mother as a young woman sitting at her aunt and uncle's table, taking in one horror story after another. Goldie was spoon-fed the painful knowledge that generations before her had been virtually wiped out. She took personal responsibility for helping to rebuild the next generation. It was a worthy goal. But, in retrospect, we learn that she is viewed as a mother who was more interested in the head count of her children than one who was nurturing and caring.

She did as she felt she ought. She gave birth to her children. As for her need to feed her own hungry intelligence, it could not be denied completely, but at a cost. Goldie was a neglectful mother. Her neighbors and her children knew that she preferred reading and teaching over mothering.

Little Peter desperately tried to capture her attention. He used the very tool for which she'd abandoned him: intellect. It didn't take him long, though, to realize that even his intellectual excellence wasn't enough to keep her entertained. So he simply gave up.

As for his father, Aaron was determined to be more generous of spirit toward his children than his own father had been toward him. But Aaron had been moved from house to house because his father didn't consider the family worthy of a comforting and familiar residence. This was a man whose father didn't deem him worthy of a new coat. Though he certainly tried, Aaron was ill-equipped to be a parent. Despite his impossible schedule, he taught, read, and talked to his son. What he didn't understand was that this boy needed something else, and it was very basic: love, hugs and kisses.

As a result, while his father talked on about the economic system, about his philosophy of early childhood education, etc., etc.,

Peter said he learned to slip out of situations, as if he were distancing himself from moments he did not enjoy. He continued to "slip out" like this, so much so in his private elementary school that his teachers asked his parents to withdraw him. Although he doesn't mention it, it's probably safe to assume that Peter was affected by those bitter fights, or wife battering, he witnessed between his mother and father. And when he felt neglected by his mother, he continued to "slip away."

What of today? Does he still perform this odd means of escape? I'm not suggesting he doesn't savor every word of the poetry he reads, but he can certainly slip away into his books and poems.

The great problem in a marriage, of course, is that the distancing would make intimacy almost impossible. But here he is married. So how does his relationship with his wife reflect the issues of his childhood? Well, consider him in their tiny apartment as he tries to capture his wife's attention. He opens a book of poetry and begins to read aloud, performing as it were.

What does she do? She shows disinterest. And how does he interpret it? As rejection. It's the same old friend that walked hand in hand with him as a child, when he used a stick to reach the elevator button marked "Street."

In the face of Roberta's unhappiness, his distancing feats, and with their fingers pointed at one another, they are in a holding pattern. Let us see if the Levines transform their marriage.

MAKING CHANGES

STEP **9** ♥ **We made direct amends to such people whenever possible, except when to do so would injure them or others.**

Taking the list compiled in Step 8, and the willingness to become ready to right our wrongs, we move forward. This step asks us to say I'm sorry, to pay back the debt, to do whatever we can to alleviate the pain we have caused.

Peter and Roberta have hurt one another tremendously with emotional distancing and put-downs. Those disparaging remarks have taken their toll and can be erased in part by heartfelt words that say "Please forgive me for hurting you. I will always strive to keep your feelings and needs in mind."

Take up this process with each person on your list. Persist until you succeed.

─────────────── ♥ EXERCISE ♥ ───────────────

1. Relax, breathe, and picture the now familiar but even more vivid light.

2. In your imagination, see yourself with your spouse as a loving, caring mate.

3. In your mind, make a list of all of the qualities in your mate that attracted you to her/him. See yourself praising your mate.

4. Each day praise your mate verbally for the qualities you enjoy. Thank her for her contributions to your life. Skip the negative comments, focus on the positive. I always keep in mind that the word "praise" spells "raise" with a "p" in front for positive. Raise the positive.

5. Affirm: "I love and respect myself and I love and respect my husband/wife."

Love saver:
Tell each other a joke or funny story.
Laughter is a great healer.

11 LEAVING THE PAST BEHIND

I met with the Levines in a colleague's apartment only a short walk from their home. Peter and Roberta seemed weighed down by the unhappiness of their marriage. Although no one in their immediate families had suffered or died in the Holocaust directly, its grisly shadow has fallen over Peter and Roberta. The deadly anti-Semitism of Russia also reaches into the subconcious of their families. It is not unlike America's ugly history of slavery and racism, and neither event can be simply shrugged off by future generations and forgotten. While not all, surely some relationships would have to be affected by the horrific nature of the crimes. In fact, I think the Levines' inherited a worldview shaped by the great tragedies of their people, transmitted by their parents and grandparents and great-grandparents, whose emotional lives bear the stamp of persecution. As a result, Peter and Roberta each fashioned their own personal escape routes, but the paths led in opposing directions.

Still, I was hopeful, for I had faith that it was more than coincidental that Roberta and Peter had found one another, two decades before, in a tent in faraway Israel.

Somewhere, deep within them, they sensed that their relationship could offer the best opportunity for healing. The biggest obstacle when we met was that I had more faith in their love than they themselves had. My job was to put them in touch with that love and allow its transformational power to heal.

(Dr. Wade sits facing the Levines, who are seated side-by-side in armchairs, at the start of a morning-long session.)

DR. WADE: Although I've read the notes Brenda has prepared on you, I have no preconceptions about what we're going to work on today. That's the way I work. So why don't we start by each of you telling me, if you could have anything you wanted happen during these hours, what would you want most?

ROBERTA: I'd want to be accepted for who I am and not what he wants me to be.

DR. WADE: When you're each talking about the other, I would like you, please, to turn and make eye contact with each other. Talk directly to one another.

ROBERTA (turning slightly in her chair but looking down when she addresses Peter): It's as if you're a parent trying to mold me. I always make it a point to do the opposite of what you want me to do.

DR. WADE: Give us an example of what you mean.

ROBERTA: Well, let's say I come home at the end of the day and decide I want to watch TV, but Peter's attitude might be that there are more valuable things to do in the world.

DR. WADE: You don't want him to give you a hard time about it, then.

ROBERTA: That's right.

DR. WADE: And what do you want, Peter?

PETER: I'd like to feel less isolated in my interests. I'd like to feel sometimes with Roberta that we can leave the everyday concerns of the world behind us, spend some quiet time together, to think. (He turns toward Roberta.) I know you're not interested in my work, but it would be nice to share my thoughts with someone I'm close to.

DR. WADE: It sounds like you two are both feeling your needs aren't met. So why are you still together?

ROBERTA: Perhaps only momentarily.

PETER (shrugging): Neither of us has the energy to get up and go.

DR. WADE: I sense there's more keeping you together.

PETER: Yes, there are things we see in each other.

DR. WADE: What are they?

PETER (after a pause of about twenty seconds): Well, there's a certain chemistry that we have and it's still strong between us.

DR. WADE: Are you still attracted to Roberta?

PETER: There's certainly something there.

DR. WADE: Peter, I'm going to ask to preface your sentences with the words "I feel." You have a tendency to globalize and that divorces you from your feelings. So I'm going to ask again, why else do you want to hang out with her? Please turn to Roberta and tell her.

PETER: Well, to a certain extent, it's comfortable being with you. We know what to expect of each other. It's all familiar, our pace of life, our body rhythms.

ROBERTA: I know what you're saying. (They make direct eye contact and hold it for about ten seconds.) We're not people who can just go and go. Neither of us has a lot of stamina. We need routine.

PETER: That's more true of you than me.

ROBERTA: When you don't sleep I feel it as much as you do.

PETER: You set these boundaries for yourself and . . .

DR. WADE: Tell me, do you two often have these discussions that lead nowhere?

ROBERTA: We seldom talk. (turning to Peter) I really respect your intelligence and your humor. The problem is that you don't always listen to me.

DR. WADE: Do you often feel when you're speaking to Peter that he's not really there?

ROBERTA: Well, I sometimes tell him a story, and when I get toward the end he just looks at me blankly and says, "What did you say?"

DR WADE: Do you agree with that, Peter?

PETER: Oh, yeah, I have trouble shifting gears from something that's very deep.

ROBERTA: I find it rather disconcerting to go on and on and you just sit there. I sometimes feel I'm disturbing you.

PETER: Often you are.

ROBERTA (dabbing at her eyes with a tissue): So what's the advantage of being married to me if I disturb you all the time?

DR. WADE: Don't stop Roberta, tell him how you feel.

ROBERTA: I'm resentful that you want to get away from the world's concerns because what that does is throw them all on me and that's a heavy burden. If you criticize me for not being interested in intellectual pursuits, maybe it's because I don't have the time or energy.

PETER: I think we could say it's a given that it's not in you to be introspective.

ROBERTA: That's not true! I may just be interested in other things.

PETER: I don't see you having any interest in self-discovery. You share your dreams with me like they're funny little stories, instead of looking at the unconscious messages that might be there.

DR. WADE: But why should she do this?

PETER: I'd like us to share greater parts of each other. To know yourself means you can share yourself more fully with the other person.

ROBERTA: I'm not so sure I want to share more of myself with you.

DR. WADE: In these last few moments you have both continued to talk from your intellect. Tell Peter what you feel, Roberta.

ROBERTA: It really hurts. I have the feeling that whatever I do is wrong. Either I betray myself or I'm not going to be what you want me to be.

PETER: I know how you feel, because I feel that same way.

DR. WADE: I've just been sitting back trying to figure out what you two are up to.

PETER (ignoring Dr. Wade's comments and gesturing toward Roberta): She puts me off in a little corner to work so that I continue to be isolated. When it comes to my passions in life all she can say is that she doesn't appreciate or care about them.

ROBERTA: What can I say? I care about the outside world. I think it's a helluva lot more interesting. That's our basic difference.

DR. WADE: More importantly, you have a lot in common.... You're masters at blaming each other. And you say it in such lively, intellectual language. Still, it's quite painful, and look what it does. Stand up, please, and let me show you. (Roberta and Peter rise from their chairs and Dr. Wade takes Roberta's index finger and aims it toward Peter.) Okay, Roberta, you're busy pointing your finger and saying, "It's not fair." So even if Peter were trying to get closer (she moves Peter toward Roberta), all he'd get was a finger stabbed directly at his chest. Then he blames back. (She points Peter's finger toward Roberta.) Look guys, now you two are only within shouting range of each other. So what if, instead of saying, "It's not fair," you used the "A" word. Anger is a good place to start, because you two are quietly seething.

PETER: Suppose I don't know how to do anything but intellectualize?

DR. WADE: But that couldn't be true. You use that same brain power to get yourself into an emotional place so you can write and read poetry. Poets think, but they must also feel. This is critical. So try switching, and tell me, Peter, our resident poet. What do you feel?

PETER: I feel despair over my marriage.

DR. WADE: And you, Roberta? Are you feeling lost? Disconnected? Alienated? What's the feeling?

ROBERTA: I feel that I'm sleeping with someone . . .

DR. WADE: Address your husband, please, not someone.

ROBERTA (still standing and looking at Peter): . . . I'm sleeping with you and I'm supposed to be intimate with you but I don't know who you are. And I have this feeling that physically, everything is perfect. You say I should be in touch with myself. But you don't want to really be in touch with who I am. The real me feels lost. (She begins crying and sits down.)

DR. WADE: Can you talk about the hurt?

ROBERTA: I'm in great pain.

DR. WADE: Where? Show me where in your body.

ROBERTA: Most of it is not physical pain.

DR. WADE: It's emotional pain but it always manifests itself on the physical level.

ROBERTA: It's my skin. I want to scratch it off. (She runs her hands along her legs, her arms.) I want to burn the flesh away on my legs. I have to stop myself in the shower. The water is much too hot. It hurts! (Her arms are wrapped around her body and she rocks back and forth.)

DR. WADE: Roberta, who made it too hot?

ROBERTA: I did. I want to get inside in my legs. To find myself . . . I need to scratch away the surface. If there's a pimple or any tiny opening I put alcohol on it. I like the burning sensation. I don't understand why.

DR. WADE: To find the answer look closely at the metaphor you've presented. What does this mean that you would scratch yourself, want to make yourself bleed?

ROBERTA (rocking in her seat, holding her legs): It reminds me of a dream I had where I was squeezing my body, like a tube of paste, and this long fibrous stuff kept coming out. There's a part of me I want to get rid of.

DR. WADE: What part?

ROBERTA: That's the question.

DR. WADE: But I think you have the answer.

ROBERTA: I want to get rid of the married part of me, the pain, the hurt.

DR. WADE: I want you to stop talking for a minute, Roberta, and begin taking deep breaths. (She walks behind Roberta and begins massaging her shoulders.)

ROBERTA: Ouch, that hurts!

DR. WADE: Interesting. I'm barely touching you. I'm doing this because I want you to be in your body, be conscious, be present to yourself. (At this point, Dr. Wade begins a three-minute session, with Roberta closing her eyes and picturing a bright star. Finally, Roberta is sitting, trancelike, breathing calmly.) Okay, Roberta, that bright light you now see is your intuition. Ask your intuition what the fibrous tissue in your dream has symbolized. Breathe nice and easy. Ask your intuition to give you the seed cause of the pain you want to get rid of. Where did it originate?

ROBERTA: I was a girl.

DR. WADE: Ask your intuition how old you were.

ROBERTA: I'm three or four years old. Some kids on my block are surrounding me. They're angry. They're throwing rocks. My mother comes up. She is worried that one stone has come so close to my eye.

DR. WADE: Is your mother yelling at these children? Is she chasing them? She's saying something to you, what is it?

ROBERTA: She doesn't show her anger. She doesn't want me to show anger. She uses the attack as a lesson. She says to me, never throw stones.

DR. WADE: Good Roberta, you're doing so well. Continue to tap into your intuition, it has been there waiting for you. Ask what you did with that pain. What did that angry little girl do with her anguish?

ROBERTA (tears streaming down her cheeks, eyes still closed): It kept piling up, each time . . . I never threw stones back . . . not at anyone. And there are wounds. They have never healed.

DR. WADE: Ask your intuition how you can bring about healing.

ROBERTA: I have to let the pain out. I can't keep it in.

DR. WADE: I'm going to ask you to, very gently, bring yourself back here, with us.

(Roberta opens her eyes and continues breathing deeply.)

PETER: I was thinking, as Roberta talked about being on that street and having her mother come out, that the lesson her mother taught her was the same lesson she gave her about her father. No matter what her father said to her, her mother expected her to not throw stones back at him.

DR. WADE: Roberta, were you able to get in touch with some of your rage toward your mother?

ROBERTA: No, I felt anger toward my father. He was always putting me down.

DR. WADE: Listen, your mother and father were colluding. Your father leaned on you until you were in tears. Why do you think your mother not only didn't stop him, but turned to you and basically told you not to throw stones back at him?

ROBERTA: She didn't want to threaten their relationship.

DR. WADE: Yes, and at the expense of her daughter? As a mother it would be hard for me to just sit by and watch someone torment my child.

ROBERTA: She meant well.

DR. WADE: I don't care what her philosophy of life was about. As a child you deserved to have a champion in that house. Someone needed to stand up to your father's abuse and say, "Leave this child alone, this is hurtful." I think her silence was sadistic.

(Roberta begins crying again.)

DR. WADE: You go ahead and cry. It has been your salvation. Crying was the only way you could express the anger you felt. It's good you can cry. Okay, Roberta, we're going to do some work. These chairs (she places two empty chairs in front of Roberta), that's Mother, that's Dad. Who do you want to talk to first?

ROBERTA (at the chair): Mom, why didn't you protect me? He was hurting me so much. What was so great about him that you refused to stop him? I love you, Mom, but I can't pretend all the blame belongs to him anymore. I've been projecting all my anger toward him. I've been telling you what a great mom you were, but sometimes you really were terrible.

DR. WADE: Our parents were neither all good or all bad. Say to her, "I'm angry with you."

ROBERTA: I'm angry. You're the one who brought me into this world. I needed you to look after me and protect me. All these years I never understood that I deserved it. (She clamps a hand over her mouth and is suddenly silent.)

DR. WADE: What happened? What's going on?

ROBERTA: I'm trying to calm down a bit.

DR. WADE: You don't want to experience those feelings do you?

ROBERTA: No.

DR. WADE: So where are you putting them, out the window? I don't think so. You're packing them into your body again. Your body is like a suit of armor for you, protects you from any real emotional experience. That's why you were turning that hot water on, that's what you were trying to rid yourself of in your dream, it was all the hurt, all the time you never fought back, because you'd been told to never throw stones. Here's your chance. You can go back. What were you starting to feel?

ROBERTA: Pain.

DR. WADE (gesturing toward the chair): Then tell her!

ROBERTA: Mom, it really hurts. I want to escape it. Only the pain I inflict on myself makes me feel alive.

DR. WADE: Keep telling her, Roberta. There's no way out of this but to go through it. Okay, Dad has been sitting there. Talk to him for a moment.

ROBERTA: You helped do this to me. You got angry with me, but it wasn't me. You had disappointments in your life and you blamed me for them. You really, really hurt me. (She begins beating the chair and continues doing so until she collapses into another chair and sobs and sobs. She finally looks up as if noticing the others in the room.) I'm feeling a sense of relief.

DR. WADE: But let's not stop here. The deal is yes, they hurt you, they were fairly sadistic, and there was this vague, painful sense of old family pain that existed long before you were born. Yes. But you, now that can be a different story. You can be the first one in your family to add a twist to this drama. You get to choose. You can let go of this notion that because your parents hurt you that you're damaged goods. It's your life and you can stop seeing yourself as a victim and start being the victor. With your great intuitive powers and strengths, you can overcome this pain. Decide right now, Roberta. Do you want to look up in the sky, and say, "There's no such thing as real peace. I can't see it, it's not there?" Or are you determined to find it? Come on, decide that you want to exist, not to hurt, not to feel put down. If you don't, you can get Peter, with your subtle cues, to stand in for your father for the rest of your marriage. So, are you the victim, Roberta?

ROBERTA: To a certain extent, I am.

DR. WADE: Okay, that's your choice. So I'm asking you to sit down here on the floor, because that's where victims belong. And every victim has a persecutor and here's yours, right here. Peter, would you come and persecute Roberta. She needs it so she can feel like a victim. (Peter stands over her.)

DR. WADE (softly): Now, I ask you, my darling victim, do you want to get up? Do you want to spend the rest of your life on the floor? Because right now, that's your marriage. It's in a pretty sad state.

ROBERTA: No, I don't want that, I want to be on the same plane. (She stands up and looks into her husband's eyes. They hold hands.)

DR. WADE: Is there anything else you'd like to do to feel better?

ROBERTA (Wiping away tears and reaching for her purse, she pulls out a large candy bar.): I'd like to have some fun.

DR. WADE (smiling): Ah, yes, I've been thinking of the "F" word myself, because now you could have a playmate. A playmate is so much more fun than a persecutor. This opens a large range of possibilities.

(After a short break, the session resumes.)

DR. WADE: Okay, Peter. You've had a head start because you've watched Roberta do her work. If you're interested in playing a new game we can get a lot done here. These chairs, you know who they are. Who do you want to talk to first? (Peter stares at the chairs; he doesn't speak.) Okay, take the deepest breath you can. I'm going to do some Reichean work with you. It's important for you to get some energy moving so you can be in touch with your body, with the present. (She massages Peter's shoulders and arms.)

PETER (with a sudden steely look at a chair and in threatening tones): I'm not going to let you control me anymore.

DR. WADE: Who just joined us, Peter?

PETER: My mother.

DR. WADE: What did you do to her?

PETER: I shut her out.

DR. WADE: That's what you've always done, and that's what you've done in this marriage. Tell me, what is it your mother wants you to do?

PETER (after a long pause, perhaps ninety seconds): She wants me to be the audience. She wants me to sit at her feet. (to the chair) I don't think you're open and honest with anybody and you think you can fabricate that kind of relationship, but it just limits the relationship.

DR. WADE: You're intellectualizing again, Peter, and as soon as you began, the energy in this room changed. You were alive for the first time since you came in here, and then you began to talk from your head.

PETER (to chair in flat tone): I don't feel like I get anything from you when I talk. It's a one-way channel and it's boring.

DR. WADE: What is it she wants you to do? Let her have it, Peter, don't talk to her with the monotone, with the blank expression. That was your way of defending yourself from her onslaught of energy and noise, so be here in the present, take her on.

PETER (to chair): No, I can't be with you, not the way you are! If that's the only way you can relate to me, I'm not going to just shut down just because I can't be a real person with you. I'm fed up and disgusted and I won't have anything to do with you.

DR. WADE: Tell her how angry you are, show it in your face and your body.

PETER (snarling): I'm just so angry with you. (He steps back quickly, as if catching himself.)

DR. WADE: You felt it, too, didn't you?

PETER: I did for a minute.

DR. WADE: You backed away from it. You were so afraid of those feelings, see how quickly you backed away from them. Come on, Peter, come back, come back. Give it back to her. Don't swallow it anymore. That's what this is about. Tell her how you feel.

PETER (with an earsplitting scream): Shut up! Get out of my space. This has never been mine. You've never let me have my own place in this world, never allowed me to feel important. It hurts to be with you. Go away. (in childlike voice) Give me my space to be me.

DR. WADE: There's something else you want from her, pull it out. (Dr. Wade pats his stomach.)

PETER: I want, I want to . . . be loved with no strings attached. (He begins crying but tries to steel himself.)

DR. WADE: Peter, please don't suck it back in. You've been wanting that for so long, so long, there's nothing wrong with wanting your mother to approve of who you are, nothing. (His sobs come out freely now, and he bends from the waist, as if there is no strength remaining in his upper torso. Roberta walks up, puts her arms around his shoulders, and leads him to a chair. He leans into his wife's arm, against her breast. With an open hand, she strokes Peter's face, from his temples, down the length of his cheek, to the chin, over and over, as he sobs.)

DR. WADE: Good, good for you, feel it and pass through it and let it go. (He continues crying.) Let it go, you don't have to carry it anymore. (Below, in the city street, an ambulance passes, with sirens wailing. This blends into Peter's wails.) Now, Peter, would you please tell Roberta what you feel inside right now. Don't shut down, stay right there. How does it feel, the way she's touching you?

PETER (to Roberta): There's a lot of anger I've been directing toward you that doesn't have a thing to do with you.

DR. WADE: Can you let your body come back to life? Feel the way she's touching you. That must feel good. (Peter raises his head slowly, as if just noticing Roberta. He puts his arms around her, and they stroke one another's faces. His legs are crossed, his feet are pulled in under the chair, and his back is bent; he is almost in a fetal position.)

DR. WADE: That's good. You two can comfort one another. You both have the same wounds, a matching set of wounds. That's why you fell in love. When you two are in your bodies, fully present that is, you can be there for each other, stroke for stroke. Roberta, tell him how it feels for you, to be with him like this.

ROBERTA: I feel so close to you. I want to be closer. I like it when you touch me like this. This tenderness has been missing in my life.

DR. WADE: Now, Peter, this is the soul of the poet that really matters, this aliveness, a sense of being in these enriching moments. The two of you together like this, it's sheer poetry. What would you need to continue this kind of closeness, and yet give you each some space? (Peter does not respond.)

ROBERTA: We have to wait until our lease runs out, but we'd like to move to a larger apartment.

DR. WADE: Oh, I don't know. When you go home today you might find that you have a lot more space right where you are. Having your mother and father there has made a huge crowd. The alienation when you came in was extreme. Roberta, you were pinched, pale, and angry; the same for you, Peter. But Peter, you've got one more piece of this puzzle to unravel. I want you to sit here by yourself again. But if you need Roberta to come over, ask her for what you need. That's an important part of the process for you. You never dreamed you could actually feel your feelings or express your feelings and have someone be there for you. I think you made a pretty good choice. Roberta came, when you let her know that you needed her. But you have to ask her or you'll run the risk of having a controlling mother all over again. Okay, Peter, it's harder to work with you because you leave your body. Do you do anything physical?

PETER: I lift weights.

DR. WADE: You know now that you do have the ability to be present. You need more than lifting weights, some way to get your energies stirred. Okay, Peter, take on your dad. Here we go, fly from your intuition. Be aware of your body.

PETER (talking to chair): Just because you have to shut down with her, doesn't mean you have to shut down to me.

DR. WADE: Peter, we have to find some way to get you back into your body. You're talking to him the only way you know, from your head. That won't do right now. You're fighting for your marriage.

PETER (animated): Wait a minute. There's one physical thing I used to do with my father. It was boxing.

DR. WADE: Well, then, let's clear the floor so you can do it.

(With the furniture pushed to the side, Peter begins moving, prancing, his fists positioned, his feet almost dancing across the floor, back and forth, and he breathes heavily.)

DR. WADE: That's so graceful, so beautiful. Now punch him, I have a feeling you'd like to, and talk to him the way guys in a ring talk to each other.

PETER (while still moving): You can be shut down. I'm not going to be shut down.

DR. WADE: Good, look at him. Tell him what you need.

PETER: Listen to me. Love me for who I am. I don't want to perform for you. I'm not a trained bear. Talk to me. (jabbing) Me! (another jab) Me! I exist, you know. Do you hear, me. Hey, I'm over here. So you won't accept me, at least recognize me. Can't you see me? I'm not going to disappear. I'll make you see me. Come here, I've got something for you. (breathing heavily, then taking wide swings) That's right, here I am. (Draws back for a walloping punch, his fist flying through the air. Then suddenly, Peter's feet stop moving. His chest heaves with the exertion. He stares down at the floor threateningly.) And you'd better keep listening!

DR. WADE (holding his hand up in the air as if proclaiming him the winner in a boxing match): You laid him out! How does that feel?

PETER: It feels good. I feel terrific.

ROBERTA: It was incredible to watch you. Your swinging and your talking was coordinated.

DR. WADE: You fought for your power, you took it back. You won, Peter. You're here and you're with us. You're with your wife. Let me be the first to make the introductions. This is Roberta, she used to be a victim but has chosen not to be. And this is Peter, he's . . . he's new to this world. (The Levines sneak looks at one another. They look slightly embarrassed.)

DR. WADE: Something tells me you two should think about getting married again.

(Roberta throws her hand over her mouth and gasps.)

DR. WADE: What is it, Roberta?

ROBERTA: Last night . . . I dreamed we were getting married again, that something was wrong with the first ceremony.

DR. WADE: Something did go wrong. You two weren't present, you used stand-ins. But now that you're here you might be ready to start for real. That dream, it was your intuitive powers working for you, and they will continue to work for you, now that you've discovered them. Congratulations on the real life you're going to have together.

DR. WADE'S FOLLOW-UP ON THE LEVINES

Behavior Therapy:

The Levines should find a marriage counselor to continue their work, a family therapist who is particularly sensitive to the great losses many immigrants suffered as they literally fled for their lives to escape religious persecution. I especially recommend therapy by someone in the AVANTA network. They are skilled at keeping the connection flowing between the mind and body and resolving intergenerational issues.

I also think it would be quite enriching for Roberta to develop an interest in some area of the arts that is of her own choosing. My hope is not only that this may help her establish some common bond with Peter, but also allow her to relax more and open herself to creative self-expression.

Most importantly, they should learn to play together, whether it's taking long romantic walks in the park, bike riding, or hiking; something strenuous enough to keep them in touch with the "poetry" of their day-to-day existences.

Cognitive Work:

I have given the Levines a daily affirmation which they can say separately: "I am fully alive and full of love. I express my love for my partner freely."

Bibliotherapy:

Roberta should read, *Codependent No More* by Melody Beattie, so she can learn to handle control issues.

Peter should read *Making Contact* by Virginia Satir, which offers tips on how to remain in the present and communicate.

MAKING CHANGES

STEP 10 ♥ **We continued to take personal inventory and when we were wrong promptly admitted it.**

This step holds the key to ongoing growth in a love union. What is my part? Am I improving my character, personality, etc? Asking these questions on a regular basis prevents sliding back into the old pattern of blaming our mate rather than looking

within. The Levines' personal inventories free them from oppositional behavior, so they can pursue fully their own creative interests. Ask yourself, Am I making progress in my efforts to become
a more whole person and a more loving spouse?

───────────── ♥ EXERCISES ♥ ─────────────

1. Take three deep abdominal breaths, relax your body from head
   to toe, then visualize a light brighter than any you've imagined
   thus far. Mentally "see" the light flowing down through your
   body and out through the bottom of your feet. Affirm: "I am
   a success, I am a success."

2. Review your first inventory and assess your progress. Renew
   your efforts to correct the character flaws as you identified
   then.

3. Make a list of strengths as well as shortcomings based on your
   actions of the past twenty-four hours.

4. Affirm: "I am a worthy and deserving person. My life gets
   better and better everyday."

───────────────────────────

 Love saver:
Do something new together, just for fun.

12 HEALING THE WOUNDS OF LOVE

If there were not a toddler crawling across their laps, as they lay stretched across the grass in New York City's Central Park, Jacques and Isabella Fortassier would look like characters straight out of the old television show, "Miami Vice." They radiate a sense of drama, high adventure, and style.

On this spring day they wear fitted, dark green leather jackets with wide, sloping shoulders. But it is more than their clothing that makes them seem like twins. In part it is their startling good looks. He is thirty-six, and she thirty-nine. Both have olive complexions, dark hair—hers near waist length and straight, his brushed back from the brow—and both have long, sleek bodies. Or perhaps it is something less tangible, such as their combined appetite for accelerated living that gives them an aura of excitement.

Despite their glamour, this is not a television sound stage. It is noisy Manhattan on a Friday afternoon and Jacques must return to work. He hastily folds the blanket on which they've been sitting as Isabella collects the scattered baby toys, readying little Alma for the stroller ride to their nearby townhouse.

Her tiny arms stretch outward to kiss Daddy goodbye. Jacques glances at his watch. He's late. A client is coming from a chain of luxury hotels to discuss the intricate wall designs cre-

207

ated by Jacques's small firm. He bends to deliver a kiss to the child's forehead. And then there is his wife. For her he makes time. As they embrace he thanks her for the surprise picnic. He loves her, he murmurs, his French accent elevating her name into a melody. "Ease-a-bella," he croons, as if he can taste her.

They part, and just before Jacques crosses the street, he turns and waves. Little Alma is crying. She wants her daddy. "You'll see him later, honey," Isabella says, then adds under her breath, "I hope."

She speaks of hope, and yet there is little left when it comes to Jacques. What she most feels these days is fear, for herself, for her daughter, and especially for her marriage. "I never know when he's going to start using it again," she says. The "it" she's referring to is cocaine.

"Sometimes when we've had bad fights," she says, "I've thought to myself, How stupid you've been. You've wrecked your life. When we do get along and it's good, it's so exciting. It seems we were meant for each other. We have so much in common: our interests in art, in the environment, in raising a family. But when we decided two years ago to get married we didn't consider that we didn't really know each other. We were thrown together by passion."

Everyone, it seems, knows or has heard of a woman like Isabella. She is a woman for whom the fates seem to conspire in her favor. She has good looks, an education, tenacity of spirit, and sparkling personality. But her record with men is a grim one. Her first husband was obsessively jealous. Jacques is saddled with this drug problem.

She doesn't often tell people her story because their response would seem inevitable. Were she to appear on one of the daytime talk shows, for instance, and tell her tale, someone in the audience would invariably rise, hands on hips, and ask: "Why don't you just pack your bags, grab your baby, and leave that man?" The question would surely be followed by raucous applause from the audience.

Isabella would understand that this is easier said than done. Because what few people in that cheering crowd would realize is that for Isabella and Jacques, the forces that bind them and the defining moments of their past keep them together, albeit painfully, as if by the strings of their hearts. It's something Jacques understood the moment he met Isabella four years ago.

"I'm devoted to her," he says. "Her fears about the drugs, the violence, it is all in the past. I wish I could reassure her that it is our lives I care about . . . us loving each other, really loving each other so there is no fear there. I am a man who likes inspiration. I get vibrations from Isabella."

He says that the cocaine is only a weekend recreation, that his wife exaggerates. "Only sometimes when I have had a difficult day," he says. He's not hooked, he insists. He can always stop.

As for his wife, he says she demands change in him but is unwilling to change herself. His chief complaint is that she holds him back from experiencing life to the fullest. He believes, for instance, that financially, they could have so much more, like that building on Long Island he wanted to buy. He complains that she is afraid of any risks. The only way to make money, he says with exasperation, is to take risks. And when he doesn't do just as she demands, he adds, she refuses to have sex with him, sometimes for as long as three or four months. This he cannot tolerate. "It's offensive," he says, "to manipulate sex, withhold it because she wants me to live the way she wants."

The key to understanding what binds them, of course, is to look back at their lives and the lives of their families before them. Let us begin then by introducing the central figures.

Isabella's family

Maternal grandparents: MARIA
LECH

Paternal grandparents: CARMEN
ENRIQUE

Isabella's mother: BONITA
father: LOUIE

Jacques's family

Paternal grandparents:	PHILLIPE
	GABRIELLE
Maternal grandparents:	ELIENNE
	CHARLES
Jacques's father:	CLAUDE
mother:	SIMONE

Family Themes: In Jacques's family, men believe that life must be lived to the fullest, regardless of who gets hurt. In Isabella's family, women believe that men must be controlled by any means necessary or they'll destroy the family.

Let's begin by looking into the maternal side of Isabella's family tree. Her grandparents are:

MARIA: born in Puerto Rico in 1912
LECH: born in Poland in 1909

Maria and Lech married in 1927, and the following year moved to the Lower East Side of New York. Lech worked construction jobs by day but loved to spend his evenings gambling. After the birth of their third child he told Maria he had to go to California for a business trip. He never returned. Maria later heard rumors that the Mafia was looking for him for unpaid debts. Over the years she received several letters from Lech begging her to join him in California and to bring the children. Maria was unwilling to go. But she did have someone in her household to remind her of her ex-husband. With her blonde hair and fair skin, her youngest daughter was a living reminder of Lech. She would grow up to be Isabella's mother:

BONITA: born in 1931 near Delancey Street in New York City

As the translation of her name implies, Bonita was quite beautiful. But at five years old she was heartbroken when her father moved away. She would have another father figure in her life, though. His name was Pablo and he was the carpenter her mother married when Bonita was eight years old. Pablo was stable and kindhearted. Concerned about Bonita being so thin, he paid for her to spend summers with a family on a farm in Long Island, where she could enjoy a healthier life. Years later, when Bonita developed a bad acne problem, Pablo came to the rescue again. He paid for her to consult one of the best dermatologists on Park Avenue. Despite his kindnesses, Bonita would never get over the loss of her father.

World War II had ended and Bonita was sixteen and working as a waitress when she met Isabella's father Louie, a handsome G.I. who'd just returned from England. She admired his devotion to his family and, like her, he loved to dance. They began competing in dance contests, bopping to swing music. They won prizes for the rollerskate/dance routine they created together. When Louis proposed to Bonita, she accepted.

Before we take a look at Bonita and Louie's marriage, let's look into his past. His family tree would include Isabella's paternal grandparents:

CARMEN: born in Brooklyn, New York, in 1910, of Panamanian heritage
ENRIQUE: born in Puerto Rico in 1903; moved to New York as a boy

Carmen and Enrique moved to Westchester County in the early thirties, where they purchased a half-acre farm. They had five children. Their oldest child was Isabella's father:

LOUIE: born in 1925 in Westchester County

As the oldest son, Louie had to work very hard on the farm. He remembers having an accident with a pitchfork while working alongside his father. One of the thick-forked prongs went through the skin between his thumb and forefinger, and he bled profusely. When he alluded to the pain, his father told him to wrap it up with a hankie and to stop complaining. The scar would always remain with him.

When Louie was growing up, Spanish was the only language spoken in his home. In elementary school, when he was unable to respond to the nuns in English, they whipped him across the back and hands.

After graduation, he enlisted in the Army, and his family was quite proud of him. While away, his sisters and mother sent him many care packages.

When he returned from the war Louie must have been overjoyed to see his family and probably thanked God he'd never have to do without them again. His two sisters had married and they all had small houses built near their father's farm.

Not all would be blissful. Those same sisters were gravely disappointed when they met the woman Louie had chosen for his wife. The lovely Bonita looked nothing like these large-boned, muscular, farm girls. Even her hair and skin marked her as different. She was fairer than most of the Puerto Rican girls they had known. They seemed to dislike her from the start.

Like his sisters, Louie was determined to build a house nearby, and he did. In the beginning there were many visits between the houses. On Saturdays, as Bonita and Louie prepared for nights out on the town, the sisters watched her enviously as she shimmied into her low-cut sequined dresses and decked herself out in rhinestone jewelry and red lipstick. They branded Bonita as vain and haughty. Bonita's entrance into the family touched off a feud that would change forever the bucolic atmosphere that Isabella's paternal grandparents had labored so hard to create. "She took our brother away from us," one of the sisters would be heard to say.

Bonita and Louie would have two children. The first was a boy, the second was:

ISABELLA: born in 1953

"I don't remember, but I'm told that my father used to get drunk and he and my mother would have terrible battles. She'd complain about something, like the house being too cold, and he could be horrible. When my mother told me she said it with such despair. Once, she said that when they were arguing he smacked her downstairs. Mom said Daddy didn't care about bettering himself, didn't want responsibility. They offered him promotions at the plant where he worked—in all those years he never missed a day from work. He would tell them, no, that he didn't want to change jobs. My mother would keep pushing him to move up, get ahead."

Isabella does remember seeing Louie raise his fist threateningly toward Bonita. "She'd throw herself on the floor," said Isabella, "and have something like a convulsive fit and would pound the floor."

One of the most explosive issues between Bonita and Louie was his family. "She was angry that the sisters would badmouth her and yet my father remained so close, so respectful to them."

When it came to the subject of her sisters-in-law, Bonita warned Isabella to be cautious. "All my cousins and I used to play together, always at one house or another," said Isabella. "But my mother told me to watch out for my aunts, not to trust them because they didn't treat me like the other nieces and that they thought the others were prettier and liked them better."

In turn, when she grew older, the aunts warned Isabella about her mother. "They said she was a born troublemaker."

The good news in Isabella's life is that some time during the late fifties, her father stopped drinking and was never violent again. The bad news is that without the liquor he became zombielike at home. He spent hours simply sitting around watching television and was very unresponsive to the family. Not surprisingly, the relationship between Isabella's parents deteriorated further. "There were only three beds in the house," said Isabella. "My brother slept in one, my mother was in the other and for about eight years, until I was thirteen, my father and I shared one. The story was that my mother liked to read in bed at night and that the light kept my father awake."

Bonita said that despite the unusual circumstance of sleeping with her dad, she was not molested nor did she feel uncomfortable about spending nights with him. "There was no hankie pankie," she said. "Believe me, I'd talk about it if there had been.

My father and I were very close but in a healthy way. At night he would tell me the story of the three pigs and I would fall asleep."

Meanwhile, her mother, still young and beautiful, longed for the excitement she'd had during her dancing days with Louie. In her loneliness she gave in to the temptation of another man, an executive in the clothing factory where she worked as a line supervisor. With her exotic looks, Bonita would have been difficult to miss. This man, Henry, began wooing her with small gifts and with rides to the train station in his fancy car. He wanted them to get to know one another, he said. Bonita gave in, agreed to meet him, but how? Her sisters-in-law had been warning Louie for years not to trust her.

Deciding that nothing would stand in their way, Bonita sacrificed Isabella's innocence. After swearing the eight-year-old to secrecy, Bonita began taking her along on her Friday night dates. She told Louie she was going to spend more time with their daughter, to begin having a girls' night out. "It hurt me so much to lie to my father," said Isabella.

Bonita's gentleman friend was kind to Isabella. "He bought me gifts, a ring, earrings, and he took us out to these nice restaurants. He was single and my mother had him convinced that she was divorced. But she told him that he couldn't come to the house because her ex-husband lived down the street. She did allow him to call the house, though. She knew my father would never answer the phone. He'd just sit there and let it ring."

Her mother's affair lasted for years, with Isabella right in the middle. "Even when this man went away for a business trip my mother and I would go over to his apartment in Manhattan and clean it for him."

Bonita apparently hoped her beau would propose, but he did not. He may have considered their relationship too stormy for nuptials. "He was a heavy drinker," said Isabella, "and he and my mother had terrible fights about it. He'd call her names, say she was crazy and a liar."

Back at home, life for Isabella wasn't happy. Her mother had always made her do a lot of housework, "from the time I was five and six years old," she said. But as she got older her work load increased. "My mother is a cleaning fanatic; we'd spend most of Saturday and Sunday cleaning, and we did everything, dusting behind the radiator, washing the windows. She's obsessed with it." The weekend work she grew to expect, but Isabella resented being treated like a house flunky. "Once I got my driver's license it really got bad," said Isabella. "One night she woke me up at one in the morning to go to the store to buy my brother's wife some cigarettes. And I had school the next morning."

"If my sister-in-law dyed her hair at our house, I was expected to clean up after that, too, as well as clean up the mud my nieces and nephews left behind during the visit," continued Isabella. "I used to think of my mother as the evil stepmother. When I was doing the laundry and scrubbing the floors I used to sing the song from the movie *Cinderella*. My favorite song was "Some Day My Prince Will Come."

After graduation and her eighteenth birthday, Isabella's grandfather, Pablo, who'd been so good to her as a child, came to visit. He quietly watched Isabella slaving away and called her aside to give her advice. "He told me not to live my life for my family," Isabella said. She realized he was right. Following her grandfather's advice she moved away as quickly as she could.

Over the next decade and a half, Isabella would support herself waitressing in Puerto Rico. She then used her savings to put herself through undergraduate school in Florida. She married at twenty-four, but was divorced a few years later when her husband proved to be obsessed with her.

Isabella moved to Manhattan four years ago to fulfill her lifelong dream to attend graduate school and study French. She hoped eventually to live in France, and was visiting the French consulate in New York when she met Jacques.

He was in the hallway waiting for a woman who, like him, was from Quebec. This woman had helped Jacques secure his graduate fellowship to Columbia University. He had dropped by to thank her. When he saw Isabella he began speaking to her in French and she responded.

"My heart started pounding," Isabella recalled. "I couldn't

believe he was so handsome. He gave me his number and suggested we get together."

When Isabella did phone him, a woman answered. "Jacques explained that he was living with a family. I knew how scarce space was in New York, so I didn't think twice about it," she said. When Jacques and Isabella began dating their nights were filled with high-speed excitement. "We'd go to reggae clubs and dance all night," Isabella said.

A few dates later they spent the night together in a hotel room and the next morning he woke up, looked at his watch, and jumped out of bed. Isabella took one look at his frightened face and said, "You're married, aren't you?"

Jacques denied that he was married, but said he was living with someone with whom he was about to break up. Isabella accepted his story. But a few weeks later, when she called his house, his 'live-in' lover answered the phone again. She said "You're Isabella, right?"

"Yes," Isabella replied.

"Well, I'm Helene," the woman continued. "And I just want you to know I'm going to fight for my husband."

Isabella hung up, stunned. She was determined to find some way to get Jacques out of her life. She packed a suitcase and headed for Florida to stay with a friend. Somehow, though, Jacques got her number in Florida and called. "He begged me to believe that it was all over between him and Helene. But later, when I called him back and he answered, he said 'Please don't call me anymore.' I knew Helene had to be in the room and that their marriage wasn't over."

Isabella remained in Miami six more months, long enough, she believed, to get Jacques out of her system. When she returned to New York, though, she called him. "He came right over. He tried to talk me into going to the beach with him. He said, 'Let's go to Brighton.' When I frowned, he said, 'I get it, you only swim in beaches in the Caribbean, right?' When I smiled he said, 'Then we're going to Jamaica.' I was so needy I couldn't refuse."

They spent two passion-filled weeks in Montego Bay. Jacques rented a motorcycle and they traveled the island, meeting the natives, swimming, sunning, and making love. "The only problem," said Isabella, "was that he liked to get high a lot and I didn't want to."

Back in New York, Jacques, swearing his marriage had ended, invited Isabella to move into his new apartment with him. She did. One night, they were in bed sleeping when Isabella heard someone enter the apartment. "All of a sudden a woman was standing over the bed, just watching us. I knew it had to be Helene. I could see her in the moonlight. She was tall and very thin with light hair. I was terrified. I kept trying to wake Jacques up but he was sleeping so deeply. Finally I just shoved him onto the floor. That's how he woke up."

Jacques took Helene outside to talk. Isabella hoped that would be the last she'd hear of her, but it wasn't. "She called constantly. She got involved in coke and was always asking for money. She was very much in love with Jacques. He said it had been a marriage of convenience, a way of sharing expenses and getting a permanent visa, but that he'd treated her well. I later learned that he'd been violent with her."

That spring Jacques completed his course work at Columbia and was awarded an MBA. His father and stepmother flew in from Quebec City for the ceremony. "His parents were polite, but they insisted on seeing Helene. They invited her to attend Jacques's graduation with them. I told him it was okay and that it wasn't necessary for me to go and I stayed home to avoid a scene."

While she was waiting for Jacques and his family to return, Isabella took everyone's dirty laundry over to her parents' house and washed, dried, and folded it. It took her hours. When she got back to the apartment, Jacques and his parents still hadn't returned. In fact, they didn't get back until the next afternoon. "They'd all gone dancing together, along with Helene," said Isabella. "I was furious."

Before returning to Canada, Jacques's father apologized, said it had been his fault, that he'd just gotten so drunk he'd lost track of the time. Isabella said she understood, she was anxious just to get on with normal life with Jacques. That never happened. Four months later she discovered she was pregnant.

"Jacques wanted me to get an abortion, but I couldn't. I was worried that maybe I'd never be able to have another baby, and I loved Jacques. I laid a guilt trip on him. I said, 'Don't worry, I'll raise the child myself.'"

Jacques called his father for advice. He told him that not having money didn't really matter, that when his mother had been pregnant they'd been so poor they'd had to live over a brothel. "And the night your mother went into labor," continued his father, "I had to borrow money from one of the prostitutes to get her to the hospital in a cab."

Next, Jacques turned to a friend, the woman at the embassy where he first had met Isabella eighteen months before. She encouraged him to complete his divorce and marry Isabella. "She seems perfect for you," she advised.

They were married three months later, and it wasn't long before Isabella realized that the man she loved had a violent side to him. "Once when we were visiting his father he threw a glass of juice at a painting his father had just completed. Jacques was on coke, I'm sure of it. I had found it and thrown it down the toilet."

"I also learned that he'd once had a fight with his mother. He'd attacked her and wrecked her kitchen." His outbursts weren't confined to his parents. After one argument with Isabella, he dragged her down a stairway, and when they argued, he often pushed and shoved her.

The most shocking incident of all occurred just before the baby was born and they were living with her parents. "My mother was in our room and found a scale and a couple of bags of cocaine," Isabella said. "We realized he'd been dealing from her house. She told him to get out and that she was going to call the police. Her brother was a policeman. Jacques grabbed her and put his hands around her neck and began choking her. I tried breaking them up. We were all fighting. My father just sat there and didn't say a word."

Isabella rushed into the bedroom, madly throwing Jacques's clothes into a suitcase. She put it at his feet and fell down on her hands and knees begging him to leave. "I was crazy, hysterical. He was pulling me to come with him, but I wouldn't go."

He left only minutes before the police arrived. "They didn't go after him, but for days I remained in shock. I felt exposed. I hadn't wanted anyone to know about my life. I went into my bedroom and sat on the bed, rocking back and forth. I was like a zombie. My mother said if I went back to him she'd be through with me."

They were separated for four weeks before the strain of being apart proved to be too much. They wanted to live together, but neither of them had much money. Then they found the perfect place. It wasn't much to look at, but the rent was cheap. "It was located right over a house of prostitution," Isabella said. "There was a long flight of stairs and, while I was pregnant, some of the women would help me carry my groceries upstairs."

After they'd had their daughter, Jacques's father helped him finance a business venture. Their financial fortunes have improved, but the arguments continue. Isabella said that she wants her marriage to work out for her daughter's sake as well as hers. She doesn't want Alma to grow up without her father. She has seen firsthand how that can affect someone.

"To this day," Isabella said, "my mother tries to get me to write to her father. She was five when he left. I've called several places. She doesn't know if he's alive or dead. Her brother doesn't want anything to do with him. She has memories of her father and I think it still hurts her."

♥

I felt it was important to tell you Isabella's story in as much detail as possible. It is not unusual. Week after week, I counsel women like Isabella. Lovely beyond words, educated, seemingly self-assured—they tell me not only of love gone awry but of the terrible humiliations.

I had one client, a striking and tremendously successful journalist, who went to her married lover's house and banged on the door, demanding that they have a showdown between him and his wife. My client described to me in bruising detail how this man called the police and how she had to be dragged away—she'd tried holding on to his ankles—as this man's wife, children, and neighbors looked on.

Another woman, equally as stunning and bright, told me of

suffering through her husband's many infidelities. Once he'd even returned from work with lipstick on his underclothes, and the shade was one she'd never worn. This client wanted so desperately to save the marriage, that as a Christmas gift, she gave her husband an all-expenses-paid solo trip to Club Med. She hoped that he'd have enough liaisons on the trip to get other women out of his system.

I call it the Little Mermaid Syndrome. Because, like the beautiful character in the fairy tale—who gave up her voice, her family, her very body—these women are willing to sacrifice everything for love. Why? They suffer from what can best be described as classic codependence. When I am asked to define codependence, I reply with this joke from the Codependent Anonymous fellowship: What happens when a codependent dies? Answer: Someones else's life flashes before her eyes. The hallmarks of this syndrome are: complete absorption in and attempts to control another's life; the idea that she can't live without him; and an inability to create boundaries, that is, a sense of just where to draw the line. These make for self-sacrificing misery for codependents.

Isabella presents a textbook picture of codependence. For the millions (usually women) who feel as she does, falling in love is often akin to drowning in the very ocean they longed for.

When, for instance, Jacques's failings and rage surfaced in front of her mother, Isabella said she felt exposed. No matter how terrible her marriage might have been, it was worth anything to her to keep feeding the false image of a stable marriage. Her parents have kept a similar illusion going to this day.

When Isabella met Jacques she was like a moth drawn to a flame, for Jacques was what she had been groomed for. She'd seen her mother submit to being used in the worst way by her executive boyfriend, so Isabella let herself be used. She'd been raised in an atmosphere of lies and artifice, so she tolerated Jacques's lies. Ironically, Jacques even told Isabella the same sort of lie her mother had told Henry: that he was not really married. She'd heard stories of her mother and father's dancing and laughter, and it was enough that she and Jacques could dance through the night. She'd heard stories of her father's violent nature. She must have sensed that anger in Jacques. Moreover, Jacques's personality must have seemed hauntingly familiar. Alcoholics and drug addicts share a common trait. Whether sitting passively while white-knuckling an armchair or flying into a rage, it is they who control the emotions of those around them.

What's more, Bonita passed her own father hunger on to her daugher. Bonita, who'd never gotten over the loss of her father, wasn't emotionally equipped to allow her daughter to really have a father. So what did she do? She put Isabella in the bed she should have been in, once again inappropriate boundaries. Isabella was the wife, cooking, cleaning, and slaving around the house and even sleeping with her father.

When Isabella grew up, she took one look at Jacques, listened to his words, and of course her heart began pounding. Finally, after all these years, that prince she'd been singing about over her piles of laundry had finally asked her to dance.

I don't condemn Jacques. Like the cocaine he's addicted to, he was the "substance" Isabella found herself unable to live without. Let's find out more about how he fits into this drama by taking a closer look at Jacques's family history. His paternal side would include his grandparents:

PHILLIPE: born in the Dijon region of France
GABRIELLE: also from Dijon

In the 1930s, Jacques's grandfather inherited his family winery. He and Gabrielle, a neighbor, married at an early age. They had three sons but, unfortunately, Phillipe died at the age of twenty from a heart attack. Gabrielle was forced to run the business. Bravely, she kept it going for three years, but was undone by unscrupulous employees, ruthless competitors, and by the bad debts incurred by extended family members to whom she'd given money. In the end, she had to sell the winery at a great financial loss and was left with enough to pay for the education of two of her three sons. The youngest son was overtaken by the disease of alcoholism, and Gabrielle, feeling fate had made the decision for her, quickly ruled him out of the picture. Her middle son was Jacques's father:

CLAUDE: born in 1931 in Burgundy

After Claude graduated from law school with honors, he pursued his interests in Impressionist art and socialism. He gave long, impassioned speeches on socialism in the village square. One of his most ardent sympathizers was a local woman named Simone, who would be Jacques's mother. She insinuated herself into Claude's life and they began dating. Simone was five inches taller than Claude and their friends referred to them as Beauty and the Beast.

By the early fifties, Claude had become disenchanted with contemporary French socialism and decided to leave for Quebec. He'd heard he would feel right at home in this Canadian city. Not only because Quebec and France shared a language and some customs, but also because the city's stone houses and crooked cobblestone streets gave it the air of an old European city. Yet he hoped enough of the new frontier remained to give him a new life.

He departed for Canada, leaving his beloved Simone. Although these two young socialists considered the idea of a legally sanctioned marriage passé, her parents felt otherwise. Her father was a religious conservative who insisted that his daughter would never leave the country without benefit of marriage.

Thus Simone and Claude agreed on a marriage by proxy. Two nearly identical ceremonies were arranged. One was held in Dijon, with Simone wearing a lavish bridal gown and surrounded by family; the other in Quebec, with Claude in a borrowed tuxedo, marrying before an audience of his new acquaintances from the local intelligentsia. Simone immediately left France to join her groom. While she travels let's take a look into her family background. This would include Jacques's maternal grandparents:

ELIENNE: born in Dijon
CHARLES: originally from San Florentin

Jacques's maternal grandfather was a carpenter by trade. He ruled his household with a firm hand and had rigid ideas about what a woman should and shouldn't do. When his wife, Elienne, did not obey him, he took the strap to her. She took the beatings but raised her children as she saw fit, and this included allowing her daughter to have secret liaisons with her lover. This daughter was:

SIMONE: born in 1933 in Burgundy

In her early twenties, Simone confided to her mother that she'd fallen in love with the young man in town who everyone was talking about. She and her mother put their heads together to plan nighttime rendezvous. Elienne would coax the father to bed early, then help Simone sneak out of the house to meet her lover. Jacques's mother, Simone, had some leftist ideas of her own that she'd developed at the college she'd attended for three years, which added an intellectual resonance to their affair d'amour.

She would run down the dark, cobblestone streets and head for the village square to join Claude at a tavern. They would sit at long tables covered in red-and-white-checkered cloths and eat baguettes and Avallon cheese with plenty of the dark rich burgundy their region was known for.

A year later when, at twenty-three, she set out to join Claude in Quebec, she must have had a head full of beautiful dreams about their life together. As we have heard, for the first years of their marriage the two were so impoverished, they lived over a bordello. Claude's paintings were not selling and he hated practicing law. Their first child was one of our two main characters:

JACQUES: born in 1956 in Quebec, Canada

"Although my father tried, he was never able to fully support himself as an artist," said Jacques. Claude tried his hand at a number of business pursuits but was only mildly successful. His painting was always his first love, and he often spent up to nine hours a day locked in his studio. One milestone exhibition of his work was held in New York. Jacques couldn't accompany his father to the opening, but he promised himself that he'd one day visit that city.

"My family attended art exhibits on Sundays the way some people attended church," Jacques said. "My parents were socialists who believed some priests could be as dirty as politicians. One of my favorite art galleries had a big fish pond, and while my parents got into long conversations with other adults, I'd crawl through the opening of the gate that surrounded this shallow pool and catch fish."

Until Jacques was ten he and his family lived in an apartment, but when the rents escalated, Simone pressed the owner to sell to the tenants. He refused and Simone began to picket the building and led a rent boycott until the owner gave in. Three years later they'd made enough profit on the apartment to buy a four-bedroom house that they could fill with Claude's artwork and antiques. In the dining room, Claude painted frescoes of flowers and built beams along the ceiling. On the sheltered patio, he added an aviary of colorful birds and lush plants so they could be surrounded by beauty.

Jacques remembers his parents being very much in love. "They read the same books and discussed them and spent a lot of time out together with their bohemian friends." Simone wanted her husband's opinions on everything, even the clothes she wore, and they spent many nights out dancing and attending parties.

It wasn't all bliss, however. Simone argued with Claude about his drinking. When he drank he seemed to slow down physically and mentally and did not seem to hear a word of what was said to him. He would lock himself in his studio and drink and paint.

It also infuriated Simone that Claude turned down so many promising business deals. Simone complained to her oldest son about these unaggressive traits in his father, and she also tried talking to Claude directly, encouraging him to get ahead in life. "He'd listen for awhile," Jacques said, then he'd say, 'Okay, that's enough.'"

One of the most frightening aspects of Jacques childhood was his mother's epilepsy. "She had seizures about once a month," said Jacques, "especially when she was stressed. I saw her have many seizures. As I got older, I would put something in her mouth so she wouldn't bite her tongue. She also had excruciating migraine headaches. She stood up slowly in the mornings to control them and this seemed to work well for her."

When Jacques was thirteen, he and his mother began to have fiery arguments. "She was especially antidrugs and was deeply upset when I started smoking grass at fifteen." What Simone didn't know and would have been even more furious about was that on one occasion Claude and Jacques, father and son, smoked marijuana together.

Jacques learned to keep secrets from his mother. "It was usually hard for me to tell my mother anything in a straightforward way," he said. "When she got angry she would throw earlier infractions in my face. I began to say to myself, 'Why not save yourself and don't tell her the truth?' So I didn't."

Meanwhile, Jacques was developing a fondness for dangerous sports, like racing cars and motorcycles. During one high school vacation he and his brother, Chuck, were invited to visit a relative who lived in Peru. The one place they were determined to visit was the pointed rock beach, Punto de Peidra, where surfers had to jump from a steep and dangerous rock to reach the water. "One night when I was surfing out there, it got late and I got lost," said Jacques. "I was frightened. My brother swam out for me, and as soon as I could reach his surfboard I clenched to it. The waves were breaking all around us. We were stranded out there for more than an hour before we could make our way back to the beach."

In 1984, Jacques's mother began calling saying she was concerned about Chuck, who at the time, was also living in New York. She'd been trying to reach him by phone but had heard nothing. When Jacques failed to get a response at his brother's apartment, he tracked down some of Chuck's friends and heard a horrifying story.

Chuck, they said, had collected eight thousand dollars from "investors" and had taken the money to Peru, where he planned to buy some cocaine. But Chuck had been gone several weeks, this friend told Jacques, and there were threats being made against his life by some of his "business partners."

Jacques, believing he might know where to find his brother, and hoping to stop him, caught a flight to Lima and quickly located him at the home of a mutual friend. Jacques learned that he had arrived too late. Chuck had already purchased sacks filled with the drug and said he planned to leave for the States the next day.

Certain that it would kill their mother if Chuck were imprisoned, Jacques devised a desperate plan. "We bought a lot of condoms, doubled them and put the coke inside them, then put Vaseline all over them and inserted them rectally. When we made it back to the States the coke was ruined. Eventually, Chuck borrowed from my father to repay his investors."

Before the money was repaid, however, Jacques returned home, relieved the trip was over. But when he listened to the messages on his answering machine, he began to worry. Several of them were from his father, asking him to call immediately. The news from home was bad. Simone had died the night before of a massive coronary. "Where have you been?" the father asked. "Your mother has been so worried about you boys." Jacques knew what had really killed his mother.

♥

I'm not going to give a lecture here against illegal drugs. I don't have to. Certainly Jacques or anyone reading this book is aware that illegal drugs, especially cocaine, are the scourge of our cities. Using it is harmful enough. Selling it is murderous. But Jacques's story is an important one because he is not alone in his addiction. Millions of other addicts and their families must struggle daily with this problem.

The path to Jacques's addiction was a clear one. With an uncle and a father who are alcoholics, it was almost inevitable that Jacques and Chuck show signs of compulsive behavior. Their mother died while they were trying to get their hands on more drugs, and eight years later, Jacques continues to insist that he is not an addict. Well, the truth is, he is every bit as addicted as a junkie on a street corner, and every bit as at risk of winding up with nothing, not even his wife and daughter.

Jacques's quarrels with his mother were also predictable. Teenage children of alcoholics often turn against the nondrinking parent.

In his relationship with Isabella Jacques was able to pick up just where he had left off with his mother, in anger, violence, and disappointment. When he met Isabella, Jacques used that unconscious mate-selection radar to match their backgrounds so perfectly. They'd both had fathers who became emotionally numbed by drink, whose wives had quarreled with them to "get ahead" and both had parents who colluded with them in activities they could not reveal to the other parent.

Jacques's tender feelings must have rushed to the surface when he met Isabella. After all, his mother died before he had had the opportunity to show her that he had changed from the wild, rageful teenager who'd wrecked her kitchen.

This was his chance. He started his marriage with the conscious intentions of being a responsible husband and father. Yet, he and Isabella even moved to an apartment over a bordello, which is exactly the way his parents began their marriage. So far Jacques and Isabella have followed many details of their old family scripts. Let's see what can be done to break out of those patterns so the Fortassiers can have a marriage on their own terms.

MAKING CHANGES

STEP **11** ♥ We sought through prayer and meditation to improve our conscious contact with God as we understand God, praying only for knowledge of God's will for us and the power to carry that out.

I call this step "the magic 11." It promotes truly living from the inside out. Jacques and Isabella can transform themselves and their marriage in the most beautiful way by using this step. Remember, most addicts have slips when they forget to ask for spiritual help to stay clean and sober. This step thwarts codependence as well, because this is the ultimate way to maintain inner focus.

In my own life, a sense of exquisite peace comes over me and

I am able to meet life's challenges in a very fluid way when I can maintain conscious contact with God. Again and again I have witnessed the same shift with clients when they begin to practice Step 11 in earnest.

I believe the purpose of life is transformation. To shed enough of the old, to bring forth of the best in ourselves. When we transform we can love deeply enough to touch the divine.

♥ EXERCISES ♥

1. Breathe deeply into your abdomen, then expel all of your breath. As you begin to inhale, tense every muscle in your body as tightly as possible and hold the deepest breath you can. Let go of your muscles and the breath at the same moment. This paradoxical exercise really helps with relaxation.

2. Visualize a radiant, clear light washing down through your body, quieting your mind. Allow your mind to become still. Experience a kind of floating sensation.

3. Prayer is talking—meditation is listening. Ask: What is your will for me———(put in whatever name you use for your spiritual practice). Listen. The answer usually comes as a very gentle "knowing" or "hunch." Some people see pictures or visions, others the proverbial "still, small voice." Find your own inner voice. Be patient if it isn't immediately clear. Above all else trust the hunch that comes to you.

4. Find a spiritual practice or ritual that you and your mate can observe together. If you're single, build your own ritual. This can be attending temple or church or medicine gatherings, walking in the woods; it's up to you. Remember, couples who reported a high degree of satisfaction in their marriage after twenty years were more likely to have a shared spiritual life.

5. Affirmations: I am a success, I will persist until I succeed. (In this case, bear in mind, "until I succeed in achieving conscious contact with God.")

Bibliotherapy: Choose a book for spiritual inspiration (any sacred text that touches your heart):

The Bible
The Prophet by Kahlil Gibran
A Course in Miracles by the Foundation For Inner Peace
Gates of Paradise (a Jewish prayer book)
Bhagavad-Gita
Koran

Love saver:
Write down your greatest hopes for your love relationship and place the slip of paper inside a book of spiritual inspiration.

13 SERVICE AS HEALER AND TEACHER

The Fortassiers were the last couple I would work with in this study, and thus they were at the tail end of a whirlwind week of cross-country travel, which of course included hours upon hours of intense therapy. So it came as a surprise to me when, upon meeting the Fortassiers, I felt my spirit rejuvenated by their vitality. Despite their serious problems, I felt from the moment I entered their home that they were prepared to do whatever was necessary to make their love work.

(Dr. Wade worked with the Fortassiers a total of ten hours, during four different sessions. This transcript is a compilation of those sessions. It opens with Dr. Wade seated in a living room chair, with the couple seated side-by-side facing her.)

DR. WADE: Jacques, one of the most important facts I am hoping that you will come to understand about yourself is that you come from a family where addictive issues are very dominant and you have manifested all those patterns: your grandfather's pattern of violence with his wife, your father's addiction. You inherited the illness. Even though it was genetically transmitted, you can do something about it.

JACQUES: I've read about this so-called genetic inclination, but I don't know if I believe all that about it being transmitted through the genes.

DR. WADE: A lot of people who grew up in addictive households have themselves become addicts. There's no avoiding that fact. You probably inherited these genes from your father. There's a chromosome that made your addiction more likely.

JACQUES: I want to change. I don't know what to do with myself. I definitely want to get off the drugs.

DR. WADE: Yes, but do you realize that with your addictive patterns, getting off the drugs is something that's virtually impossible for you to do alone? It will only work if you have a support group. There is a saying at Narcotics Anonymous that the disease is cunning, baffling, and powerful, and it is. It is cunning and it gets you by the throat, especially because your father had the same patterns. I am convinced your brother is an addict even if he's not using drugs right now. What's more, you may be able to get the coke handled only to find yourself more attracted to alcohol. Keep an eye on it, you're genetically predisposed to the disease of alcoholism.

JACQUES: I usually only have a glass of wine with my dinner.

DR. WADE: I can't say it strongly enough. If I could brand it inside your skull I would. There are certain diseases that you have a predisposition for. If you two can handle your addictions, your daughter is not going to have two addicts for parents and she will have a much better chance for a healthy life.

ISABELLA: If he goes to his meeting and I go to mine I think we will really have to go together to be sure he gets there.

DR. WADE: He will have an easier time healing his problems if you will take care of yours and leave him alone. Leave him completely alone about those meetings. Don't ask him if he attended one. The more pressure you put on him, the more it triggers the dynamic he had with his mother.

JACQUES: I have found that when people are behind my ass I have a tendency to rebel. I have a very rebellious soul.

DR. WADE: Yes, but you're also an adrenaline junkie. This is why you like cocaine so much and why you don't prefer pot and the alcohol. They slow you down. Cocaine kicks you into overdrive. That's what you like. You like life to be exciting, like those escapades in Peru. But you can have an exciting life that is positive, too. You can have excitement by taking your wife and your daughter on a fabulous vacation. You can have your excitement by avoiding the cocaine and going out dancing instead. How about learning the lambada together? That's exciting. That's sexy. Or how about a great business deal?

JACQUES: Yes, yesterday I worked from 10 A.M. until midnight. I do like working.

DR. WADE: Be careful, because you know what I am going to say next. We have a disease called workaholism.

JACQUES: Never, because I'm also a guy who loves to relax.

DR. WADE: I hate to force this down your throat, but you, my dear, have an addictive personality. It could be anything. Some people only go up to their knees in life, you're always in up to your eyebrows. Work can be positive for you or it can become one of your greatest weaknesses. Even though you say you want a calm life with Isabella, part of you prefers the upset. It gets your adrenaline going and it's more like the home you grew up in.

JACQUES: Yes, we both know that.

DR. WADE: Can you two work something out so that when you

get home at night, Jacques, Isabella can share the excitement with you? Can you two plan and dream together? Or can you put on some music and dance and hold the baby between you?

JACQUES: Yes, but part of the problem is that we haven't been having sex whatsoever. I am a physical person and I love her and I like being involved with her physically.

ISABELLA: I'm scared. I think it has to do with my background and being afraid of trust. I have to deal with all that.

DR. WADE: Let me ask you about that. You shared with us that you slept in bed with your dad until you were thirteen. And as far as you knew there had been no sexual contact. But were you comfortable with that arrangement?

ISABELLA: I guess since I was doing it since I was a child, I was. The only thing that I wasn't comfortable about was that it was another secret I had to keep from my friends.

DR. WADE: Listen to what you're saying. If you had to keep it a secret, then you knew it was wrong. So your parents had you keeping secrets about your sleeping arrangements. They had you keeping secrets about your mother's boyfriend. They had you keeping secrets about the drinking and fighting. Why do you think they wanted you to keep where you slept a secret? Certainly not because it was something they were proud of. And so, by being in that bed you were in a bind. It would be difficult for you to be comfortable with your sexuality. This is an issue for you to work on as a woman. Your father gave you some very mixed messages by sleeping with you and you associated the message with secrets and shame. So when your husband sleeps with you, it's going to bring up some unresolved issues with your father. These are things for you to work on.

ISABELLA: We didn't have problems sexually when we first started dating. It was only after the baby.

DR. WADE: Often these dynamics don't come out until people are in the roles of mother and father. What happens to you, Isabella, when he approaches you sexually?

ISABELLA: There's a part of me that can really let go and enjoy it. He likes to get a little kinky. With all the problems going on I just can't deal with that. I just want the two of us making love romantically. I can't get into any stories or anything like that. He would start saying something and it would immediately trigger something in my mind and I would freeze up.

DR. WADE: My hunch is that the problem isn't just between the two of you or what he's saying. I think this is more of an issue of your problems with intimacy. When you are intimate and you're close, there's also an emotional vulnerability.

ISABELLA: That sounds just right, because I am afraid of being vulnerable. I'm afraid of betrayal. I'll start seeing him doing something awful like when he tried to strangle my mother.

DR. WADE: That sense of betrayal is key for you. When you and Jacques are close it taps into this reservoir inside you. All the betrayals of your life are in there, all the lies. Your mother, your father, all the hurt in the family, and when you start to feel deep feelings when you are close to Jacques, suddenly you hit that reservoir and you have a vision of him strangling your mother. Don't you see the connection? Here you are making a connection with your heart and then you get a vision of the first people you had an emotional connection with. All your hurt and anger is suddenly triggered.

ISABELLA: Yes, that's right.

DR. WADE: So what you have to do is make a separation. You might say to yourself, "I am safe in my love and my intimacy with my husband." And just keep telling yourself that. And when you feel frightened say to your soulmate, "I feel frightened. I need to connect with you and know that I am safe."

ISABELLA: I think I need more reassurance from Jacques on the fact that it is going to work and we are going to make it.

DR. WADE: Listen, what is possible is for you to exist today and only today. That is how we all have to live our lives. If you continue to worry about what the future might be you will never be able to relax in your husband's arms. Live with him today, tonight. But first let's do some work that can help you get through the day a little better. . . .

Let me tell you what I see. You're locked in a classic power struggle. I could get you a textbook and say, here, this is you. You've got some underlying issues fueling your power struggle.

ISABELLA: All I've done is try to make him change, stop using the drugs.

DR. WADE: Isabella, your mother is as codependent as they come and you learned at her knee.

ISABELLA: What's codependent?

DR. WADE: Your husband is addicted to cocaine. You're addicted to your husband and to getting him to quit. You're not that way because you're bad but because you were taught to be that way. Your mother's message to the family, and especially to you, was that you, my dear, are powerless. So you learned to steal power any way that you could. You were forced to betray the father you love. Your mother was doing something wrong. You couldn't stop it, you were powerless. And in a way it was kind of nice and fun. You had to make a choice about which parent you'd be most like. You chose her because children would rather identify with the parent who appears to be stronger. But in this kind of struggle, it's the passive one who always wins.

I want you two to try something, so I can make my point. Jacques, please sit on the rug and cross your legs, lotus position sort of, and fold your arms in front of you. Isabella, I want you to grab his arm and start pulling him. Jacques, resist her with all your might. (Isabella begins to pull, tugging at Jacques's arm.)

More resistance, Jacques. Show her how much strength you really have in this relationship. Now, Isabella, I want you to say to him, "Stop taking drugs! I'll make you stop! I'll make you see things my way! I'll make you the way I want you to be!"

(Isabella repeats some of these lines.)

DR. WADE: Now keep shouting and pulling him.

ISABELLA (with fury): I want you to change. You must change!

DR. WADE (crouched over, looking into Jacques's, then Isabella's, face): Now tell me, who's in control? Who has the power here?

JACQUES: Me, of course.

DR. WADE: You've got her hanging on, alright. Isabella, he can make you do this for the rest of your life. Meanwhile, look at the picture. (Dr. Wade grabs Isabella's other arm and begins pulling.) While you're busy pulling on him, guess who's pulling your other arm, needing the rest of your time and energy?

ISABELLA: My daughter?

DR. WADE (still pulling): That's right. Rather exhausting, isn't it? You must feel so weary.

ISABELLA (weakly): I am. I am.

DR. WADE: So, Isabella, how do you get out of it?

ISABELLA (crying): I don't know, I don't know. I want to get out. I want out . . . (She begins crying quietly and Jacques rises and holds her in his arms.)

DR. WADE: Jacques, I'm going to ask you to continue to comfort her. Okay, just be with that for a minute. Isabella, here, hug him back, put your arms around him, too. Now how does that feel for you, Isabella? Why did you have your arms folded across your chest when he was hugging you?

ISABELLA: I'm scared he's going to screw something up. I'm afraid we'll lose what we have.

DR. WADE: You're about to push him out the window as it is. What message do you think you're communicating to him by holding back? Tell him.

ISABELLA (to Jacques): I'm telling you that I've let you in so many times before and each time you've betrayed me. My mother used to betray me like this, too. She did it to my father, too.

DR. WADE: Isabella, let me explain what went on in your family. Your mother was over there across the room. On the other side there was you, your father, and your brother. Your mother was in her own private world. She never really let the family in or really connected with you. Please sit on the floor, alone. Imagine that you're seven years old. (Dr. Wade does some relaxation massages and exercise with Isabella, then continues.) Okay, you're a little girl. This chair I'm placing next to you is your father, because just like this inanimate object, he just sat there and did nothing. Pretend I'm your mom. I'm all dressed up here and I've got her Mr. Rockefeller Center at my side. I'm on my way out the door, but just as an afterthought, I turn my head, notice my little Isabella, and I say, "Okay, you come along, too." What's the message to this little girl?

ISABELLA (looking frightened and childlike): I don't know. I don't understand.

DR. WADE: You didn't understand then, either. But listen, hear her voice. Your mother is calling, "Come with me, honey. Your father is rotten. This guy is great."

ISABELLA (still with child's voice): I feel so guilty. My father thinks it'll just be the two of us.

DR. WADE (still in the role of Isabella's mother): "Oh, come on, honey, come with us. You and I can make up something."

ISABELLA: I always felt torn between my mother and father. I loved them both. I was never sure what to do.

DR. WADE: What was the solution you hit upon? You found an answer to the dilemma, what was it?

ISABELLA: That I had to be like my mother and not depend on my father, that my father could never be counted on. I'm afraid. I'm feeling so angry at my father.

DR. WADE: Well, tell him, tell him about that. You're not eight anymore. You can stand up, take your power back. Tell him why you're angry.

ISABELLA (looking at the chair confusedly, then back at Dr. Wade): But he didn't know we were lying to him.

DR. WADE: It's okay, you're not a little girl anymore so you can stop making excuses for him. He was not innocent. On some level he knew about your mother and her boyfriend. He couldn't have continued in that relationship for so many years without knowing. But because he needed your mother, his decision was to do nothing.

ISABELLA (to the chair): Daddy, why didn't you do something? (She shoves the chair.) Why didn't you stop her? Look what she did to us. You betrayed us. (Isabella places her head in the seat of the chair and sobs. Jacques comforts her.)

DR. WADE (stroking Isabella's back in an upward motion): Let it come up. Feel that pain coming up and out. Release it, Isabella, release it. (For a few minutes only the sound of Isabella's sobs can be heard.)

DR. WADE (softly): At some point, when the hurt became too much for you, you began to believe that no man would ever be there for you, that you couldn't trust men or let yourself depend on any man. So with great care you selected Jacques. You took one look at him and decided he couldn't be trusted. And, eureka. You'd found Mr. Right. You wanted the chance to go back, present Daddy with an opportunity to change, and, in the guise of Jacques, he has failed you again. The same words you've used to talk to your father were the same you used to Jacques—that he has betrayed you. You're trying to change your father, get him to give you the love and support you needed. You set Jacques up. This girl who was disappointed by her father couldn't possibly find a husband who could please her.

JACQUES: I always told her I knew I couldn't do anything to please her. I was in a no-win situation.

DR. WADE: Yes, Jacques, but at the same time, who'd be on that chair for you?

JACQUES: My father. He did nothing. He always scrambled behind my mother to please her. But believe it or not, who I dislike is my mother.

DR. WADE: Oh, I believe it. But first, tell me about your father.

JACQUES: Well, one thing I didn't like was that he would never go with me. I asked him to go with me to the motor-cross races, to athletic events. When he said no, I had to ask someone else's parents instead.

DR. WADE: Alcoholism is a disease of isolation and emotional disconnection. He had nothing left for you. Jacques, do you know why you fought so much with your mother?

JACQUES: Because I couldn't do anything right?

DR. WADE: Because she couldn't win with your father. She was frustrated, so she tried to control you, she yelled at you, "Go tidy your room. Stop racing motorbikes. Concentrate on your studies!" You were all colluding. You were his stand-in. You protected your father from your mother's anger. You were like a lightning rod.

JACQUES: I've been used. I had to finagle my way through my mother and father.

DR. WADE: You were pretty willing. All you had to do was screw up and she could dump her anger on you again. Which is exactly what you do in your marriage. Every time you take a drug and screw up, what does your wife do?

JACQUES: She yells at me that I've screwed up again . . . I dealt with my mother the only way I could.

DR. WADE: By being angry back at her. But the only way out of this three-way entanglement is to allow yourself to express some anger about this man who was not available for you, to protect you and accept the anger that was rightfully his.

JACQUES: When he came to visit us here recently, I saw it more than ever. Instead of going out to play with our daughter he remained inside, here in the dark, finishing a liter of Scotch. This woman he married after my mother died, she is so stupid. Just like my mother, she caters to him a lot. After my mother's funeral I could have brought him here to live with me, but there was that woman allowing him to drink. I could have killed that woman one day.

DR. WADE: Look what you're saying. You're angry with her and you're letting passive Daddy off the hook. I want you to talk to your father (She points at the chair.) about your feelings about him.

JACQUES (to Dr. Wade): You know, I've done it already by eliminating him out of my life.

DR. WADE: That's what you think, Jacques. But believe me, he's still there, you're still caught in the same old net, acting out those feelings.

JACQUES (to the chair): When I wanted you to go with me, you were not there. When I needed you to protect me, you were not there. You were not there. You were not there.

DR. WADE: Go on Jacques, take your power back. Tell him.

JACQUES: I wanted someone to comfort me, say you're good at this racing, your work is getting better, to say that I am a good person.

DR. WADE: Well, your mom sure paid attention. She said, "Why did you do this, why are you failing me? Why can't you organize your life?" Jacques, in your own words, can you say to your mother, "I'm willing to forgive you and I let go of you." (She places a large Raggedy Ann doll on the couch.) This is your mother. Talk to her.

JACQUES (looking at the doll): You know, I never got to show you what I became. When I left you it was as a reckless person. You had your doubts.

DR. WADE: Tell her what you've become.

JACQUES: I'm a very sensitive person who cares about friends and family and wants to achieve something. I didn't like it when you kept after me. You made me the scapegoat in the family. To keep my father, and so you could pretend you had a happy marriage, you directed the anger toward me. That's why we fought so much, not because I wasn't good. It wasn't me who was bad. My father wasn't connecting to you as a woman in a marriage, or to me as a son.

DR. WADE: Give that anger back to your parents. Tell them both about it. (Dr. Wade picks up another doll and places it on the chair that has represented Jacques's father.)

JACQUES: Mother, there he is drinking, doing nothing. You want me to substitute for him, but I won't, not anymore.

DR. WADE: Good, take your power back. Turn your back on them.

JACQUES: I'm out of the middle. I'm not your husband. I don't have to do this anymore. I have a wife I love. (He grabs Isabella by the shoulders, encircles her as he turns his head and talks over his shoulder to the chair and sofa.) I have a wife and I want to be happy with her.

DR. WADE: Are you willing to let your parents break up if they have to, so you can save your family?

JACQUES (crying): I don't care about your marriage anymore, Mother. You've had your chance. I care about mine, about Isabella and our child. (to Isabella) I love you so much. I love you. Will you be my wife? I want you to be my wife. I want you to be happy.

DR. WADE: Jacques, you've had your mother, and Isabella, you've had your father—you both brought along companions in this marriage. Four people make for a crowded bed.

JACQUES (to Isabella): No more scapegoat. I'll beat these drugs. I love you. I want to be your husband. I want you to be my wife. I want us to be with our child.

DR. WADE: Isabella, I want you to try something. Say to Jacques: "I trust you."

ISABELLA: But what if I don't feel that way?

DR. WADE: You're still projecting your mother to your father. Give all that away. Take a pillow and beat it every day if you have to, but give it back and maybe you'll have room for your husband. You were like Jacques, trying to keep it together for them. What do you think would have happened if your father had confronted your mother?

ISABELLA: She'd have gotten a divorce.

DR. WADE: She didn't want a divorce. That's obvious or she would have gone with Mr. Rockefeller Center years before. In the meantime, you could take her place with your father. And Jacques, your mother got you, instead of your father.

JACQUES: I was a challenge to my mother. I stood up to her.

DR. WADE: Yes, but who do you and Isabella have to take care of now?

JACQUES: Ourselves.

DR. WADE: Then walk away. (Jacques puts an arm around Isabella's shoulder and they walk away from the dolls and across the room.)

DR. WADE (She moves chairs and the dolls to the opposite corner of the room and speaks to the dolls.): You guys can have a ball, but Jacques and Isabella are out of here.

ISABELLA (looking into Jacques eyes): I trust you. I trust you. I want my husband and my family. I want to start over. I want to start over. I'd die without you.

JACQUES (still crying): Please don't leave me. I love you.

DR. WADE: You guys aren't leaving each other. This is your first chance to see what it's like to be alone. You've just been divorced from your parents.

DR. WADE'S RECOMMENDATIONS
TO THE FORTASSIERS

For Jacques, ongoing attendance and participation in Narcotics Anonymous is imperative. Nothing in his life or marriage will work until he gets the distinctive affects of drugs out of his system.

For Isabella, attendance in either Codependents Anonymous or Al-Anon will provide badly needed tools to assist her in living her own life. Her attempts to control Jacques have only led to more conflict and intense frustration for her.

Any twelve-step program can be reached by checking your local phone directory. Alcoholics Anonymous in particular is now available in almost every country.

Just eliminating the addictive behavior doesn't bring about recovery. Working the steps and practicing the principles they set forth does yield healing.

MAKING CHANGES

STEP 12 ♥ Having had a spiritual awakening as a result of these steps, we tried to carry this message to others and to practice these principles in all our affairs.

If only, if only we could all practice these steps in all of our affairs. Can you imagine the way our world would be? All individuals striving always to bring their highest and best to every situation, looking to improve ourselves instead of blaming others. A world in which we are all spiritually awakened and willing to give service to one another. Service, that's what this step really means to me.

Carrying the message by helping and giving whenever we can. Service was a factor cited in the University of Denver study when couples who had been happily married for twenty years described their relationships. They participated together in a community or creative project. This allows more focus on your strengths and what you have to offer rather than what you think isn't right. The Fortassiers would benefit tremendously by setting aside an hour or two per week to offer their many talents at a neighborhood shelter or charity. Service really keeps us humble and appreciative of our own circumstances.

♥ EXERCISES ♥

1. Practice breathing, tensing, and releasing—visualize light and ask: What kind of service would be best for me to give?

2. Find a service project that is right for you. If you are a harried parent of young children, taking your children to a senior citizen facility might be ideal for everyone's benefit. The hour or two you spend each week can become a joyous one. If you have more time available give it.

3. Continue working with your affirmations from earlier chapters—refer to your notebook.

4. Read a passage from your inspiration book to one another each night before bed. Take turns reading. Of course, read out loud to yourself; if you're single, this makes sleep all the more peaceful and refreshing.

♥ | *Love saver:*
 | **Give service together; contribute something to the lives of others.**

14 LIVING THE LOVE LESSONS

There is a part of ourselves that only love calls forth, a part of ourselves we don't use except in an intimate relationship. The intimacy provides the proximity needed for your mate to be your mirror, bouncing back to you the images of your family, the patterns they acted out, the wounds these actions made. These are the actions and feelings we need to acknowledge and work through in order to heal the wounds, the unresolved hurts, resentments, negative beliefs, etc., that we trip over again and again with our life partner.

The wounds act like the monkey traps used in India. This trap is made with a long-necked glass bottle. Inside the bottle are a few brightly colored baubles and the monkey's favorite kind of nuts. When the monkey sticks its hand in this treasure-filled bottle and closes its fist around a treat, the fist is too fat to fit back through the bottle's neck. The monkey is trapped, because it simply will not open its fist. It's trapped by its own refusal to let go of trinkets and a few bits of food.

We are like the monkey, with our family issues and patterns. Rather than see our outmoded points of view and behavior as the traps they really are, we keep our fists closed and refuse to let go of what is familiar. All of our couples exhibited this behavior at the beginning of their work with me; they were caught in a cycle of blame, counterblame. They said to their partners verbally and nonverbally, "You change, I'm fine." But they worked for and accomplished change as they began to look within and face their own feelings and meet their own needs.

Transformation. That's what life is all about. We are always growing, learning, changing, adapting no matter what. In this final chapter, I want to summarize the most important concepts of *Love Lessons* and give you an update on our five couples. The five couples we have come to know in this book clearly illustrate that love can prompt us to triumph over our human flaws and foibles. Our triumph in response to the prompting of love can be likened to the transmutation of a lump of coal, which in the end becomes a diamond.

The Twelve Steps clearly point the way to real transformation, but it must occur on the inside first. We are often tempted to say, if only things were different, I would be happy. Better still if only my mate were different, I would be happy. The Twelve Steps confront us with the reality that we can be content. We can experience the serenity we wish and pray for. We can do so by learning to master ourselves, by learning who we are. Self-mastery means owning up to our faults, making amends, looking for higher (spiritual) guidance and help, and giving to others. What a challenge. Yes. But what a reward. You become a diamond and your marriage becomes a celebration of love. Your partnership becomes a satisfyingly warm haven instead of an ever-worsening and failing struggle.

Surrender. Let love guide and heal you, and when you find yourself filled with resentment toward your mate, ask, "How is it that I feel this way? What in me is causing me to feel this way? What do I need to do to change this negative pattern?" I outlined appropriate communication tools and anger release techniques in *Love Lessons*, as well as conflict resolution and forgiveness methods. They can help you in the actual process of relating if you use them.

Don't forget the importance of daily practice; use your affirmations and meditation. You can't fall too far off the mark if you create for yourself an inner sunrise each morning. The daily renewal insures that a positive focus remains uppermost in your mind as you experience life with and without your partner. Let me again remind you that studies focused on predicting divorce clearly demonstrate that a couple needs five times as many positive as negative comments and thoughts about and to one another to keep a marriage strong. On the other hand, only one and a half times as many negatives can sink the ship and lead to divorce. This sounds so simple, but is yet so powerful. Speak positively to and about your spouse, even be careful that your thoughts about your loved one are positive. Know that negative familial belief systems can be defeated by facing them and changing them for the better.

Sharing a spiritual life with your mate adds the final polish and luster to your love life. This is like the polishing and faceting of the diamond. Say to yourself, Now love shines through us. We have become the treasure, we are love. Our own efforts to grow, aided by our love for that special other person, have led us down the same path to the deepest love. The deepest, purest love of which we are capable is truly divine.

♥ *Love note:*
Walk into your yard or a nearby park together; experience nature.

TWO YEARS LATER: OUR COUPLES

Two years after my intervention, I'm happy to say that four of the couples have chosen to remain together, though their marriages have had to withstand a great deal of pressure.

The Kinkaids:

Five months after our sessions, the Kinkaids adopted a little girl. They felt their marriage was stronger and that they were ready to make more of a commitment to one another. Frank has found more work but is still struggling to increase his income. He has also consistently attended Alcoholics Anonymous and has been clean and sober for two years. Rebecca has not attended Al-Anon meetings. A year ago, when pressures of their marriage began to overtake them, Frank became physically abusive toward Rebecca again. She began proceedings for a legal separation, but they have since decided to call a halt to the legal actions. Frank has agreed to seek help for his violent inclinations, and when we last talked, the Kinkaids, though living apart, were going to begin seeing a marriage therapist. They are saying there is a chance they will reunite.

The Bonadonnas:

A few weeks after their therapy session, Monica said to me, "I can't believe the change in us. We both feel so much freer and so much closer, like we're on a high." Two years later they continue to feel close and loving. Jimmy's outbursts have ended. Last year Monica's mother apologized to her for her selfishness toward her when Monica was a child. "Mom and I drove out West together," Monica says. "My mom said, 'I was really in over my head with you kids. And you seemed to be the one who least needed me. I'm sorry.'" Monica says she was shocked, but that her mother's apology was a relief. "The sun was just coming out. I rolled down the window for fresh air and I thanked her, adding 'Let's move on now.'" That next Christmas her mother gave her a "terribly ugly" skirt. Monica thanked her, then promptly went out, and with money her parents had given her for practical items, she bought herself a new necklace. "I told myself it was from my mom." she says. Jimmy and Monica have discussed moving closer to Monica's parents, but the issue causes conflict. Neither of them have joined a support group. Jimmy enjoys listening to audiotapes by the popular therapist John Bradshaw.

The Ogots:

Bernard Ogot recently said, "I'm a happily married man." He sounded that way during our most recent follow-up conversation.

He has been clean and sober for a year. Although he and Constance have not joined a support group, the family attends a church regularly and prays for, among other things, his continued sobriety.

The day before we talked Constance received a letter informing her that the daughter she'd left behind in Africa, and her new grandchild, had just been given visas. They will arrive in Atlanta shortly to begin new lives with the Ogots.

The Levines:

The Levines have been in marriage therapy. Roberta has been taking art classes and thoroughly enjoys painting in oils. The couple remains committed to the relationship. They also enjoy exercising together and nights out on the town. "One of the most important lessons we learned from Dr. Wade was to have fun," said Roberta.

The Fortassiers:

Jacques joined Narcotics Anonymous but only attended a few meetings. He has had relapses. Although they reported a few weeks after our session that the quality of their marriage had improved greatly, five months later, Isabella insisted on a separation when she discovered that Jacques was using cocaine again. They have since reunited, and Jacques, who has started attending N.A. meetings again, continues to struggle against his addiction. He recently asked me for advice for his younger brother, who is now a cocaine addict. I referred him to a therapist in their area. Isabella has joined Al-Anon and attends regularly. She recently wrote us the following letter.

Dear Brenda: Hi!

Sorry it took so long to write. We are doing great! I'm working my program and I love it. I actually look forward to that night. Jacques is fine, too, and is waiting to hear about a recent real estate purchase, so for now we're in limbo. (But at least it's

a happy limbo.) I hope all is well. Give my regards to the other Brenda. I love you both. You've saved my life.
Sincerely,
Isabella
P.S. Jacques's brother is one-month in counseling now.
    Thanks again.

    Thanks, Isabella, for proving that the recovery programs and therapy can make a difference. To all our couples, God bless you all.

Selected Bibliography

Bhagavad Gita. Long Beach Publications, 1990.

A Course In Miracles. Foundation for Inner Peace, 1975.

Gates of Paradise. Central Conference of American Rabbis, 1975.

Barbach, Lonnie. *For Yourself: The Fulfillment of Female Sexuality*. Garden City, New York: Doubleday, 1976.

Beattie, Melody. *Codependent No More*. San Francisco: Harper-Collins, 1989.

Bradshaw, John. *Healing the Shame That Binds You*. Health Communications, 1988.

Brown, Les. *Live Your Dreams*. New York: William Morrow, 1992.

Kahlil Gibran, *The Prophet*. New York: Random House, 1923.

Ray, Sondra. *I Deserve Love*. Berkeley: Celestial Arts, 1987.

Satir, Virginia. *Making Contact*. Berkeley: Celestial Arts, 1976.